MACARTHUR
as Military Commander

MACARTHUR

as Military Commander

Gavin Long

COMBINED PUBLISHING
Pennsylvania

This edition published in United States of America and North America in 1998
by Combined Publishing, Pennsylvania, by arrangement with B.T. Batsford, Ltd.

For information, address:
COMBINED PUBLISHING
P.O. Box 307
Conshohocken, PA 19428

E-mail: combined@dca.net
Web: www.dca.net/combinedbooks
Orders: 1-800-418-6065

ISBN 0-938289-14-4
Cataloging-in-Publication Data available from the Library of Congress.
Printed in The United States of America.

Contents

Maps

War in the Pacific

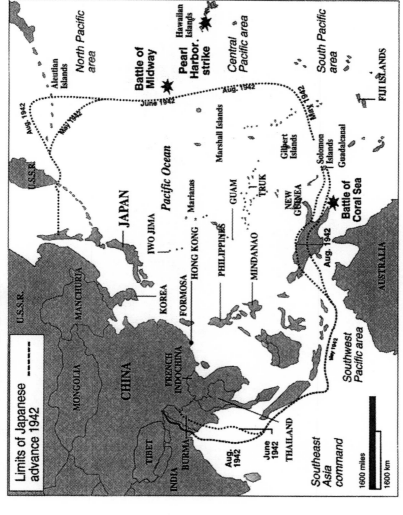

Limits of Japanese advance 1942

Acknowledgment

My debt to the authors of books about General Douglas MacArthur and his campaigns and particularly to the authors of relevant volumes of the United States and Australian official histories is made evident in the following pages. In the final stages of this work I was given generous help by Mr. A.J. Sweeting, formerly Senior Research Officer in the Australian War History Section.

G.L.

Grateful thanks are due to Time Inc. of New York for permission to reproduce extracts from MacArthur's *Reminiscences*.

To my wife

Born in the Purple

1880–1917

On an early September day in 1945 the clouds were low over Tokyo Bay where a great grey-painted fleet lay at anchor. An American destroyer, steaming back from the shore, went alongside the battleship *Missouri*, where she towered over other ships of the motionless fleet, and from it a group of 11 impassive-seeming Japanese climbed the gangway. The visitors were lined up in three rows on the quarter-deck under the eyes of a parade of admirals, generals and air officers dressed in their best, and a congregation of cameramen and ant-like sailors crowding every point of vantage.

After a few minutes General Douglas MacArthur strode on to the deck and to a table with microphones before it. He was dressed more simply than most of the others near by: a braided cap, open shirt with no medal ribbons, sharply creased trousers. Using his fine voice, as though trained as an actor, he told the microphones:

> We are gathered here, representative of the major warring powers, to conclude a solemn agreement whereby peace may be restored. The issues, involving divergent ideals and ideologies, have been determined on the battlefields of the world and hence are not for our discussion or debate. Nor is it for us here to meet, representing as we do a majority of the peoples of the earth, in a spirit of distrust, malice or hatred. But rather it is for us, both victors and vanquished, to rise to that higher dignity which alone befits the sacred purposes we are about to serve, committing all our people unreservedly to faithful compliance with the understanding they are here formally to assume.
>
> It is my earnest hope and indeed the hope of all mankind that from this solemn occasion a better world shall emerge out of the blood and carnage of the past—a world founded upon faith and understanding—a world dedicated to the dignity of man and the fulfilment of his most cherished wish—for freedom, tolerance and justice. The terms and conditions upon which the surrender of the Japanese Imperial Forces is here to be given and accepted are contained in the instrument of surrender now before you.

After a few more words he gestured to the Japanese to sign. First, Mamoru Shigemitsu, the Japanese Foreign Minister, lamed by a Chinese bomb, limped forward and wrote his name on the documents, and then General Umezu, the Japanese Chief of Staff. With Lieutenant-General Jonathan M. Wainwright of the American Army and Lieutenant-General A. E. Percival of the British Army, both recently released from prison camp, standing behind him, the Supreme Commander Allied Powers signed his name to the documents, using five pens. One of these was given to Wainwright, one to Percival, one to the *Missouri*, and one would go to President Truman. Representatives of nine Allied nations then signed.

All this done, MacArthur stepped forward, and the resonant voice spoke again: 'Let us pray that peace be now restored to the world and that God will preserve it always. These proceedings are closed.' But they were not quite closed. As the delegates and their retinues moved away, 400 heavy bombers and 1,500 carrier aircraft swept over the idle fleet. And in a few minutes MacArthur was broadcasting to the people of America a speech that began: 'Today the guns are silent', and, after traversing 'the long, tortuous trail' to Tokyo Bay, reported that their fellow countrymen were homeward bound. 'Take care of them.'

Here, patently, was a great commander. An architect of victory over a Power that had for a while mastered South-East Asia and the western Pacific (otherwise why was he there?), a man of high ideals (the Japanese had listened to his address with high hopes), eloquent (in that accomplishment far beyond the ambition of most soldiers), austere (observe his dress and demeanour).

He was 65 when he presided over the fall of the Japanese Empire in Tokyo Bay on 2 September. It was just ten years since he had relinquished the highest appointment in the American Army and had gone to the Philippines as military adviser to the nascent republic. Defeat in the Philippines had led to the transfer of this eminent soldier, too exalted by far to be allowed to fall into the hands of the enemy, to Australia to command the base whence one prong of the inevitably successful counter-offensive would be directed. Now he was accepting the surrender of the Asian Power that had for a few years guided the course of Far Eastern history. After the ceremony was over he would control Japan with supreme power over government and people.

His fellow countrymen between 1918, when he first came into the public gaze, and 1945 had been divided in their attitude toward him. At one extreme distinguished admirers had portrayed him as a soldier-statesman of lofty stature, whose strategy and tactics, they declared, rivalled those of Alexander the Great, Hannibal, Julius Caesar and Napoleon. At the other extreme denigrators pictured him as a dangerous militarist and an enemy of democracy. In between were those who saw him as a pretentious person, easy to poke fun at.

MacArthur's aim, zealously pursued since boyhood, had been to win the sort of esteem his father, General Arthur MacArthur, had earned. This intent, partly by accident, partly by design, caused the graph of their achievements to run together now and then: fame as bold regimental officers, senior service in the Philippines, deep absorption in the affairs of Asia, conflict at times with political authority.

Arthur MacArthur's life as a soldier covered 45 years of the history of the United States Army, from the Civil War in which massive armies were manœuvred, through the period of Indian wars waged by an army dispersed among dozens of forts throughout the moving western frontier, to the sudden demands of a large-scale encounter with a decadent European Power.

Arthur MacArthur was 15 when the Civil War began. In May 1862 he was recommended to President Lincoln for entry into the Military Academy, but all vacancies for that year had been filled. The eager youth promptly obtained a commission in the 24th Wisconsin Volunteers; in October at Perryville in Kentucky his regiment was in action as part of General Sheridan's division, and he behaved coolly and was promoted captain. In the battle of Murfreesboro in late December and early January he again won the commendation of the doughty Sheridan. After having been invalided for a time with typhoid he rejoined late in 1863, and was with his regiment again in the desperate encounter with General Bragg's Confederate force at Missionary Ridge. In sight of Sheridan he led his regiment with great valour in the charge that won the ridge and put the Confederates to rout. The regiment voted MacArthur into the rank of major on the spot and soon afterwards he was given command. He was 19.

In a gallant but unsuccessful assault on entrenched Confederates at Kenesaw Mountain in June 1864 2,500 men in his division were killed or wounded. Young Colonel MacArthur was one of the wounded; another was Lieutenant Ambrose Bierce. MacArthur was wounded again, charging at the head of his regiment at Franklin, Tennessee, in November. Twenty-five years after the end of the war Congress awarded him, for his gallantry at Missionary Ridge, the Medal of Honour, the highest decoration an American soldier can win.

When he was demobilized in June 1865 MacArthur began to study law, but in February 1866 obtained a commission in the regular army, becoming a captain in July.

By that time most of the volunteers who had served in the Civil War had been demobilized. Perpetual peace was to reign in the New World, it was supposed, and the President had signed a Bill fixing the maximum strength of the regular army at 54,000. This was a puny force with which to impress the restless Mexican Empire of Maximilian to the south, and in the west to subdue the Red Indian tribes who had become more confident and aggressive during the years when white Americans had been fighting one another.

Arthur MacArthur served seven years on the western frontier in a dwindling army barely able to hold its own against the Indian warriors. Each year there were 30 or more actions against the luckless 'redmen'. But the army 'was unseen, unknown and unpopular. It was difficult for the service to get even the most mediocre recruits. . . . And the country seldom looked beyond the Mississippi to hear the ominous sounds of massacre and depredation that the troops were trying vainly to suppress.'[1] The leaders of the neglected army from the generals down to the junior ranks during these years were hardened soldiers forged in the furnace of the Civil War (though no Confederates were admitted). Ulysses S. Grant was General-in-Chief until 1869 when he became President, then W. T. Sherman until 1883 and then Sheridan, Arthur MacArthur's old commander, until 1888.

Captain MacArthur had been fairly constantly on active service for 12 years when he was posted to New Orleans, where he met and married, in May 1875, Mary Pinkney Hardy, a Virginia girl whose brothers had fought for the South. There were three children: Arthur, born in 1876, Malcolm born in 1878 who died as a child, and Douglas, born on 26 January 1880 at the Arsenal Barracks, Little Rock, Arkansas. When Douglas was four the family moved to Fort Selden on the Mexican frontier, and there, in a garrison of about 50 men, they spent the next three years. 'It was here', wrote Douglas MacArthur in his *Reminiscences*, 'I learned to ride and shoot even before I could read or write. . . . My mother, with some help from my father, began the education of her two boys. Our teaching included not only the simple rudiments, but above all else, a sense of obligation. We were to do what was right no matter what the personal sacrifice might be. Our country was always to come first. Two things we must never do: never lie, never tattle.'[2]

In the 1880s the United States Army, under Sherman and Sheridan, began to experience something of a renaissance. Thus, in 1881 a school for the higher training of officers was established at Fort Leavenworth, Kansas. The two-year course was quite elementary by later standards, but a foundation had been laid. Officers back from the frontier service where they had been leading little sub-units began to learn what was happening and what was being thought in the big armies of Europe. The world-wide depression of the 1890s gave the army the additional and distasteful task of policing civil disturbances, and at the same time brought into the ranks a fine body of men

[1] W. A. Ganoe, *The History of the United States Army* (Ashton, Maryland; rev. ed., 1964).
[2] Douglas MacArthur, *Reminiscences* (London, 1964), p. 15.

who had fallen out of work; so many were seeking a livelihood as soldiers—anything would do—that at last the army could pick and choose. But Congress continued to resist military expenditure as stridently as in the 1870s and 1880s, and in 1898 the army was still fewer than 25,000 strong, in a population of 73,000,000.

Meanwhile from 1886 Captain MacArthur and his company of the 36th Infantry served at Fort Leavenworth and there Douglas went to school. School opened 'new vistas'. And so did life at a larger post. For Douglas,

> it was a never-ending thrill to watch the mounted troops drill and the artillery fire on the practice range. I learned there the vital value of 'hits per minute'. There was extra excitement when my father commanded the afternoon parade, with the cavalry on their splendid mounts, the artillery with their long-barreled guns and caissons, and the infantry with its blaze of glittering bayonets.[1]

In January 1897 Colonel MacArthur was transferred to St Paul, Minnesota. Soon the family decided that young Douglas should study for a competitive examination to be held in May 1898 for a vacancy at West Point in the nomination of a Congressman of Milwaukee. The boy worked hard and came top, and was due to enter West Point in June 1899.[2]

Meanwhile, in April 1898 war with Spain had broken out, and the diminished American Army was faced with large-scale operations in Cuba and the Philippines. It had dwindled to fewer than 25,000 with 25 regiments of infantry and ten of cavalry, each of 500–600 officers and men, and a total of about 4,000 artillerymen. The Spanish army in Cuba numbered five times as many. The American staffs had managed to look after their army's multitude of scattered detachments, but for more than 30 years had had no experience of assembling, training and deploying anything larger than a regiment. Congress authorized a wartime increase in the strength of the regular army to 62,000 and President McKinley called for 125,000 volunteers in April and another 75,000 in May. Seven army corps were organized. In late June a corps of some 16,000 men made confused landings on Cuba: fortunately the American Navy had bombarded the objectives so vigorously that the defenders had hastened inland. Meanwhile Commodore Dewey's squadron had destroyed the Spanish men-of-war at Manila, in the Philippines, and another army corps, hastily assembled under Major-General Wesley Merritt, was on its way thither across the Pacific to confirm the naval victory. Its leading brigade, about 2,500 strong, landed at Manila Bay at the end of June. Two more were to follow, the last and strongest of them (4,800 men) being commanded by Brigadier-General Arthur MacArthur.

[1] *Reminiscences*, p. 16.
[2] His biographer Lee says that his entry was delayed for a year because of 'a spinal complaint' but the *Reminiscences* do not mention this.

By the end of July Merritt had some 11,000 troops round Manila. He attacked towards the city on 13 August and after a show of resistance the sensible Spaniards surrendered. But the Filipinos had no intention of exchanging one lot of overlords for another, and their 'liberators' now had to pacify 40,000 resolute nationalists led by the crafty and resolute Amilio Aguinaldo. MacArthur was now a major-general commanding the 2nd Division of the VIII Corps, which was led by General Otis who had succeeded Merritt. The corps was 20,000 strong, about 15,500 of these being volunteers not over-eager to soldier on now that the war was formally over. In February the Filipino *insurrectos* attacked and in a few days the American forces lost twice as many men as in the polite fight with the Spaniards.

In the mopping-up operations against Aguinaldo, MacArthur played a vigorous part. It proved a long and gruelling campaign that demanded the commitment of increasingly larger forces, until by the end of 1899 there were 51,000 Americans in the field; 500 had been killed and 1,000 had died of illness. In June 1900, when MacArthur succeeded Otis as commander and governor-general, there were 63,000. MacArthur introduced more drastic measures, deporting some 50 Filipino nationalist leaders and influential sympathizers, and in March Aguinaldo, in a bold raid led by General Frederick Funston, was captured and brought to Manila.

The nationalists thought that the announcement of the capture of Aguinaldo was a ruse and sent to Manila a Major Manuel Quezon to find out the truth. There he was taken to MacArthur and learnt that Aguinaldo was indeed a prisoner and, what is more, had taken the oath of allegiance to the United States. By July the resistance on Luzon was collapsing (though guerilla warfare continued elsewhere in the archipelago for another decade or more). William H. Taft, with whom MacArthur had had sharp words, succeeded him as civil governor and General Adna R. Chaffee in command of the troops. MacArthur returned to an appointment at home.

In June 1899, just a year after his father had sailed for the Philippines, Douglas MacArthur was enrolled as a cadet at the Military Academy. His mother moved with him to West Point and established a home nearby. Her husband was in the Far East, her elder son at sea.

By general European standards, discipline at the Academy was extremely strict. Much later MacArthur was to write that the cadets were 'cloistered almost to a monastic extent'. Three years before MacArthur was enrolled Second-Lieutenant, Winston Churchill of the 4th Hussars, on his way to Cuba with another English subaltern to observe Spanish operations against Cuban insurgents, had visited the institution. Churchill wrote to his brother in England that he was sure that he would be 'horrified' by some of the regulations of the Academy. 'The cadets enter from 19 to 22 and stay four years. . . . They are not allowed to smoke or have any money in their possession. . . . In fact they have far less liberty than any private school boys in our country. . . . Young men of 24 or 25 who would resign their personal liberty to such an extent can never make good citizens or fine soldiers.'[1] This remained to be seen.

At intervals in the history of the Academy 'hazing'—the bullying of the junior class by the seniors—became a subject of national concern. Since the avowed intention of hazing was to reduce newly arrived cadets to a common level from which they might aspire to become worthy members of their corps, MacArthur, son of a general now winning distinction in the field, and Ulysses S. Grant III, grandson of a general who had become a President, were given special treatment intended to take them down a peg. In the December of MacArthur's second year a Congressional committee investigated the hazing problem and Cadet MacArthur was summoned to appear before the court as a principal witness in a case in which he had been a 'so-called victim'. More than 60 years later he wrote a highly emotional account of the incident. If he was asked to reveal the names of the upper classmen involved he would refuse to do so. Would he then be expelled and his long-cherished ambitions dashed? His mother, sensing his dilemma, had during a court recess sent him a letter in rhyme. In part it read:

> . . . *Remember the world will be quick with its blame*
> *If shadow or shame ever darken your name.*
> *Like mother, like son, is saying so true*
> *The world will judge largely of mother by you.*
> *Be this then your task, if task it shall be*
> *To force this proud world to do homage to me . . . .*

Standing in court, the cadet experienced the 'dreadful nausea' he had felt when he faced his competitive entrance examination at Milwaukee. When the order came to name the offenders he 'pleaded for mercy'—apparently at some length and with much feeling. He was taken to his quarters. 'For hours I waited for that dread step of the adjutant coming to put me in arrest. But it never came. The names were obtained through other means. . . . Only once again was the old nausea to strike.'

MacArthur worked hard and purposefully and was top of his class in his first, second and final years, though 'there were a number of my classmates who were smarter than I'. He held the highest rank in the corps in his final year, and had played in the baseball team for two seasons. He was the most handsome cadet at West Point just as, later, he was the best-looking senior officer of the AEF in France and, later still, perhaps the most photogenic

---

[1] Randolph S. Churchill, *Winston S. Churchill*, Vol. I (London, 1966), p. 270.

commander-in-chief in World War II. He was sought after by girls—not only, it seems, for his good looks but because his father was General Arthur MacArthur. According to one biographer he fended off one girl who asked him wide-eyed if he was really the son of General MacArthur with: 'Yes 'm, General MacArthur has that proud distinction.'

In June 1903, when MacArthur was commissioned as a second lieutenant in the engineers—then the *corps d'élite* of the United States Army—his father had been home for two years and was in command on the Pacific coast. His son's first appointment was in the Philippines, where he was engaged on survey and construction work. As guest of Captain James G. Harbord he met two interesting young Filipino lawyers, Manuel Quezon and Sergio Osmena. While leading a party to cut timber he was set upon by two guerillas. 'Like all frontiersmen, I was expert with a pistol. I dropped them both dead in their tracks, but not before one had blazed away at me with his antiquated rifle. The slug tore through the top of my campaign hat.'[1]

In 1903, while young MacArthur was in the Philippines an American general staff had been created. Hitherto the army had been subject to dual control. The 'General-in-Chief of the Army', despite his resounding title, was responsible to the President as Commander-in-Chief for operations and discipline but not for administration.[2] The Secretary of War was in charge of supply, recruiting, and finance, and directly controlled some ten bureaux such as those of the Adjutant-General, Quartermaster-General, Inspector-General, Surgeon-General, Chief of Engineers, Chief of Ordnance. The system lent itself to the development of a cluster of little bureaucracies each on the defensive against the others and each determined to resist coordination. Under new legislation the senior commander of the army was named Chief of Staff. He headed a general staff to comprise two other generals, four colonels, six lieutenant-colonels, 12 majors, 20 captains.

In the same year a law was passed providing that the organization and equipment of the National Guard—the States' militia—should be the same as those of the regular army, which would provide instructors for these State forces. But the Secretary for War, Elihu Root, who sponsored the new legislation, envisaged that in war the army would be made up not of two components—regular army and National Guard—but three. 'Whenever we come to fight a war', he said in May 1903, 'it will be fought by a volunteer army, as the war with Spain was fought.'[3]

Already in 1900 the establishment at Washington of an Army War College for the higher education of officers of all branches of the service had been

[1] *Reminiscences*, p. 29.

[2] The first General-in-Chief had been George Washington, from 1775 to 1783. But he was also the President.

[3] Quoted in E. Colby, 'Elihu Root and the National Guard', *Military Affairs*, Spring 1959.

authorized; and in 1904 an Army Staff College was developed at Fort Leavenworth, Kansas, to train General Staff officers at courses preliminary to those offered by the War College.

Douglas MacArthur returned to California in October 1904. Next year his father was sent to Japan to report on the Russo–Japanese War and soon Douglas was ordered to join him as aide-de-camp. As a result of earlier reports Arthur MacArthur was instructed to extend his reconnaissance to China, South-East Asia and India, and for nine months father and son travelled and talked to leading people in Hong Kong, Singapore, India— they visited the North-West Frontier—Colombo and the Dutch East Indies. 'The experience was without doubt the most important factor of preparation in my entire life,' the son wrote afterwards. 'It was crystal clear to me that the future and, indeed, the very existence of America, were irrevocably entwined with Asia and its island outposts.'[1]

In 1908 MacArthur graduated from the Engineer School of Application and in this period served as ADC to President Theodore Roosevelt and mixed again among political leaders. After his Asian tour Arthur MacArthur, now a lieutenant-general, was considered by some to be in line for appointment as Chief of Staff, but from 1904 to 1908 William H. Taft, with whom MacArthur had clashed in the Philippines, was Secretary of War, and this may have spoiled his chances. Arthur MacArthur retired in June 1909; three years later he fell dead while addressing the fiftieth reunion of his old Civil War regiment.

At 28 Douglas MacArthur was a well-educated and experienced young engineer officer, had seen the world and listened to stimulating conversations, but his regimental and staff experience had been limited and there seemed little time for him to remedy this lack, headed as he was for instructional work. How would he prove in command of troops in a substantial unit? In April 1908 he went to the 3rd Engineer Battalion at Fort Leavenworth. As junior captain in the battalion he was given the 'lowest-rated' of its 21 companies. 'I had watched my father and First Sergeant Ripley too long not to have learned the trick. By praising them when they were good and shaming them when they were bad, by raising their pride and developing their sense of self-respect, I soon began to convince them that they were the best of the lot.'[2] Under MacArthur they became 'champions'. And MacArthur had proved something about himself: he was a capable manager of men. He was made adjutant and, never at a loss, contrived a tour of duty in the Panama Canal Zone, where the engineers under Colonel George Goethals had not only completed the Canal with immense efficiency but

[1] *Reminiscences*, pp. 31–2.
[2] *Ibid.*, p. 34.

had greatly raised the already high repute of the corps of engineers, of which MacArthur was a member.

During MacArthur's term at Fort Leavenworth Lieutenant George C. Marshall, born in the same year as MacArthur, passed the Staff College there. When Robert L. Eichelberger was commissioned from West Point in the following year, 1909, he was told that the coming men in the army were MacArthur and Marshall. This was guessing far ahead, but within ten years the crystal gazers of 1909 could begin to congratulate themselves on their foresight.

In 1910 a strong and imaginative Chief of Staff was appointed. He was Leonard Wood. Aged only 49, he had achieved the remarkable feat of proceeding from the medical corps of the regular army by way of the volunteers to high rank in the regular army. He had served in Indian wars, led the 'Rough Riders' in Cuba (with his friend and ally Theodore Roosevelt as his second-in-command), governed Cuba, and later the rebellious Moro province in the Philippines. Wood had clear ideas about some of the steps needed to prepare the army for a war against an organized and heavily armed enemy. He set about trying to gain control over the bureau chiefs who had ignored the intentions of the 'general staff' legislation of 1903, produced a paper on the organization of the army, disposed among its 50 posts and 'forts', into three divisions, and initiated training camps for potential citizen officers. In 1911 he succeeded in temporarily assembling a division—the 'Maneuver Division'—for exercises in Texas, where incidentally it was intended to make a show of strength to the restless Mexicans. MacArthur spent four months as an engineer officer with the division and gained his first experience with a body of troops larger than a battalion. After the manœuvres Wood published an article in which he declared that the exercises had 'demonstrated conclusively our helplessness to meet with trained troops any sudden emergency'. Foreign observers agreed with him.

It was a particularly useful experience for MacArthur, who would soon be called upon to concern himself with larger problems than hitherto. After his return from Texas he was transferred from his engineer battalion and appointed head of the department of engineering at Fort Leavenworth. In September 1913 he was posted to the general staff at Washington, where his mother joined him. This staff then comprised 38 officers, of whom MacArthur was the junior. His only postgraduate course had been at the Engineer School and his work as an instructor had been in the engineers. Unlike a number of his contemporaries who seemed destined for senior posts he had not passed through the staff college, and thus there was something of a gap in his education for the sort of appointments that seemed to lie ahead.

At this time about half the regular army was overseas, mainly in the

Philippines (where a Captain John J. Pershing was leading operations against the Mohammedan Moros still waging guerilla warfare against the American occupation). At home the General Staff was wrestling with the problems that had been starkly revealed during the concentration in Texas.

Douglas MacArthur had been with the General Staff only eight months when he was sent into the field and had his first experience of active service. Tension between the Mexican government of General Huerta, which President Wilson refused to recognize, and the United States had been increasing. In April 1914 Huerta arrested several sailors, on shore from an American warship. The American admiral, Mayo, demanded that Huerta apologize and salute the American flag. Huerta refused, marines landed and occupied Vera Cruz, and war seemed imminent. Brigadier-General Funston was sent to Vera Cruz, which he held with a force of about 4,000 army troops and about 3,400 marines. Leonard Wood sent MacArthur to Vera Cruz to observe and report, and with instructions that if war broke out he was to join the staff of a field army operating from Vera Cruz under General Wood himself. MacArthur found that Funston was immobilized for lack of transport. Around him was a big and well-armed Mexican army. MacArthur decided that if the field army arrived it would need to use the railway. There were trucks and passenger cars in the town but the locomotives had been driven away. MacArthur learnt from 'the maudlin talk of a drunken Mexican' that there were engines along the line towards Alvarado. He wrote afterwards that, without informing Funston, he set out in a hand-car with his Mexican informant, who had agreed to take him to another hand-car manned by two other Mexican railwaymen. They would locate the engines and would be paid $150 after MacArthur had been safely returned to the American lines. The first hand-car was halted at a broken bridge. The two men made their way on foot, by river boat and on ponies to the second car and in it reached a town where they found five engines. On the night journey home MacArthur and his companions had several running fights with parties of armed Mexicans; one of his group was wounded but not severely. They reached Vera Cruz safely. MacArthur wrote later that General Wood recommended him for the Medal of Honour, but the War Department disagreed.

War with Mexico was avoided. MacArthur returned to Washington, and was there when war broke out in Europe. On 11 December 1915 he was promoted major.

By 1915 almost all of the mobile part of the American regular army was on active service, mainly along the Mexican frontier. These forces, as distinct from static garrisons and depot troops, numbered about 25,000. Cold reasoning suggested to a few leaders that the time had come to prepare for involvement in the larger war among the European nations. There was the fact that the isolation of the United States in her own hemisphere had decisively ended when in 1898 she became one of the great colonial Powers; indeed, since 1898, she had been engaged in colonial police operations more continuously than any other nation. There was the fact, apparent long before 1914, that major wars would henceforth be fought by nations in arms. There was the evidence that Britain, dependent like the United States on a regular army just about large enough to comfortably cope with colonial policing, would need years to organize fully her military power, and that modern arms and equipment took a long time to develop and produce. But American isolationism was dying hard. For such military readiness as the United States acquired before they were drawn into the world war, Congress was largely indebted to a Mexican revolutionary-cum-bandit, who in a few months of 1916 brought about a doubling of the establishment of the regular army, caused to be exercised the regulars and about 150,000 National Guardsmen under active service conditions of a kind, and required the staffs to assemble and manœuvre substantial bodies of troops.

This benefactor was Pancho Villa who, in March 1916, led 1,500 of his followers into New Mexico where they looted the town of Columbus and killed some 20 troops and civilians. Promptly two American forces were organized to march into Mexico and capture Villa and his band. From Columbus Brigadier-General Pershing led two regiments of infantry and two of cavalry across the border; farther west Colonel George A. Dodd rode into Mexico with a cavalry force. General Funston, the area commander, controlled the whole frontier region. The soldiers were under orders from Washington to avoid any clashes with the government troops, who were little less hostile than Villa's men. In March, April and May there were numerous small-scale actions against the forces of Villa and the government troops. By May all mobile units of the regular army that had been stationed within the United States were in Mexico or along the border. President Wilson called out increasing contingents of the National Guard. By the end of 1916 about 65,000 men were in the frontier zone, and in 1917 about 150,000.

Meanwhile on 3 June an alarmed Congress had passed a Defense Act that would produce dramatic changes in the size and organization of the army. It authorized a regular army of more than double the existing size—an increase from a maximum of 5,000 officers and 128,000 other ranks to 11,000 officers and 287,000 other ranks—but this was to be achieved gradually in five annual instalments. The mobile troops were to be organized into divisions of three brigades, each of three regiments. The Act provided for bringing the National Guard, about 425,000 strong, into the federal service when needed; and for an officers' reserve corps composed of civilians who had passed the necessary examinations. In short, at the end of five years the regular army should be able to place about five infantry divisions in the field, including the overseas garrisons. Other measures aimed more directly at preparing for the seemingly-inevitable involvement in the European war followed: in August a big naval programme was adopted and in September a plan for acquiring a fleet of merchant ships.

The Secretary for War who would be responsible for implementing the new Defense Act was Newton D. Baker, who seems quickly to have been impressed by Major MacArthur's powers of persuasion. On 30 June he appointed MacArthur as one of his military assistants, in charge of the War Department's Bureau of Information, and later also press censor and liaison officer between the newspaper correspondents and the army. It is difficult for military censors and public relations officers to win the favour of news-papermen, but MacArthur was so successful in this task that after nine months the 29 leading correspondents signed a letter to Baker praising MacArthur's 'unfailing kindness, patience and wise counsel' and predicting that 'rank and honors will come to him if merit can bring them to any man'.[1]

MacArthur was now 37 and a major of but 15 months' seniority. He had seen little active service and had commanded nothing larger than a company; nor was he an academically-trained staff officer. On the other hand he had moved in high places, and had won the regard of his senior colleagues, the Secretary of War and the Press. He was proud, confident, eloquent and convinced that he was a man of destiny.

[1] *Reminiscences*, p. 44.

II

'My Martial Vanity'

1917–18

Because in the 1940s General Douglas MacArthur was to become the commander-in-chief of a multi-national force there is reason for sketching the background of the coalition army in which he gained his first experience of front-line warfare against a formidable foe, and of some of the problems that faced his seniors in his first war, a war in which he was at the outset a fairly junior staff officer in Washington, and at the end a divisional commander elect.

The United States severed diplomatic relations with Germany on 3 February 1917, three days after the German ambassador had announced that submarines would sink without warning all merchant ships in a defined zone round the British Isles and the Mediterranean. Next day President Wilson and Secretary Baker decided to take steps to introduce conscription for military service, and within 24 hours a Selective Service Bill had been drafted. War was declared in Washington on 8 April, and a long and heated debate on the Bill followed in Congress and the Press. For the support that the provisions concerning conscription received from the Press the handsome Major MacArthur's winning words to the Washington correspondents seem to have been largely responsible.

The Bill provided not only for conscription but for the establishment of officers' training schools, for immediately bringing the regular army to the strength authorized by the 1916 Act, for the drafting of National Guard reserves and the raising of a National Army of 500,000. The President was empowered also to raise four divisions of volunteers, but wisely did not use this power. Already there were to be three components in the new army, and that would be more than enough.

While the Bill was being debated it became evident that without conscription the United States would not be able to maintain an effective army in France. Despite a vigorous recruiting campaign, only 4,355 men volunteered for the regular army in the first ten days after the declaration of war. Baker announced that recruits need serve only for the duration of the war (hitherto they had enlisted for three years plus four in the reserve) but even so only 32,000—one-sixth of the number needed to fill the establishment— had enlisted by 24 April; and men were coming forward for the National Guard no faster. At this rate months would pass before the ranks of the regular and National Guard regiments had been filled, and if only those two components of the army were sent into action provision of replacements would be a constant problem. 'The showing was poorer than it had been in the Spanish War or the Civil War. . . . The War Department waited, with increasing concern, for the passage of the Draft Bill.'[1] It was 18 May before the Act, with amendments, was passed, and 5 June before 'registration day'.

MacArthur recorded later that a majority of the general staff had approved a study which proposed that the United States army on the Western front should comprise 500,000 men organized in 16 regular army divisions, but that he had opposed this plan. Baker had agreed, and together they had won the President over to the employment overseas of the full strength of the National Guard.

So far as demands on manpower went, the raising of 42 divisions (later the objective was greatly enlarged) from a population of 100,000,000 was less ambitious than the British undertaking of more than two years before, now achieved, to recruit 65 divisions from a population of 46,000,000. But a comparison must take into account that the British War Office's problem of finding experienced commanders and staff for an enlarged army, though exacting, was far less onerous than the American War Department's. Only a dozen years before 1914 the British Army had deployed army corps and divisions in South Africa in battles against an expert and well-armed enemy; she had a corps of trained staff officers who had long been planning to send an army to France; and she had deployed two army corps in action there about a fortnight after war broke out. Also, she officered and controlled in India a second big professional army able to provide major formations at short notice.

Furthermore, by 1917 the British Army in France contained large and high-spirited formations from the independent Dominions: there were five Australian divisions, four Canadian and one New Zealand (and in Palestine two divisions of Australian and New Zealand mounted troops). Not until June 1918 would the American divisions in France equal in number those of the new Dominions, though the total American strength—873,000 in- cluding 175,000 in the Services of Supply—would be far greater. Haig's

[1] Frederick Palmer, *Newton D. Baker, America at War* (2 vols, New York, 1931), Vol. I, p. 145.

armies in France were then some 1,900,000 strong, about 1,500,000 being fighting troops.

The American decisions in 1917 closely resembled, but on a more modest scale, those that Britain had made in 1914 and 1915. Whereas then Britain had organized 11 regular infantry divisions, mobilized 24 Territorial Army divisions (the equivalent of the National Guard) and formed 30 'New Army' divisions, the enlarged American Army would eventually comprise eight regular divisions, 17 National Guard and 17 'National Army' divisions. There had been criticism of Kitchener's decision to raise his New Army, built round minute cadres of experienced soldiers, instead of expanding the framework of the Territorial Army. And it is arguable too that in 1917-18 a smaller American Army with a larger proportion of experienced officers and men, trained and dispatched with greater speed, would have been more effective. In the event fewer than half the 42 American divisions were heavily engaged.

One of the United States War Department's first major problems was to produce officers. At the first series of training camps, opened late in May with 40,000 candidates, the average instructor had to teach, train, select and recommend for commission about 150 men in less than three months.[1]

The regular units had to be ruthlessly robbed of officers and men to staff the schools and provide cadres for the new formations. Less than a year before there had been about 3,200 regular combatant officers. These had to be spread among the staffs, the schools and the 42 divisions.

The intention had been to appoint General Funston to command an American Expeditionary Force when the time came, but he died in February. It had fallen to MacArthur, as night duty officer of the general staff, to carry the news to the President and Baker. Baker asked MacArthur whom the army would choose to lead an overseas force and MacArthur said that his choice would be General Pershing. In May Pershing was appointed and on the 28th of that month sailed for France with a staff of 190 including 59 officers. His chief of staff for a force that was likely in 1918 to comprise a group of armies was a major, J. G. Harbord, aged 51.

John J. Pershing had been born in September 1860 and commissioned from West Point in 1886. He had held the rank of major in the Spanish-American War, but when promoted brigadier-general in 1906 over the heads of 862 of his seniors after his distinguished service against the Moros in the Philippines, his rank had been captain. He had been a major-general only since September 1916. MacArthur described Pershing as 'the very epitome of what is now affectionately called the "Old Army"'. An American military historian wrote of him as 'a dashing figure, popular with women, capable of

[1] Ganoe, p. 465.

self-dramatization, a skilled diplomat despite the tough and distant mien he usually assumed'.[1] A British military historian described him as 'capable, calm, determined and hardworking . . . a considerable personality, though he resembled Haig in lacking personal magnetism and inspired more confidence than affection'.[2] He was dourly determined to prevent the dispersal of his force among the Allied armies, and to dispense with inadequate commanders and bring the ablest men to the top, regardless of seniority and political niceties.

Each new division in the growing army was eager to be among the first to reach the front. To hold back the National Guard and National Army divisions until all the regulars had been sent away might displease public sentiment. Baker decided that the 1st Division should embark first, then the 2nd (which would eventually include two regiments of marines), and then a National Guard division. But which one? Baker discussed the problem with MacArthur, and later wrote:

> I said to Major MacArthur that I wished we had a division in which there were components from every State so that each State could take pride in the fact that some of its own boys were among the first to go. Major MacArthur suggested that in the formation of National Guard divisions there were frequently minor elements left over which were in a sense unattached to any divisional organization, and that these might be grouped together.

Baker sent for General Mann, the Chief of the Militia Bureau, and said that he wanted to form a division that would if possible 'cover the United States'. MacArthur said, 'like a rainbow!'. In a few hours Mann had prepared a plan for a 42nd ('Rainbow') Division. Baker told Mann that he wanted him to command the division with MacArthur as his chief of staff. On 5 August MacArthur was promoted colonel of infantry (not engineers) in the National Army; 'and that', he wrote later, 'is how I became a doughboy'. In August, September and October the 42nd Division trained hard. Mann reigned, it seems, but MacArthur ruled. 'No frills and fancy gadgets were employed (such had been over-propagandized by the trench-warfare methods of the Western Front), but the sound basic principles which from time immemorial have laid the solid foundations for victory.'[3]

This was in keeping with the doctrine that permeated the new army from Pershing downwards that the American Army should train for and initiate a new phase of open warfare. The doctrine had its dangers because the change to open warfare, which both sides on the Western front had been striving to bring about for years, might not be achieved as soon as the new army

[1] *Reminiscences*, p. 52.
[2] C. Falls, *The First World War* (London, 1960), p. 338.
[3] *Reminiscences*, p. 52.

entered the line, and it tended to carry with it a feeling that there was not much to be learned from the tired and hidebound French and British armies, as the Americans believed them to be.

Indeed in February the German withdrawal to a shorter line between Arras and the Aisne had initiated three weeks of semi-open warfare—and incidentally upset Allied plans for a vast two-pronged offensive north and south of the Somme. And in April, when the British attacked at Arras and later the French, under General Nivelle, appointed in December Commander-in-Chief of the armies of the north and north-east, attacked on the Aisne, the French had been trained in new open-warfare tactics, based on those employed at Verdun in the previous year. The infantry were equipped with 16 automatic rifles to a company, with long-range rifle grenades and light guns, and were drilled to advance firing their small arms from the hip.

Nivelle planned to break through and advance eight kilometres a day. But the Germans were forewarned and ready, and the great offensive was halted with a loss of about 34,000 French dead. Nivelle's failure caused a partial collapse of morale in the French Army and in May, when Nivelle was replaced by Pétain, it was evident that it would need a long period in which to recuperate. Meanwhile the British continued to batter the Germans forward of Arras.

Thus in the middle half of the year, while the Americans were throwing their regular army into a melting pot from which a big national army might perhaps be poured in time for an offensive in the late summer of 1918, the Allies were eager for the immediate support of American contingents. Both the British and the French leaders appealed for shiploads of recruits who could be trained at their depots and drafted into their armies. The leader of the British Mission in the United States suggested that America could 'do both': raise her national army and at the same time send to England half-a-million men who would be trained for nine weeks at English depots, drafted into British units, and at some later stage returned to the American Army as seasoned soldiers and organized in their own formations. This plan had obvious virtues: it would give the war-worn Allies the manpower they sorely needed and at the same time provide a big body of American troops with the experience they lacked. But the American leaders were resolved to concentrate on building a national army and also feared it would prove difficult later to regain the men, or units, lent to the armies of their allies.

On this point the President's instructions to Pershing ran:

> In military operations . . . you are directed to cooperate with the forces of the other countries employed against [the German Government]; but in so doing the underlying idea must be kept in view that the forces of the United States are a separate and distinct component of the combined forces, the identity of which

must be preserved. This fundamental rule is subject to such minor exceptions in particular circumstances as your judgment may approve. The action is confided to you, and you will exercise full discretion in determining the manner of cooperation. But, until the forces of the United States are in your judgment sufficiently strong to warrant operations in an independent command, it is understood that you will cooperate as a component of whatever army you may be assigned to by the French Government.

By December Pershing and his embryo staff had been in England and France for six months. There had been a few days in England, where the British Chief of the General Staff, General Robertson, had urged that the Americans should serve with or near the British armies; but Pershing had said that it seemed logical that they should serve beside the French since they were using French ports, railways and equipment; and the United States Navy was working with the British. From 13 June onwards Pershing was in France, where the first wave of the 1st Division—headquarters plus six battalions, including one of marines—arrived on the 28th. Major-General William L. Sibert was in command, with Brigadier-Generals R. L. Bullard and Omar Bundy leading the brigades; Captain George C. Marshall was an operations officer on the staff. The regiments were nominally regular army formations, but in fact two-thirds or more of the men were raw recruits and many of the officers were fresh from the reserve. The division's first month in France was spent in elementary drill 'to improve the appearance, military bearing and spirit of the officers and soldiers of this command'.

Pershing had soon reached agreement with the French leaders that the American Army should land at the south-western ports from St Nazaire southwards and be moved along the railways running thence to a sector in Lorraine, these ports and railways not being greatly used to supply the British and French armies. Pershing saw the eventual role of his army as making a decisive drive on the right flank along a front stretching from the Argonne to the Vosges. Thus the American Army would have its own sector, its own task and its own lines of communication. Pershing conceived his first major attack as one aimed at reducing the deep salient at St Mihiel, to be undertaken in the following spring or summer.

Pershing reported to Washington in July 1917 that few British or French divisional commanders were over 45 or brigade commanders over 40, whereas his divisional commanders (still at home or visiting France as observers) were in their late fifties and brigade commanders in their middle fifties. In November he earnestly requested that 'only divisional commanders who have strong mental and physical vigor be sent here as observers', and he listed six major-generals then in Europe whom he considered unfit. 'Their physical infirmities', he wrote bluntly, 'disqualify them to stand the cold, the discomfort, the continuous strain and the nerve-racking bombardments.'[1] One of the six was General Mann of the 42nd Division. To the names of the six Pershing added 'and probably Liggett of whom I will report later'. But Liggett, though portly, survived to command the I Corps from January 1918 and the First Army from October. He was of the opinion that fat does not matter 'if it does not extend above the neck'.

Early in September Pershing established his headquarters at Chaumont, central to the Lorraine sector and about 70 miles from the front. His army now had its own system of schools, and French and British officers were attached as instructors, but Pershing found 'difficulty in using these Allied instructors' because in his view they held that preparation for open warfare was no longer necessary. 'In order to avoid the effect of the French teaching it became necessary to take over and direct all instruction ourselves.' The British method of teaching trench warfare appealed to him more since 'they taught their men to be aggressive and undertook to perfect them in hand-to-hand fighting with bayonet, grenade and dagger'. The American training doctrines laid emphasis on open warfare methods, offensive action and rifle practice.[2]

The build-up of the army in France proceeded by painfully slow degrees. At the end of September 4,406 officers and 57,125 other ranks were in France, including parts of the first National Guard division to arrive—the 26th, from New England. In October General Bundy was appointed to command the 2nd Division, organized in France from regular brigades; on the 21st the 1st Division went into a quiet sector of the French line east of Nancy.

Four days later the Austrian Army, reinforced by German divisions, broke through the Italian front at Caporetto, and by 2 November had advanced 70 miles and taken 275,000 prisoners. Anxious lest their ally should be put out of the war, the British sent five divisions and the French six to Italy, and they were soon in the line along the Piave. While the Italians were rallying, the Bolsheviks seized power in Russia and it seemed that though Italy had been saved Russia had been lost. In the event the Russian leaders signed an armistice agreement with the Germans on 16 December. There were 141 German, Austrian and Turkish divisions on the Eastern front, including 99 German. Many of these would now be free to reinforce the Western front, where 141 German divisions were already deployed. Throughout the late summer the British and Dominion armies on the Western front had borne the main burden, in the long offensive named Third Ypres, inflicting huge casualties on the Germans and suffering bigger losses themselves. Eighty-six

[1] Palmer, Vol. 2, p. 228.
[2] J. J. Pershing, *My Experiences in the World War* (London, 1931).

of the best German divisions were engaged and were hard-hit beyond any early recovery. Despite the losses and disappointments of these months Haig in November launched an ambitious breakthrough attack towards Cambrai with 19 divisions supported by 324 tanks, with five cavalry divisions in reserve to exploit if the attack succeeded. Much ground was gained but the attack was halted and the Germans took back most of the ground they had lost.

This was the gruelling year for the British armies. While waiting for the French to recuperate and the Americans to arrive 'the infantry of the British divisions suffered, in proportion to their strength at the end of [the year], 88 per cent of casualties, the New Zealand 95, the Australian 97 and the Canadian 103'.[1] The total British casualties in 1917 were 448,000. As the winter settled down the prospect for the following spring was ominous. Pershing wrote to Baker on 2 December:

> With Russia out of the war it is possible for the Central Powers to concentrate 250 to 260 divisions on the Western Front. . . . Against these . . . the Allies have 169 divisions, some of which are under orders for Italy. . . . In view of these conditions it is of the utmost importance to the Allied cause that we move swiftly. The minimum number of troops that we should plan to have in France by the end of June is four army corps, or twenty-four divisions. . . .[2]

By the end of December only 175,000 American troops had landed and only four divisions were complete: the 1st and 2nd, the 26th (National Guard) which had arrived in September and October, and the 42nd which had arrived in October and November.

General Mann took the 42nd Division to France, but on 19 December he was replaced by a younger and more active officer, Major-General Charles T. Menoher, a gunner, who, according to one of MacArthur's biographers, taught his chief of staff the uses of artillery. At first the infantry of the 42nd Division were concentrated in training areas about Toul, and the artillery sent to the artillery training centre in Brittany to receive the 75s and 155s with which the French were arming their allies.[3] Soon after arrival in France MacArthur lost most of the officers of his staff—all picked regulars. But he had sagely seen to it that in each important appointment there was an understudy ready to take over. In December (before Mann had been replaced) the organization had begun of a I Corps under Hunter Liggett, whose 41st Division was then arriving in France. (It became a depot division.) The corps

[1] C. E. W. Bean, *The AIF in France 1917* (Sydney, 1938), p. 948.
[2] Pershing, p. 227.
[3] The division comprised the 83rd Brigade (165th, 166th Regiments and 150th Machine-Gun Battalion), 84th Brigade (167th, 168th Regiments and 151st Machine-Gun Battalion), three field artillery regiments (two armed with 24 75s and one with 24 155-mm howitzers), and divisional troops including a third machine-gun battalion.

was to comprise the 1st, 2nd and 26th Divisions, and the 42nd would be used to provide replacements. Mann protested in vain. MacArthur, who had already demonstrated the advantages to be gained by dealing directly with the man at the top, went to his old acquaintance Harbord and invited him to have a look at the division in training and decide whether such a likely formation should become a depot division. Harbord came and saw and was persuaded.

The division had been complete in France for about two months and a half when, on 16 February, it was placed under the command of the VII French Corps in the Lunéville area east of Nancy for battle training. Here after ten days MacArthur, more interested in what went on at the cutting edge than in staff work, persuaded the corps commander to allow him to join a French raiding party being sent out to capture prisoners for identification. With the raiders he crawled across no-man's-land to the enemy's trenches where they drew fire from machine-guns and artillery but overcame a post and seized their prisoners. On his return the corps commander straightaway pinned the Croix de Guerre on MacArthur's tunic. Later he was also awarded the American Silver Star. 'The award seemed a bit much to me, but I was, of course, glad to have it.'[1]

Soon afterwards the 42nd organized a raid by a detachment of the 168th Regiment. MacArthur obtained leave from Menoher to join in the action. Before dawn on a drizzling winter morning the troops went into the attack in the face of heavy German artillery fire, with MacArthur in the forefront. The raid succeeded. MacArthur and the commander of the company involved were both awarded the Distinguished Service Cross, a newly-instituted decoration evidently intended to be equivalent to the British Military Cross. Then and later Menoher 'preferred to supervise operations from his command headquarters, where he could keep in constant touch with the corps and the army, relying on me to handle the battle line'.[2] This was a reversal of the more usual arrangement whereby, once the plan is made and the troops deployed, the general regards himself as free to go forward and watch the battle, leaving his chief of staff to mind the shop. But it seems that any other course would have been most unwelcome to MacArthur. Emotional, bubbling over with martial ardour penned up during 20 years in which his experience of battle had not amounted to a fraction of his father's, he had to be where the issue was decided by men with weapons in their hands.

There was enough of the actor in Douglas MacArthur to tell him that the good commander needs to be not only an able manager but a figurehead to whom the troops can look up with interest and admiration. In this second

[1] *Reminiscences*, p. 55.
[2] *Ibid.*, p. 54.

role a shrewd leader often cultivates some eccentricities of behaviour and dress, and particularly of headdress. MacArthur made himself a quickly recognizable figure by removing the wire from his stiff-crowned cap and wearing the cap at an angle, and by carrying a riding crop and wearing a turtleneck sweater and muffler. These garments served also to alleviate the throat trouble from which he suffered intermittently during 1918. Indeed he seems to have been in imperfect health during much of the year and to have had to drive his body to respond to the demands of his nerves and will. 'It was hard for me to conceive', wrote a fellow officer who knew him in comfortable quarters after the war, 'of this sensitive, high-strung personage slogging in the mud, enduring filth, living in stinking clothing and crawling over jagged soil under crisscrosses of barbed wire to have a bloody clash with a bestial enemy.'[1]

By mid-March only the 1st Division (Bullard) was in the line as a complete division. The 2nd, 26th and 42nd had yet to enter the line as integral formations: the 3rd, 5th and 32nd were arriving but the 3rd and 5th would not be complete until May. There were some 300,000 men in France, including 100,000 depot troops, but the immediate support they would be able to give in opposing the expected German offensive would be small.

In anticipation of a German blow in the early spring the Allied leaders had been renewing their suggestions for using detachments of Americans to strengthen British and French formations. For example, in January Pétain proposed the assignment of American regiments to French divisions for two or three months after which they would be reassembled under their own commanders. Pershing opposed this on the grounds of language difficulty and the lack of provision for training of senior officers and staffs, and because the eventual removal of the regiments would cripple the French divisions concerned. To Haig's somewhat similar plan, mentioned above, Pershing did not offer 'serious objection', hoping to commit the British to providing more shipping. (About 56 per cent of American troops were transported in British ships.) But it was now somewhat late for such measures.

In retrospect it is evident that provision of more shipping in 1917, the earlier dispatch of more of the regular divisions, and the acceptance of some such measure as Haig's would have produced a substantial and reasonably trained American army in time to take an important part in meeting the German spring offensives. The obstacles in the way of the earlier adoption of the last two of these courses had been sentimental and political. It oversimplifies the problem to picture on the one hand Allied politicians and generals eager only to fill their ranks with American manpower, and on the other a wise and resolute Pershing determined to build up an all-American

[1] W. A. Ganoe, *MacArthur Close-up* (New York, 1962).

army. The Allied proposals were indeed aimed at bringing substantial contingents of American manpower into the line in time for their weight to be felt in the inevitable spring offensive, but also at accelerating the training and seasoning of independent American formations.

The blow fell on 21 March, when the Germans attacked the British Fifth Army and part of the Third Army on Haig's right, along a 50-mile front. In this crisis Washington authorized Pershing to allow the temporary service of American units in Allied divisions, and agreed for the present to send only infantry and machine-gunners to France.

At this stage, partly as a result of Haig's conviction that the melancholy Pétain had lost his nerve, General Foch was appointed supreme commander of all armies in France. The March crisis caused Pershing, to his great regret, to postpone the planned concentration in the American sector of Liggett's I Corps. For the next three months the American divisions were dispersed along the Allied front, mainly in quieter sectors where they relieved veteran divisions that were moved into the vast battle area.

While the 42nd Division was gaining experience east of Nancy four German offensives had been halted. The great drive towards Amiens and Paris was already losing impetus when on 28 March the Germans attacked at the northern hinge of the advance, towards Arras, where nine German divisions attacked four British divisions but were swiftly halted. This was virtually the end of the opening battle which finally ceased in the first week of April. The Germans had advanced up to 50 miles, had taken 90,000 prisoners and killed or wounded 163,000 British and 77,000 French troops, but their own battle casualties had been of the same order. Ludendorff promptly struck again, this time in Flanders on a 12-mile front, hoping to reach the coast and cut off a great part of the British Army. The offensive made dangerous progress. It was then that Haig, his reserves practically exhausted, issued his famous order of the day including the words 'With our backs to the wall and believing in the justice of our cause, each one of us must fight on to the end'. Foch sent French divisions northward to help him. A German effort to revive the Somme offensive late in April was defeated and soon afterwards a renewed thrust in Flanders was finally broken.

Ludendorff now decided to deliver a great blow at the French and, before they had recovered, to strike the British again. Thus on the Aisne on 27 May the Germans attacked a lightly held Allied sector. In the first day they advanced ten miles, and by 3 June were on the Marne at Château Thierry, and Paris was only 50 miles away. The day after the new offensive opened the 1st American Division had made a carefully prepared and successful attack which had taken the village of Cantigny near Montdidier, to the west of the battle area. After this demonstration of his troops' mettle Pershing was ready to respond with some confidence to Pétain's urgent request on 30 April to reinforce the line about Château Thierry. The 3rd and then the 2nd Divisions were hurried forward and helped valiantly in halting the offensive, and by 6 June were making successful local attacks. The 1st and 2nd Divisions took part in the defeat of a renewed offensive on the Matz from 9 June.

Pershing now proposed that an American corps should at last be put into the line, preferably about Château Thierry, and obtained Pétain's agreement to transferring his two most experienced National Guard divisions, the 26th and 42nd, from their inactive fronts to join the 2nd and 3rd. He hoped to employ them and perhaps other divisions in a counter-attack against the salient between the Aisne and the Marne.

The 42nd Division had relieved a French division about Baccarat in its quiet Lunéville sector on 21 March and had been in the line there for 82 days when on 21 June it was withdrawn, rested for about a fortnight, and moved west, but not yet to the Château Thierry salient. It joined General Gouraud's Fourth Army east of Reims. Its departure from Baccarat was marked by a glowing citation by its French corps commander who wrote of its 'offensive ardour, the spirit of method, the discipline shown by all its officers and men' and mentioned the 'staff so brilliantly directed by Colonel MacArthur'. In its new sector, round Souain, the 42nd was again given a gentle introduction, one brigade being deployed in support of the 170th French Division and one in support of the 13th. MacArthur found Gouraud a 'heroic figure', 'with one arm gone and half a leg missing, with his red beard glittering in the sunlight, the jaunty rake of his cocked hat and the oratorical brilliance of his resonant voice, his impact was overwhelming'. Among modern French commanders 'he was the greatest of them all'.[1]

He was indeed the sort of picturesque fighting leader that MacArthur was determined to become; and MacArthur was impressed by his defence-in-depth tactics whereby the forward trenches were held by a light picket line and the main strength held in the line of resistance ready to surprise, confuse and destroy the enemy attack. But it was in fact on the order of Foch, whom MacArthur regarded as 'too inflexible' that the defence in depth had been adopted all along the line. The next big German attack, of which the French had good warning, opened on 15 July and was two-pronged, one thrust being made along a 20-mile front west of Reims and the other along a similar length of front against Gouraud's army east of the city. On the west they advanced some four miles before they were halted. On the east they were stopped on the first day. Four German divisions attacked the two French divisions to which the 42nd was attached. The barrage opened at 12.10 a.m. and the infantry advanced at 3.50. On the right they penetrated

[1] *Reminiscences*, p. 57.

the French line but by 8.30 had been driven back by the French and companies of the 167th American Regiment. Later in the morning more companies of the 84th Brigade and a battalion of the 83rd were sent into the line. On the 16th a further attack was repulsed. That was the end of the German offensives. On the 19th the 42nd was withdrawn. Its units had been in a hard-fought and successful defence and had made determined counter-attacks; they had suffered 1,638 casualties. MacArthur as usual had been forward during the fighting. When it was over he was awarded a second Silver Star. After a few days' rest the division moved east to join the I Corps.[1]

No sooner had the final German thrust been halted than the first of what was to prove a series of Allied counter-offensives opened. That day Ludendorff was at Mons arranging a renewed drive in Flanders that, he hoped, would decisively defeat the British armies. There he learnt that a French attack opening in the early hours of 18 July round the Marne salient had driven his Seventh and Ninth Armies back more than four miles with the loss of more than 12,000 prisoners. The salient was being evacuated and heavy equipment was being hurried out of the threatened area. The 1st and 2nd American Divisions, with a Moroccan division in between, took part in the opening phase of this offensive, and elsewhere round the salient were, from the left, the 4th, 26th, 3rd and 28th. At the same time two divisions were in the British line, the 42nd, as mentioned, was east of Reims and five American divisions were in quiet sectors east of Verdun. Including three divisions behind the British lines, there were now 17 divisions, equal in strength to 34 Allied divisions, in action or more or less ready. 'Thus at this time the American combat reinforcements to the Allies more than offset the reinforcements which Germany had been able to bring from the Russian front.'[2]

After a spell of five days the 42nd Division entered the Marne salient on 25 July when it relieved the weary 26th Division near the tip of the salient. It was under the command of I Corps. The Germans were withdrawing and the 42nd was ordered to press them closely. On the 27th it attacked towards the Ourcq River and took the heights beyond. The German rearguards fought back skilfully. Of this engagement MacArthur later wrote:

> We reverted to tactics I had seen so often in the Indian wars of my frontier days. Crawling forward in twos and threes against each stubborn nest of enemy guns, we closed in with the bayonet and the hand grenade. It was savage and there was no quarter asked or given. It seemed to be endless. Bitterly, brutally the action seesawed back and forth.[3]

---

[1] This account of the operations of the 42nd Division is derived mainly from: American Battle Monuments Commission, *42nd Division: Summary of Operations in the World War* (Washington, 1944).
[2] Pershing, p. 489.
[3] *Reminiscences*, p. 59.

In the early hours of the 28th a battalion of the 42nd crossed the Ourcq River and gained the crest beyond. A fierce fight began for Sergy, which was taken next day. MacArthur was frequently up with the forward infantry, and on the night of the 30th, convinced by the sound of vehicles and explosions from the German lines that they were about to make a big withdrawal to the Vesle, he moved along the line and ordered each regiment to advance in the morning. About dawn he went to divisional headquarters and found Liggett there with Menoher and told them what he had done. Then, worn out by four days and nights of feverish activity, he fell asleep. The division gained little ground that day. It was withdrawn into reserve on 2 August having suffered 5,518 casualties in what was to prove its costliest battle. After it MacArthur was again awarded the Silver Star and was made a Commander of the Legion of Honour and given a second Croix de Guerre. Before the division next went into action he had been promoted to command its 84th Brigade.

When the Allied advance was halted the Germans were behind the Vesle and the Aisne. They had lost 168,000 men, including about 30,000 prisoners and 793 guns, and soon broke up ten divisions for reinforcements. The next blow fell on 8 August when the First French and Fourth British Armies attacked astride the Somme, with 19 divisions forward, supported by a gun about every 50 yards. The battle continued until 3 September, with a lull from the 12th to the 20th, and ended with the Germans withdrawn to the Hindenburg Line. In the first phase 30,000 German prisoners were taken and in the second 46,000.

The time had now come for the realization of Pershing's long-cherished ambition; an offensive by a newly-formed First American Army aimed at reducing the St Mihiel salient. The main attack was to be made in the southern side by the I American Corps (four divisions) and the IV Corps (89th, 42nd and 1st Divisions). Four French divisions held round the tip of the salient. A secondary attack was to be made at the western hinge of the salient by the V Corps (three divisions). The salient, which had existed since 1914, was 18 miles across the base and 13 miles deep. Behind the front line was a second position and across the base a third one—part of the Hindenburg Line with much wire and many concrete posts. The Germans were already preparing to withdraw to this line. MacArthur established his command post in the jumping-off trench on the 11th. The artillery opened fire at 1 a.m. on the 12th. When the infantry advanced at dawn MacArthur was with the forward troops of his brigade. At the end of the first day the 42nd Division had advanced about five miles, farther than the divisions on either flank. Next day there was little opposition. On the 14th MacArthur made a daring reconnaissance towards Metz and urged that his brigade should press on to that city at once. Menoher and Dickman agreed but Pershing did not. He wrote afterwards:

> Reports received during the 13th and 14th indicated that the enemy was retreating in considerable disorder. Without doubt, an immediate continuation of the advance would have carried us well beyond the Hindenburg Line and possibly into Metz, and the temptation to press on was very great, but we would probably have become involved and delayed the greater Meuse–Argonne operation, to which we were wholly committed.

By the 16th the salient had been eliminated, and nearly 16,000 prisoners and 450 guns had been taken. The First Army's casualties were about 7,000, 1,207 being in the 42nd Division. Patrolling and probing continued along a line into which the Germans had now deployed strong reinforcements. On 1 October the 42nd was withdrawn to prepare for its part in the next offensive—Meuse–Argonne. After St Mihiel Brigadier-General MacArthur was awarded two more Silver Stars.

The Meuse–Argonne offensive would be the first of four which Foch planned to launch in quick succession between 26 and 29 September along wide sectors of the front between Verdun and the sea. The first onslaught would be delivered between the Meuse and Reims by the First American Army (15 divisions) and the Fourth French Army (22 divisions); the second on the 27th between Péronne and Lens by two British armies with 27 British divisions; the third on the 28th from Armentières to the sea by armies comprising 12 Belgian, ten British and six French divisions; the fourth on the 29th between the Oise and Somme by a British and French army, with 17 British, 14 French and two American divisions. At this stage Allied Intelligence considered that only 51 of the 197 German divisions on the Western front were ready for heavy action. Against them were deployed (excluding reserves and formations in quiet sectors) 52 British divisions (among them ten from the Dominions), 42 French, 17 American (equivalent to 34 Allied divisions), 12 Belgian.

Pershing deployed the III, V and I Corps, each of three divisions with one in reserve, for the big offensive. The now-veteran 1st, 2nd, 26th and 42nd Divisions needed rest and would not be used in the first phase. The offensive, begun on a front of 24 miles which gradually extended to 80, was to last 47 days. The advance was rapid on the first day but slowed down as German reinforcements were drawn in. The 42nd Division entered the fight on 11 October when it relieved the 1st in General Summerall's V Corps and was given the immediate task of seizing the dominating and strongly fortified Côte de Chatillon opposite the American centre. Frontal attacks had failed. MacArthur organized an enveloping attack and after three days of fighting the stronghold was gained. For 'his field leadership, generalcy and determination during three days of constant combat in front of the Côte de Chatillon' Menoher recommended for a second time that MacArthur be made a major-general. Secretary Baker later endorsed the recommendation 'the greatest front-line general of the war'—words, wrote MacArthur later, that were 'quite unrealistic and partial'. 'I was also recommended for the Medal of Honour, but the Awards Board at Chaumont disapproved. It awarded me, however, a second Distinguished Service Cross, the citation of which more than satisfied my martial vanity.' The citation recorded MacArthur's 'indomitable resolution and great courage in rallying broken lines and reforming attacks, thereby making victory possible'.

After three weeks in the line the 42nd Division went into reserve to I Corps, commanded by General Dickman, Liggett having been promoted to First Army in mid-October. About the same time Bullard, from III Corps, was given command of a new Second Army. There were now seven American Army corps in the field. The 42nd Division went into the line on the extreme left of the American armies on 5 November. The Germans were now in retreat, and the smell of victory was in the air. That day Brigadier-General Fox Connor, Pershing's chief of operations, went to the office of Colonel George C. Marshall, his opposite number on the staff of the First Army, and dictated a message saying that Pershing desired that the honour of entering Sedan should fall to the First Army. Marshall added a note that the corps commanders involved—Dickman of I Corps and Summerall of V—should consider pressing on during the night. Later Hugh A. Drum, Chief of Staff of First Army, added the exuberant but ill-advised note: 'Boundaries will not be considered binding.' Thereupon Summerall spurred on General Frank Parker of his 1st Division and Dickman spurred on Menoher. Summerall ordered the 1st Division to advance that night (6th–7th) and assist in the capture of Sedan next morning. His units abandoned their positions and at midnight began to march in five columns towards the heights south-west of Sedan. The division announced a 'zone of action' that included the left half of the 42nd's area and the right of the French corps on the left. When Dickman learnt of the 1st Division's move he instructed the 42nd to resume the pursuit and take Sedan that night 'regardless of boundaries'. At 9 p.m. the 42nd Division issued orders to that effect. But before the leading regiments had resumed the advance three columns of the 1st Division were moving into their areas.

Later the other two columns moved into the zone of the 40th French Division. The French promptly halted the intruders. MacArthur was with his forward troops that night when he learnt that a brigade commander of the 1st Division was leading his brigade into his area. MacArthur hastened to warn his regimental commander in the neighbourhood not to fire on the newcomers. He encountered a patrol of the 1st Division whose leader recognized him. MacArthur sent him back to his commander to explain the danger that his men might fire on men of the 1st Division if they continued to move across the 42nd's zone. (The story that the patrol arrested MacArthur, thinking that he was a German officer because of his floppy cap, appears to be apocryphal.) Meanwhile I Corps had directed the 42nd Division 'to halt the movement of all 1st Division transportation and take command of all troops in its zone regardless of division. The 1st Division continued to carry out the instructions received from the V Corps.' At 9.28 a.m. I Corps asked First Army to direct V Corps to recall the 1st Division. About 11 a.m. this order was telephoned to V Corps and at 11.15 it issued orders that the 1st Division withdraw to a line specified. But the 1st Division had been out of communication with its corps since it began its move on the previous night, and the order was delivered orally about 2 p.m. By this time First Army had by radio ordered the 1st Division to withdraw to the south, and the divisional staff promptly began to comply. About 10 a.m. the French had informed the 42nd Division that they had been ordered to fire on any troops obstructing their advance on Sedan. As a result the boundaries between the French and the 42nd were redefined.

That evening MacArthur's 84th Brigade took over the whole forward position of the division. On the morning of the 8th a company of the 42nd joined the 40th French Division and that night combined French and American patrols were sent towards Sedan but were driven back by fire. On the night of the 9th–10th the 77th Division took over the front. The 42nd Division's war was over.

The story has often been printed that the Sedan affair led to hard feelings between Marshall and MacArthur, with unfortunate results later when MacArthur was Chief of Staff at Washington and later still when Marshall was Chief of Staff and MacArthur one of his principal commanders in the field. But in an interview in 1961 MacArthur denied that he paid attention to the matter.[1] It does seem to have caused ill will between Summerall and Dickman for long afterwards.

MacArthur's success in the field and the attention and multitude of medals it had attracted evidently aroused some jealousy back at Chaumont, and an officer was sent out to interview officers round MacArthur about his failure to wear a helmet or carry a gas mask, and his habit of going unarmed and of declining 'to command from the rear'. One of MacArthur's former staff officers sent him copies of some of the reports that were collected by the investigator. 'They were so laudatory that it took out all the sting of the

[1] F. C. Pogue, *George C. Marshall, Education of a General 1880–1939* (London, 1964), p. 411.

investigation.' And, MacArthur wrote later, when Pershing was informed he said: 'Stop all this nonsense. MacArthur is the greatest leader of troops we have, and I intend to make him a division commander.'[1] On the eve of the Armistice Menoher was given command of VI Corps and it was proposed that MacArthur should command the 42nd Division, but it was too late for him to be given the promotion, because at the cease-fire Washington had ordered that advancement of generals must cease. He was in command for 12 days.

Honours continued to come MacArthur's way: the Distinguished Service Medal and foreign decorations were added to the seven Silver Stars (which were awarded with far greater frequency than the British 'Mention in Despatches') and two DSCs he had won since February. In a few months he had been awarded more American decorations than Pershing himself, and in this field had left all his American contemporaries far behind.[2]

The 42nd Division had suffered 4,254 casualties in the long Meuse–Argonne offensive. From the beginning 2,713 men of the division were killed, more than in any National Guard division except the 32nd; the 2nd was the hardest-hit American division, losing 4,742 killed in battle or died of wounds. When Menoher left the division he wrote Pershing a letter in the course of which he said that MacArthur had, he believed, 'actually commanded larger bodies of troops on the battleline than any other officer in our army, with, in each instance, conspicuous success. He had developed, combined and applied the use of the infantry and correlated arms with an effect upon the enemy, a husbandry of his own forces and means and a resourcefulness which no other commander in the field has.' He had 'filled each day with a loyal and intelligent application to duty such as is, among officers in the field and in actual contact with battle, without parallel in our army'. Menoher sent a copy to MacArthur's mother who 'cherished it to the day of her death, saying it was the greatest gift she had ever received'.[3]

The achievements of this extraordinary man of 38—somewhat too old by Western front standards for front-line leadership—between late February and early November had been spectacular. In this period, though he was more often out of active operations than engaged in them, he had been decorated ten times by his own army, and had earned lavish praise and respect from seniors and juniors alike. A war correspondent described him as the

[1] *Reminiscences*, p. 70.
[2] Among much-decorated British commanders Lord Gort (born 1886, then a lieutenant-colonel), for example, had the VC, DSO and two bars, MC; the New Zealander Bernard Freyberg, a brigade commander, had the VC and DSO with three bars; the Australian Harry Murray, a lieutenant-colonel, the VC, DSO and two bars, and DCM. Their decorations of course had been won during years of service in battle.
[3] *Reminiscences*, p. 71.

'd'Artagnan of the AEF'. It was no wonder that people at headquarters at Chaumont thought of taking him down a peg.

Justifiable pride in American achievement in the last few months of the war tended to blur the truth that in an army of such dimensions organized so rapidly round so small a nucleus of trained soldiers and, for the most part, with such brief experience of battle, the general level of staff work and unit efficiency remained far below that of their allies and enemies. Full awareness of this came gradually. Fifteen years after the Armistice MacArthur would write:

> The writings of our Allies and of our opponents in the late war are particularly revealing in their comments upon American battle operations. Foch, Hindenburg, Ludendorff and many others have praised without stint the courage and dash of American units in the Western Front. But even while these veterans of many battles were lost in admiration for the bravery of troops that could sustain appalling numbers of casualties and still keep on attacking, they were aghast at the useless and costly sacrifices we made because of unskilled leadership in the smaller units.[1]

One result of the brevity of service of most formations would be that for the next quarter of a century or so the United States would lack the great reserve of expert and thoroughly tested officers, regular and citizen, that the other combatant nations possessed.

[1] Annual report of the Chief of Staff, United States Army, for the fiscal year ending 30 June 1933.

III

West Point and Chief of Staff

1918–35

The 42nd was one of nine American divisions that took part in the occupation of Germany. It moved into an area on the Rhine, where on 22 November
MacArthur reverted to the command of the 84th Brigade. He was tired and
ill with the throat infection that had long pestered him and had been
worsened by poison gas. On the Rhine 'the division thoroughly enjoyed
those days of rest and relaxation. The warm hospitality of the population,
their well-ordered way of life, their thrift and geniality forged a feeling of
mutual respect and esteem.' An American journalist, William Allen White,
visited MacArthur in January 1919 at his headquarters in a fine house overlooking the river. White, who had hobnobbed with everyone who was anyone
in the United States for years past, 'had never before met so vivid, so
captivating, so magnetic a man. He was all that Barrymore and John Drew
hoped to be. And how he could talk! . . . good eyes with a "come hither"
in them that must have played the devil with the girls. . . . His staff adored
him, his men worshipped him, and he seemed to be entirely without vanity.'[1]

In April, 18 months after its departure from Hoboken, the division began
to sail for home. Soon after arriving MacArthur was summoned to the Chief
of Staff, General Peyton C. March, and told that he had been appointed
Superintendent of West Point. He took command there on 12 June.

After a big war, reduction of rank, even premature retirement, is the lot
of many regular officers in all armies. Thus, to follow the experience of a few
officers who had won esteem in the AEF and were to gain senior rank later:
George C. Marshall (born 1880), who as a colonel had been Assistant Chief
of Staff of the First Army, was not promoted to the rank of major in the
peacetime regular army until 1920; George C. Patton (born 1885), a colonel
commanding, briefly, a tank force in 1918, was a major again in 1920 and not
promoted colonel until 1938; Lieutenant-Colonel Joseph W. Stilwell (born

[1] *The Autobiography of William Allen White* (London, 1946).

1883) of IV Corps headquarters, reverted to the rank of captain in 1919 and did not become a lieutenant-colonel again for ten years; Alexander M. Patch (born 1889), a lieutenant-colonel in the 'United States Army' in 1918, had to wait until 1935 before regaining that rank in the regular army.

But the good fortune that had pursued MacArthur in France followed him home. He retained his wartime rank of brigadier-general until it was made permanent in January 1920. This gave him a little seniority over some shining lights who were both older than he was and had carried greater responsibility in France. Among these were Frank Parker (born 1872), who had commanded the 1st Division in 1918; Fox Connor (born 1874), Assistant Chief of Staff for Operations on Pershing's staff; Malin Craig (born 1875), Chief of Staff of I Corps; Hugh A. Drum (born 1879), Chief of Staff of First Army. These men became brigadier-generals in the regular army in 1920, but later than MacArthur, whose seniority in that rank was now within about a year of that of two leading corps commanders of 1918—John L. Hines (born 1868) and Charles P. Summerall (born 1867). It seemed evident that unless MacArthur fell dramatically from favour he must become Chief of Staff of the United States Army, and at about the age of the young generals who had filled the corresponding post in the two decades after the Civil War, when first Ulysses S. Grant and later W. T. Sherman had been appointed generals of the army in their forties. Meanwhile at 39 MacArthur had become Superintendent of West Point at an earlier age than any other since 1871. His immediate predecessor had been 71.

West Point in 1919 was sorely in need of a leader of energy and vision. Normally the academy held four classes each about 250 strong, the senior class graduating and a new one coming in each summer. But in the war the first class had been graduated at the end of its third year, and on 1 November 1918 the cadets of the next two classes had been prematurely commissioned, leaving at home one class of about 280 cadets, who had been there only since the previous June. After the Armistice a new class was admitted six months ahead of the normal time, and the men of the class that had been graduated in November after less than 18 months of training were sent back, as officers, for a further six months' schooling. Thus, when MacArthur took over, there was one class that had been in training for a year, another that had been in training for six months, and a third class just arriving. Influential American academics were arguing that West Point should be abolished and regular officers, if needed, drawn from reservists trained at the universities.

When General March had informed MacArthur of his appointment he had declared bluntly that West Point was 40 years behind the times. Almost without exception the professors were West Point graduates. The professor of English had a university degree but he and only one other on the staff had ever 'exposed themselves to civil education'.[1] Normally an instructor, though not the heads of certain departments, would teach for four years, having a subject in which he had received no training except what he had gained as a cadet, and then return to a military appointment. There were other problems: not the least was how to deal with the bullying of junior cadets by cadets of the upper classes; after graduation young officers from West Point had to learn promptly and painfully that the hectoring and ill-mannered style adopted by seniors to juniors at the academy was not acceptable to enlisted men in the regular army.

In his first report as Superintendent of West Point MacArthur declared that modern war would be fought not by small professional armies but by nations in arms, and that in future 'improvisation would be the watchword'. These conditions would demand an officer 'with an intimate understanding of his fellows, a comprehensive grasp of world and national affairs, and a liberalization of conception which amounts to a change in his psychology of command'. He proposed to achieve these rather foggily stated aims by developing initiative and character rather than 'automatic performance of stereotyped duties', by instituting a broader curriculum including economics and government, by treating the cadets as 'responsible young men' and abolishing the cloistered life, by sending them to train in units of the regular army for the summer period, and by introducing compulsory participation in team games so that all graduates and not only the natural athletes would be competent to supervise games. (Previously gymnastics, fencing, wrestling and boxing but not team games had been compulsory.) With the object of broadening the teaching of cadets MacArthur sent members of the staff to visit other colleges and universities for a month at a time and regularly brought in university teachers to lecture to the cadets. First-year cadets had still to address their seniors as 'Sir' and were not socially recognized in their first year, but otherwise treatment not appropriate to an enlisted man in the army was out. MacArthur converted the camp site where the cadets had drilled in comfort in the summer into a sports ground, and sent the cadets to exercise for two months with regular army units at Fort Dix. He described the old camp site as 'a rich man's summer resort with all its luxuries'.

Naturally there was indignant opposition to these reforms from old graduates and the more hidebound members of the staff, but MacArthur, as ever, won the support of the officers who were closest to him and they worked for him 'with the zeal of apostles'.[2] One of these was Captain Matthew B. Ridgway, his director of athletics. Another was W. A. Ganoe, his adjutant, and a leading historian of the United States Army, who was inspired long

[1] Ganoe, *MacArthur Close-up.*
[2] *Ibid.,* p. 79.

afterwards to produce in *MacArthur Close-up* a vivid portrait sketch of MacArthur in this phase. The commandant never scolded his subordinates or showed impatience but gave them full trust and maximum responsibility. He worked at a clear desk, without in-tray or out-tray; files were dealt with immediately and went straight back to the clerks. He wore no ribbons on everyday occasions. He would welcome a visitor with formal courtesy and ask him to tell what was on his mind. Then he would rise and pace up and down while he repeated, and unravelled if need be, what he had been told. 'The reasoning', wrote Ganoe, 'took its course in such clear fashion that, when he would come to the end, the conclusion or decision was self-evident, so that he was able to utter it as a sort of aside.'[1] He had a photographic memory and could repeat a visitor's five-minute discourse almost verbatim.

Elsewhere Ganoe declared that MacArthur had given the academy its 'first big going over' since the time of Sylvanus Thayer, the 'father of West Point', in 1817; and that at West Point he 'showed his moral courage was not one whit lower than his physical'.[2]

In the three years that MacArthur spent at West Point the United States Army had been put on a sound legislative basis by a National Defense Act of June 1920, which took account of the lessons of 1917-18; but soon afterwards it began to fall into disrepair again as a result of successive cuts in its budget. The new Act had declared that the Army of the United States would comprise the regular army, the National Guard when called into the Federal Service, the Officers Reserve Corps and an enlisted reserve corps. The regular army was limited to 280,000, with 16,630 officers—about the strength laid down by the Act of 1916—and would be organized in corps and divisions. The officers would be placed on a single gradation list so that the rate of promotion would not be greater in one corps than another. Plans were made for the progressive training of National Guard and reserve officers. But pacifist sentiment was growing, and with it the notion that if armies, navies and armaments were reduced war would become less likely. Some influential leaders argued that professional armies should be abolished; that if soldiers were ever needed again they could be drawn from the militias. In 1922 Congress fixed the maximum strength of the regular army at 175,000, with 12,000 officers. The protests of Pershing, who had succeeded March as Chief of Staff in July 1921, were unheeded, as were the arguments of the Secretary of War, John W. Weeks, who pointed out, for example, that the nation was then maintaining one soldier to each $2,500,000 of national wealth.

Towards the end of his term at West Point MacArthur married Louise

[1] Ganoe, *MacArthur Close-up*, p. 49.
[2] Ganoe, *The History of the United States Army*, p. 498.

Cromwell Brooks, a rich and vivacious divorcee. The marriage was a failure and there was a Reno divorce in 1929. Meanwhile in October 1922 MacArthur had been posted to command the district of Manila in the Philippines. The governor-general was General Leonard Wood, the same who had been Chief of Staff when MacArthur was appointed to the general staff. The Filipinos were moving towards independence. MacArthur's old friend Manuel Quezon was now Speaker of a House of Representatives. MacArthur was sympathetic with the Filipino aim to win self-government, but 'the old idea of colonial exploitation still had its vigorous supporters' and there were those who resented his friendliness with Filipinos.[1]

He was given the task of drawing up a plan for the defence of the wild Bataan Peninsula, which encloses Manila Bay on the western side, and he 'covered every foot of rugged terrain, over its trails, up and down its steep mountainous slopes, and through its bamboo thickets'.

In May 1925, now a major-general and after commanding the Philippine division for a few months, he was transferred to the command of first one and then another corps area in the United States. While at the III Corps area with headquarters at Baltimore he was made a member of a court martial established to try an old friend, Colonel Billy Mitchell, on charges arising from Mitchell's blunt and unrelenting criticism of the government's failure to recognize the destructive power of aircraft and, as in Britain, to establish an independent air force. The court sentenced Mitchell to suspension from duty for two years and a half, whereupon he resigned. MacArthur was denounced far and wide by Mitchell's supporters for having let his friend down, but the evidence suggests that he did not vote for a conviction. 'That he was wrong in the violence of his language is self-evident; that he was right in his thesis is equally true and incontrovertible',[2] MacArthur wrote later.

In 1927 the president of the American Olympic Committee died, and, in search of an acceptable successor, the committee, torn by factions, elected MacArthur in his place. He was released from his army appointment, threw himself into the leadership of the team with his usual vim, and it won at the Games at Amsterdam in 1928.

In October 1928 MacArthur was again sent to the Philippines, this time as commander of the Philippine Department, as the United States army command there was named. Again he saw much of Manuel Quezon and 'became fast friends' with Henry L. Stimson, a one-time Secretary of War (1911–13) who was now governor-general. With Quezon he discussed the threat from Japan. This was the year in which Chiang Kai-shek gained

[1] *Reminiscences*, p. 84.
[2] *Ibid.*, p. 86.

control of China, firmly establishing his government at Nanking. Before and during the northward sweep of Chiang's Kuomintang armies there had been attacks on foreign concessions and missions. In 1927 Britain had deployed a division of British and Indian troops in defence of the International Settlement at Shanghai, and Japan had sent troops into Shantung in north China to protect her nationals and her interests, and had extracted satisfactory concessions from Chiang. Thus the Japanese Army had asserted its claim to a special interest in north China and its readiness to back its claims by force. In Manila Americans and Filipinos were learning with anxiety of the wave of Japanese immigration into Mindanao, the big southern island of the archipelago.

The Chief of Staff, now General Summerall, informed MacArthur in July 1929 that President Hoover wished to appoint him Chief of Engineers, which he planned to reorganize 'along broad lines to conform to the magnitude and diversity of its activities, greatly increased by the flood control and inland waterway projects' which had followed the great Mississippi floods of two years before. MacArthur declined, on the ground that he lacked the engineering ability the task demanded and was unlikely to have the confidence of the engineering profession.

This refusal did his career no harm. In August of the next year Hoover announced that he had been chosen as Chief of Staff in succession to Summerall whose four-year term would expire in November. The appointment carried with it the rank of general. Later MacArthur wrote that his first inclination was to decline. 'I knew the dreadful ordeal that faced the new Chief of Staff, and shrank from it. I wished from the bottom of my heart to stay with troops in a field command. But my mother, who made her home in Washington, sensed what was in my mind and cabled me to accept. She said my father would be ashamed if I showed timidity. That settled it.'[1]

In October 1929 the trade depression had descended. The army, which had been starved year by year in response to anti-war sentiment, was soon put on even shorter rations. In his final report Summerall declared that 'the funds provided have been insufficient for even an appropriate approximate realization of the military system contemplated in the National Defense Act'. The incoming chief of staff could look forward only to an even harder struggle to keep the military machine in working order.

'When this military slough of despond had reached its lowest and gloomiest level', wrote Ganoe, as an historian of the United States Army, 'General Douglas MacArthur was called to head the army. . . . Never did the service so need a champion of his caliber: young, vigorous, courageous, at once benignly gentle and properly severe, dynamic, attractive and re-

[1] *Reminiscences*, p. 89.

sourceful.'[1] He was the youngest chief of staff since that office, as distinct from the old appointment of General of the Army, had been established 27 years before; and indeed he had displayed in France and at West Point every one of the qualities this admirer listed.

Among the tasks that faced the new Chief of Staff, in common with all his collaterals throughout the world—outside the totalitarian circle—were to obtain enough money year by year to maintain at least an efficient nucleus army and continue the training of civilian reservists, to take steps towards the reequipment of an army that had few weapons beyond those it had possessed in 1918, and in particular to plan for increased mechanization. During MacArthur's five years in the appointment he used his considerable powers of persuasion to the utmost to convince Congress and the people that the army was being dangerously reduced. In 1930 the regular army numbered some 12,000 officers and 125,000 men; in 1935 the numbers were little different. The annual expenditure decreased each year until 1935 when there was a slight gain. In his final year he managed to win approval for an increase, by instalments, in the number of cadets at West Point from 1,374 to 1,960. Such an increment was the more necessary because of the big hump in the officers' list comprising officers who had entered the regular army in and soon after the war, with the result that soon the upper age groups would be crowded and the postwar age groups, the key leaders in a new war, relatively empty.

In 1932 MacArthur pointed out that Britain's active army numbered 232,000, Japan's 230,000 (soon to be greatly increased), Russia's 624,000. In proportion to population, and taking into account that the United States maintained overseas garrisons totalling 36,000, the United States Army was smaller than the one to which Germany had been limited by the Treaty of Versailles.

When MacArthur took office the army had acquired nine modern Christie tanks to experiment with, and there was a little independent armoured force at Fort Eustis where enthusiastic tank men were testing equipment and tactics. In his first report in June 1931 he declared his policy towards mechanization:

There have been two theories advanced to govern the application of mechanization. . . . The first is that a separate mechanized force should be so organized as to contain within itself the power of carrying on a complete action, from first contact to final victory, thus duplicating the missions and to some extent the equipment of all other arms. The other theory is that each of the older arms should utilize any types of these vehicles as will enable it better and more surely to carry out the particular combat tasks it has been traditionally assigned. . . .

[1] Ganoe, *The History of the United States Army*, p. 497.

In the initial enthusiasm of postwar thought the first method was considered as the ideal one.... Continued study and experimentation have since resulted in its virtual abandonment.... Accordingly during the last year, the independent 'mechanized force' at Fort Eustis has been broken up. The cavalry has been given the task of developing combat vehicles that will enhance its powers in roles of reconnaissance, counter-reconnaissance, flank action, pursuit and similar operations. One of its regiments will be equipped exclusively with such vehicles. The infantry will give attention to machines intended to increase the striking power of the infantry against strongly held positions.... I feel that the continued observation of [this] basic doctrine now promulgated to our Army will have far-reaching and beneficial effects in future training and readiness for emergency.

Again in 1933 he affirmed that in peace the army should develop pilot models of new equipment, including tanks, and secure small quantities for tactical tests but otherwise it should 'insure that upon the outbreak of any major war a manufacture will be initiated in the most modern rather than in obsolete types'.

In the field of higher organization he resisted in 1932 a proposal for the amalgamation of the army and navy departments within one department of defence—'the line of demarcation between the Army and Navy is clear-cut and permanent', but 'tactical operations by air are not separated from those on land and sea by any such line of demarcation. Air units trained entirely independently of the Army and Navy, and acting under an independent commander, would be of little if any use to the land or sea forces engaged in a particular battle ... the setting up of an independent air force could not contribute to actual fighting efficiency but would in fact diminish it.'

In his last three years he introduced two major reforms in organization: the formation of four armies whose areas embraced the whole of the United States; and the setting up of a mobile 'GHQ Air Force' directly under the Chief of Staff. These arrangements would enable the senior commanders and staffs to work on problems of higher command in large-scale operations, and indeed in 1934 a tactical exercise without troops involving two armies and their component corps and divisions was carried out in New Jersey. But the biggest exercise on which the army was engaged in MacArthur's period was the non-military one, mentioned below—the organization and control of the Civil Construction Corps.

MacArthur accompanied his official pleas for military preparedness with off-duty denunciations of 'pacifism and its bedfellow Communism'. Pacifism, he declared in a speech in June 1932, 'hangs like a mist before the face of America, organizing the forces of unrest and undermining the morals of the working man. Day by day this canker eats deeper into the body politic....' For voicing such sentiments, he wrote afterwards, he was 'slandered and smeared almost daily in the press. . . . It was bitter as gall and I knew that something of the gall would always be with me.' It was in that month that his unpopularity with 'anti-militarists' of all complexions reached its height.

Since the early 1920s the veterans of the AEF had been seeking grants of money from the government to help make up the difference between their soldiers' pay and what they would have earned if they had not been conscripted. After much agitation the principle of such grants had been accepted and in 1924 an Act was passed providing compensation in the form of endowment and insurance policies. When the depression descended and tens of thousands of former soldiers were out of work there was a demand for immediate payment of the face value of the policies. In June an army of Bonus Marchers began to advance on Washington to present their case. MacArthur from Washington instructed his nine corps area commanders to ascertain whether the marchers passing through their areas included Communists and to report leaders with Communist leanings. General Malin Craig on the west coast reported that there was no evidence of Communist leadership and the men were well disciplined. Only one corps suggested the possibility of serious trouble. The intelligence staff at GHQ reported that three of 26 leaders were Communists or affiliates.[1]

About 12,000 marchers camped in Washington, some in partly demolished city buildings, some across the Anacosta River in tents provided by the army. When the government offered the men the cost of their fares home about half of them accepted. According to MacArthur those who remained contained few veterans (which seems improbable) and fell increasingly under the influence of Communist agitators. On 28 July the police, after a warning, began to evict those marchers who were living in the area between the Capitol and the main business district. There was a clash with police in which the police shot and killed one marcher. The local authorities then told the President that the situation was out of control, and that afternoon Hoover ordered the army to disperse the demonstrators. The orders which the Secretary of War, Patrick J. Hurley, issued to MacArthur read in part:

> You will have United States troops proceed immediately to the scene of the disorder. Cooperate fully with the District of Columbia police force. . . . Surround the affected area and clear it without delay. Turn over all prisoners to the civil authorities. . . . Insist that any women or children who may be in the affected area be accorded every consideration and kindness. Use all humanity consistent with the due execution of the order.

MacArthur had been warned that such an order was coming, and about 600 infantry and cavalry and a platoon of tanks were ready. He informed Brigadier-General Perry Miles of the 16th Brigade that he would accompany

[1] J. W. Killigrew, 'The Army and the Bonus Incident', *Military Affairs*, Summer 1962.

the troops 'to be on hand as things progressed, so that he could issue necessary instructions on the ground', and, in uniform, he moved with the troops, accompanied by two officers of his staff, Majors D. D. Eisenhower and George S. Patton. By 8 p.m. the troops had herded the demonstrators out of the business area and across the Anacosta River to the site of their main camp. Some of the marchers threw brickbats; some of the cavalry used the flat of their sabres. No shot was fired and nobody was seriously hurt. At 9 p.m. the troops were ordered to clear the Anacosta flats. Miles gave the marchers until 11.15 to collect their gear and move out. Here rocks were thrown at the troops and the troops used tear gas. Next morning the marchers had gone from the flats. Some who remained in the south-west of the city were ejected that day. It was ascertained that there were Communists among the leaders of the marchers; indeed the Communist hierarchy would have been neglecting its self-appointed duty if it had not sought to infiltrate the movement. The use of troops in support of the civil power inevitably excites much indignation, and this incident 'played directly into the hands of the anti-militarists and the pacifist groups throughout the country. MacArthur . . . received the continuing opprobrium of liberal critics.'[1] In retrospect he seems to have acted with common sense and propriety.

Stung beyond endurance by published criticism, MacArthur at length filed a suit for libel seeking $1,750,000 damages from a pair of author-columnists, Drew Pearson and Robert S. Allen, who had been treating him as a figure of fun. In the atmosphere of the times it was an ill-judged step and he eventually dropped the case.

The depression soon brought the army a larger and more constructive task. Franklin D. Roosevelt and the Democratic Party were swept into power with a promise of a 'New Deal' for the common man. Unemployment was at its height. In March 1933, the month in which Roosevelt became President, with George H. Dern as his Secretary of War, one of the new administration's relief measures was to provide money to employ some 300,000 on reafforestation work throughout the country. The army was to organize these men into units, equip them and transport them to their places of employment, where the appropriate civil departments were to establish camps and supervise their labours. But the departments could not cope with their part of the task and in the event the army was called on to conduct the whole project, with technical help from civilian officials. This it did with great promptness and efficiency. In seven weeks 1,315 camps were established and 3,100 regular army officers and 2,300 from the reserve and the navy had been allotted to the Civilian Construction Corps. While it was engaged in organizing the CCC, the Bureau of the Budget cut the army's

[1] Killigrew, in *Military Affairs*, Summer 1962.

appropriation by $80,000,000. MacArthur declared that this would result in

the retirement of some 3,000 to 4,000 regular officers; the discharge of about 12,000 to 15,000 enlisted men of the Regular Army; the elimination of field and armory drill training for the National Guard; of all active duty training for the Reserves Officers' Training Corps and of field training for the Regular Army; the almost complete dismantling of the technical services of the Army. . . .

And he recalled 'the useless and costly sacrifices' in France in 1918 'because of unskilled leadership in the smaller units. Training—professional training —and the skill and knowledge and morale resulting therefrom are the first indispensables to efficiency in combat.'

At the suggestion of Dern, MacArthur was given a private audience with Roosevelt to protest against the cut. He took with him his assistant Chief of Staff, Major-General Drum, and the Chief of Engineers, Major-General Lytle Brown. MacArthur later wrote a dramatic account of the interview. Roosevelt was obdurate and 'turned the full vials of his sarcasm' on MacArthur.

The tension began to boil over. For the third and last time in my life that paralyzing nausea began to creep over me. In my emotional exhaustion I spoke recklessly and said something to the effect that when we lost the next war, and an American boy, lying in the mud with an enemy bayonet through his belly and an enemy foot on his dying throat, spat out his last curse, I wanted the name not to be MacArthur, but Roosevelt.

The President was 'livid' and roared that MacArthur must not speak to him that way. MacArthur told him that he had his resignation. But Roosevelt cooled down and said 'Don't be foolish, Douglas; you and the budget must get together on this.' 'You've saved the Army', said Dern. 'But', wrote MacArthur afterwards, 'I just vomited on the steps of the White House.' Thenceforward, MacArthur wrote, Roosevelt was on the army's side, and in 1934 it was Roosevelt who extended MacArthur's term for a year, a unique event at that time.[1]

The peroration to his final report as Chief of Staff has the genuine MacArthur ring:

The Army extends its analytical interest to the dust-buried accounts of wars long past as well as to those still reeking with the scent of battle. . . . Were the accounts of all battles, save only those of Genghis Khan, effaced from the pages of history, and were the facts of his campaigns preserved in descriptive detail, the soldier would still possess a mine of untold wealth from which to extract nuggets of knowledge useful in moulding an army for future use. . . . The successes of that amazing leader, beside which the triumphs of most other commanders pale into insignificance, are proof sufficient of his unerring instinct for the fundamental qualifications of an army. He devised an organization

[1] *Reminiscences*, pp. 100–1.

appropriate to conditions then existing; he raised the discipline and morale of his troops to a level never known in any other army, unless possibly that of Cromwell; he spent every available period of peace to develop subordinate leaders and to produce perfection in training, and, finally, he insisted upon speed in action, a speed which by comparison with forces of his day was almost unbelievable . . . he clearly understood the unvarying necessities of war. It is these conceptions that the modern soldier seeks to separate from the details of the Khan's technique, tactics and organization, as well as from the ghastly practices of his butcheries, his barbarism and his ruthlessness. So winnowed from the chaff of mediaeval custom. . . they stand revealed as kernels of eternal truth, as applicable today in our effort to produce an efficient army as they were when, seven centuries ago, the great Mongol applied them to the discomfiture and amazement of a terrified world.

Twice during his term as Chief of Staff MacArthur had visited Europe, where he talked with political and military leaders and saw the armies of France, Yugoslavia, Turkey, Hungary, Romania, Poland; and, to the French 'stated frankly the . . . opinion that sooner or later Germany would try again'.

It has been written that Colonel George C. Marshall's promotion was held up by MacArthur because of differences between them dating back to the advance on Sedan, mentioned earlier. Marshall's biographer states that this 'is not borne out by the record at any point. The truth seems to be that MacArthur was reluctant to listen to Marshall's claims only as he was reluctant to listen to all claims that required setting aside promotion by seniority, perhaps because of the resentment aroused by his own spectacular jump up the ladder. For whatever reason, he preferred not to seem to play favourites and chose to risk the shortcomings of the seniority system. These were glaring and damaging.'[1] In fact MacArthur, at Pershing's suggestion, recommended Marshall for promotion to brigadier-general in 1935 and planned to appoint him Chief of Infantry, 'a post that carried the rank of temporary major-general but which would not be vacant for several years' unless the incumbent who was ill resigned sooner.[2]

When he rejected the concept of a separate tank arm and an independent air force MacArthur was swimming against the tide. By the 1930s his decision to distribute light tanks among the cavalry and heavy tanks among the infantry made as little sense as a proposal to amalgamate the field artillery with the cavalry and infantry would have done. And the right answer to the airmen's demand for independence was to grant it, yet strive to develop sound systems of cooperation.

[1] Pogue, p. 312.
[2] *Ibid.*, p. 313. In the event Marshall was promoted brigadier-general on 1 October 1936, appointed Assistant Chief of Staff in July 1938, Deputy Chief of Staff in October and Chief of Staff on 1 September 1939.

MacArthur's insistence that in peace the army should limit itself to designing and testing pilot models of new equipment, tanks in particular, but not commit itself to large-scale manufacture until a major war broke out had attractions for a country such as the United States which was not likely to be invaded across its land frontiers, though he did not advance it as a policy appropriate only to his own army. But, for a European Power, plenty of yesterday's tanks in the field would be more useful than the tanks of tomorrow still on the drawing board.

The task of Chief of Staff during the depression was bound to be frustrating. MacArthur, in common with his opposite numbers in other democratic countries, could hope to do no more than maintain an efficient nucleus round which to expand the army when better times returned or sudden danger threatened. Wisely he emphasized that military plans and preparations made today take years to reach fruition; and he devoted great eloquence to warning that the military establishment was falling to a level from which recovery would be a long and hazardous process. In addition he introduced some important organizational reforms. The citation for an Oak Leaf Cluster to his Distinguished Service Medal, awarded on his retirement as Chief of Staff, mentioned his reorganization of the land forces, the creation of the GHQ Air Force, and the initiation of a comprehensive programme of modernization. In 1934 Pershing said that he had 'only praise' for MacArthur as Chief of Staff. 'He thoroughly comprehends the requirements necessary to develop . . . a unified fighting force for the national defense. He is progressive without being radical. His courageous presentation to high authority of his sound views has been admirable.'

When his extended term as Chief of Staff ended and he was succeeded by Malin Craig, who was five years his senior, MacArthur was 55, but already he knew that a big task lay ahead. While he was still Chief of Staff, Manuel Quezon, now president elect of the coming Commonwealth of the Philippines, visited him in Washington and asked him whether he would undertake the task of organizing the defence of the Archipelago in preparation for the time in 1946, when, under the Tydings–McDuffie Act of the previous year, the Philippines would gain independence and all American military forces (but not necessarily naval forces) would be withdrawn. MacArthur agreed to become Military Adviser to the Philippine government, and told Quezon that it would take all of the ten years, with much help from the United States, to build up adequate defence forces. Soon afterwards Roosevelt summoned MacArthur and offered him the new post of High Commissioner in the Philippines, which with the inauguration of a more independent government, would replace that of Governor-General. 'It was a flattering proposal but involved my retirement from the army. So I declined, stating that I had started as a soldier and felt that I should end as one.'[1]

In his new appointment MacArthur would be a servant of the Philippine Government, whose army and other defence forces would be developed independently of, but in cooperation with, the American garrison—the Philippine Department of the United States Army, which MacArthur had once commanded and was now led by Major-General Lucius R. Holbrook, who was instructed to give the utmost assistance to General MacArthur.

Thus in 1935 the eminent soldier whose promotion had outstripped his years faced the agreeable prospect of a challenging and congenial post-retirement appointment in the faraway country which was his second home, and a task that seemed likely to keep him busy until a second retirement at the age of 66, when he might be expected, in the conventional way, to accept a few company directorships, and, with the help of some industrious amanuensis, to write his memoirs.

[1] *Reminiscences*, p. 102.

IV

View from Manila

1935-41

MacArthur's staff as Military Adviser of the Philippine Commonwealth comprised four officers: Major Dwight D. Eisenhower and James B. Ord of the general staff, a medical officer and an aide. Eisenhower, aged 45, when on MacArthur's staff in Washington had greatly impressed him with the lucidity and fluency of his reports and appreciations. With the help of a committee formed at the Army War College, Eisenhower and Ord drafted a Bill for a Philippine National Defense Act, and drew up a plan to provide by the end of ten years a militia about 200,000 strong mainly organized into small divisions of about 7,500 men 'with a minimum of transport and with services largely improvised'; a small air corps; and a Marine Force equipped with motor torpedo boats.[1]

To achieve these aims they planned the establishment throughout the archipelago of about 150 camps where batches of conscripts would be trained: privates for six months, non-commissioned officers and specialists for a year, and candidates for commissions as reserve officers for 18 months. A military academy modelled on West Point would be established, with an annual intake of about 100 cadets; but it would not begin to produce officers until four years after the programme had begun. Meanwhile the camps would be staffed by officers and NCOs drawn from the Philippine Constabulary. 'Administrative and logistic groups' were to be formed, manned principally by officers who had been similarly engaged in the Constabulary.

President Quezon had agreed with MacArthur that the government would provide each year 15,000,000 to 20,000,000 pesos ($7,500,000 to $10,000,000) for military purposes, including the Constabulary. Part of this sum was to be saved in the early years, and later spent on additional equipment.

[1] Louis Morton, 'The Philippine Army, 1935-39. Eisenhower's Memorandum to Quezon', *Military Affairs*, Summer 1948.

Under the National Defense Act, approved in December 1935, there would be a nucleus of 10,000 regulars, with 930 officers. The militia would initially be organized into ten divisions and eventually 30. MacArthur was convinced that by 1946 this army, plus a flotilla of 36 motor torpedo boats and an air force including 100 bombers, would be powerful enough to defend the archipelago against 'any conceivable expeditionary force'. The absence of a battle fleet, MacArthur explained, was due to the defensive mission of the military establishment. The major duty of a large navy, he declared, was to protect overseas possessions (a view not shared far and wide); therefore round the Philippines, which had no colonies, the only naval task was that of inshore defence, to be provided by the torpedo boats and air force which would 'deny the enemy an opportunity to bring its forces close enough to Philippine shores to debark his troops and supplies'.[1] MacArthur expressed these opinions in a speech in 1936.

The notion that 36 torpedo boats and 100 bombers could prevent invasion by Japan, possessor of the third largest navy in the world and of a highly trained and growing army, was naive. And Quezon, introducing the Defense Bill in the National Assembly, had implied not that the Commonwealth did not need a fleet but that it could not afford one. Also, the Tydings-McDuffie Act had authorized the United States President to negotiate with the Philippines for the retention of American naval bases there. Thus the situation in 1946 might simply be that an entirely local military force had been substituted for the American garrison, for the land defence of the archipelago in general and the United States naval base in particular.

It was evident that a major problem in the early years would be to produce an adequate number of efficient officers. In the Constabulary, which had the strength of about two regiments, were (according to Eisenhower later) 'some commissioned individuals who were natural leaders and who possessed a rather good background of military training'; but 'in the main … the Constabulary was trained as a police force'. The Philippine Scouts were members of the regular army of the United States, but during two decades only a handful of Filipinos had been commissioned in the Scout regiments: by July 1941 only 26 of the 1,434 officers of the United States Army in the Philippines were Filipino Scout officers as distinct from American officers serving in the locally-raised force. When the training plan was begun the Filipino Scout officers (all 26 of them) were lent to the new national army and these largely provided the central staff. In addition a few American officers were lent to MacArthur by the Philippine Department as instructors and inspectors and to fill administrative appointments. Artillery and other

[1] Louis Morton, *The Fall of the Philippines* (Washington, 1953), a volume of the official series *United States Army in World War II*.

technical training was given to Filipino troops at American Army establishments.

The general staff would comprise a Filipino Chief of Staff, with one Assistant Chief in charge of personnel and supply, another in charge of intelligence, operations and training, and a third in charge of plans. A Provost Master General would control the Constabulary, and heads would be appointed to the technical services.

This was a meagre cadre round which to build an army at first of ten, and later of 30, half-size divisions. The machine could soon begin to turn out substantial numbers of basically trained privates, but, with such a half-hearted approach and such slender resources, the time when adequately officered units could be exercised and would begin to develop confidence and *esprit de corps* lay far ahead. A major problem was posed by the wide number of dialects used in the archipelago. Not only did American officers have difficulty in communicating with Filipinos who could not speak English, but in some districts Filipino officers could not make themselves easily understood by their men.

The year 1936 was spent in planning and in preparations to receive the first intake of recruits on 1 January 1937. MacArthur had proposed an initial call-up of only 3,000, but Quezon insisted on the full quota of 20,000, with the result that in 1937 instructors were spread very thinly and the plan to save money in the early years and spend it later on equipment was not realized.

Each of the camps had an officer and some 12 NCOs as instructors of groups of about 150 men. The idea was to form only platoons in the first four or five years and then organize the regiments.

A more realistic plan would have given priority not to training batches of recruits and then sending them home but to forming cadres adequate in quality and quantity, and to building up at least skeleton regiments and divisions from the outset so that effective training and retraining could proceed at all levels. To do this would have demanded larger numbers of borrowed American officers and NCOs, and the intensive training of substantial quotas of Filipino officers to help fill the gap before the military academy produced its first lieutenants in 1941.

In an eloquent exposition of the plan MacArthur gave high priority to the 'professional instruction of all elements with first emphasis upon the Regular Officer Corps', and placed 'organization of Reserve Cadres' last, but in practice it seems to have worked the other way.[1]

The tactical principles behind the decision to organize half-size divisions with 'a minimum of transport and services largely improvised' were

[1] F. C. Waldrop (ed.), *MacArthur at War. His Military Writings* (London, 1943), p. 344.

described by MacArthur in 1936.[1] He explained that 'to hold the enemy under destructive fire, to concentrate upon him the maximum volume of fire at every point where he is operating at a disadvantage, particularly at the moment he attempts to effect a lodgement on shore, is the mission of every unit of the defending force. A war of relentless attrition, of resistance from the water's edge to the furthermost retreat left available to the defending army, is the doctrine and purpose of any military unit that finds itself in the inescapable situation that faces the Philippine military establishment.' Consequently units should be relatively small, free of all impediments that cannot be easily transported over difficult country, and trained to a minimum of dependence upon elaborate supply establishments and a maximum utilization of local resources for transportation and subsistence. 'Conservation of ammunition, simplicity in supply, messing and camping arrangement, and development of the utmost endurance and hardihood among the soldiery of the command are all important tenets in the doctrine of the land elements of the new Army.'

These principles might work if the army was comprised of highly-trained, and resolute troops led by junior leaders of exceptional enterprise and independence and the whole army from top to bottom indoctrinated in guerilla tactics. Lacking these advantages, it was likely to produce a defending force that would have only nuisance value against an expert and fully equipped invader.

MacArthur had taken his mother with him to Manila. She was already in ill health and died a few weeks after their arrival. His brother Arthur had died in 1923 and now, of the little family of four that had been so closely knit when the boys were growing up, only Douglas remained. Quezon gave him spacious quarters at the top of the government-owned Manila Hotel and (the *New York Times* reported) a salary of $31,500. His principal relaxation appears to have been going to the movies, which he did almost every night. In April 1937 he married Jean Marie Faircloth, the 38-year-old daughter of an old Southern family of Murfreesboro, Tennessee; she remained thereafter, he wrote in 1964, his 'constant friend, sweetheart and devoted supporter'.

In that year, MacArthur wrote later, a 'growing coolness between Roosevelt and Quezon made my position almost untenable'.[2] Soon Roosevelt offered MacArthur a newly-conceived command embracing Hawaii and the West Coast, but MacArthur had promised Quezon that he would remain as adviser throughout Quezon's six-year term as president, ending in 1943. MacArthur weakened the link with the United States administration by

[1] Waldrop, pp. 326–7.
[2] *Reminiscences*, p. 107.

retiring from the active list as from 31 December 1937. He was appointed to the rank of field-marshal in the Philippine Army and donned an appropriate cap which he wore thereafter.

Also in 1937 he travelled with Quezon to Japan, Mexico and the United States. The Japanese generals had been on the march in China since 1931, and in 1937 had begun full-scale operations there. Having won China, where would they go next? MacArthur reached the conclusion that Japan coveted and would seek to gain the minerals and oil of the Dutch East Indies and Malaya and the rice of Burma and Siam; Quezon hoped that the Philippines would escape their attention, since the Philippines had nothing that Japan needed in the way of raw materials. But its strategical position might tempt them. In later years, in public and in private, MacArthur strengthened his opinion that Japan was overspending her powers in China, and successful attack on the Western nations was beyond her strength.

In the first three years at Manila MacArthur made some additions to his staff. In 1937 it was joined by Captain Hugh J. Casey as engineer adviser and Major William F. Marquat as anti-aircraft officer. When Colonel Ord was killed in an aircraft accident in January 1938 he was replaced by Major Richard K. Sutherland, a highly-trained staff officer who had been commissioned in the regular army from the National Guard in 1916 after graduating at Yale.

Generally MacArthur seems to have won the admiration and devotion of the little staff over which he presided, although his chief of staff, Eisenhower, did not find his postures entirely congenial. Clark Lee has recorded a remark of Eisenhower's, much later on, to a gushing woman who asked whether he had met her 'real idol' MacArthur. 'Not only have I met him, madam, but I studied dramatics under him for five years in Washington and four in the Philippines.' Few of his subordinates, however, seem to have been immune to his charms. General Lewis H. Brereton, who joined him later, described MacArthur as 'one of the most beautiful talkers I have ever heard, and while his manner might be considered a bit on the theatrical side, it is just a part of his personality and an expression of his character. There is never any doubt as to what he means and what he wants . . . immaculate . . . always looked fresh in a tropical climate.'[1]

His role in the Philippines made it desirable for MacArthur to appear before the people as a picturesque figure and something of an oracle. Two of his severest critics later wrote:

His defense programme would never succeed unless the Filipinos developed an active and unquestioning confidence in his wisdom. He therefore had to impress them with a sense of his authority, if not of his infallibility. The rhetoric,

[1] L. H. Brereton, *The Brereton Diaries* (New York, 1946), p. 25.

the military swagger, the remorseless gold braid were, in part, the response of a naturally histrionic personality to a situation where histrionics became almost a part of policy. Yet . . . in the long run, the public personality may begin to swallow up the private, the actor may begin to believe in his own role. The danger is doubtless the greater when the actor lacks humor and succumbs to the spell of his own rhetoric—greater still when there are no dramatic critics. Manila exposed MacArthur to fatal temptations while relieving him from the restraints once imposed by his contemporaries in the Army.[1]

When Lieutenant-Colonel Eisenhower's four-year term was finishing at the end of 1939 he decided, despite the urgings of Quezon, not to seek re-appointment. MacArthur did not press him to stay. Lieutenant-Colonel Richard J. Marshall was sent out to fill the gap. Sutherland, whose seniority in the regular army was the same as Richard Marshall's—both had been promoted lieutenant-colonel in July 1938—became the new chief of staff; he would remain at MacArthur's right hand until 1946. Sutherland had defects of character and temperament that were inappropriate in a chief of staff. Clark Lee found him 'brusque, short-tempered, autocratic, and of a generally antagonizing nature'.[2] General George C. Kenney, later Mac-Arthur's senior air commander, who had known him since they were at the Army War College together in 1933, wrote of him: 'While a brilliant, hard-working officer, Sutherland had always rubbed people the wrong way. He was egoistic, like most people, but an unfortunate bit of arrogance combined with his egotism had made him almost universally disliked. However, he was smart, capable of a lot of work, and from my contacts with him I had found he knew so many of the answers that I could understand why General MacArthur had picked him for his chief of staff. . . . I decided that I'd get along with him.'[3] Sutherland was the wrong kind of chief of staff for MacArthur, whose foibles he would not offset but nourish.

By the end of 1939, after the outbreak of war in Europe and when Japan was successfully persuading the Western belligerents to remove their troops and naval ships from Chinese waters, training of the new Philippine Army had been in progress for three years and some 100,000 recruits had received their six months of training. For about 18 months young third-lieutenants had been graduating from an Officer Candidate School, and there were 4,800 officers in all, several times the total number of officers in the Philippine Department of the United States Army and, in mere numbers, more than enough to officer in the lower grades the ten small divisions proposed as the initial objective.

[1] R. H. Rovere and A. Schlesinger, *The General and the President* (New York, 1951), pp. 41–2.
[2] C. Lee and R. Henschel, *Douglas MacArthur* (New York, 1952), p. 161.
[3] G. C. Kenney, *General Kenney Reports* (New York, 1949), pp. 26–7.

During the second half of the next year Japan came closer. Japanese troops marched into Indo-China. The United States began to impose economic 'sanctions' on Japan. In September President Roosevelt signed a Selective Service Bill which in effect authorized an American Army of 1,400,000 men and the mobilization of the National Guard began.

The task of directing this expansion of the army fell upon General George C. Marshall, who had become Chief of Staff on General Craig's retirement in September 1939, having already acted in that capacity since July. MacArthur had hoped for the appointment of Hugh A. Drum, who had been Deputy Chief of Staff in 1933-35, but once again the President, in Mac-Arthur's view, picked the wrong man. After his brilliant staff service in France in 1918 promotion had come slowly to Marshall, but from 1936, when he was promoted brigadier-general, his advancement was rapid: Assistant Chief of Staff in July 1938, Deputy Chief of Staff later that year. He was only 11 months younger than MacArthur, who had gained the appointment of Chief of Staff nine years earlier. In the next two years Marshall, looking ahead, secured accelerated promotion for a number of officers of talent, notably George S. Patton, Eisenhower (brigadier-general in September 1941), Mark Clark (promoted from major to brigadier-general between July 1940 and August 1941), and others.

It would have been logical at this stage for the Philippine Government, on MacArthur's advice, to have called its army together, or at least to have carried out a trial mobilization for a period long enough to test the organization and make unit- and formation-training possible.

A new commander of the Philippine Department, Major-General George Grunert, had been appointed in June 1940, and he promptly began to ask for more men and equipment, and in particular for an increase in the strength of the Philippine Scouts from 6,400 to 12,000. There was at first no response from Washington. Grunert pressed on with a warning that the Philippine Government believed that the United States no longer intended to defend the islands and a recommendation that 'a really strong air force and a strong submarine force' be established in the Philippines, United States Army units built up and officers sent out to train the Philippine Army. Quezon had already asked for funds to enable the Filipino troops to be given the same kind of training as was then being organized for Americans in the increased army at home.

In November Grunert sent Marshall a newspaper report implying that the Philippine Army possessed 12 divisions totalling 120,000 well-trained men. He accompanied this with a statement that the Filipino regular army had 468 officers and 3,697 men, the largest unit being the 1st Regiment with 286 men. The reserves possessed 6,416 officers and 120,000 men, but 50 per cent of the officers had had no training, 15 per cent of the remainder had had no field training and none had commanded anything larger than a company. No unit larger than a battalion had ever been assembled for field training. There was no ammunition. He proposed, in the event of an attack, to use Filipinos in companies or battalions, with an American officer commanding each company. He recommended that the Filipino units should be mobilized immediately, and asked for 500 American officers, including 300 for the infantry.

In response to this request 75 officers were sent; the proposal to mobilize the army was rejected for lack of funds. But in January 1941 the President approved an increase in the strength of the Philippine Scouts to 12,000. And already the War Department had decided to reinforce the United States units and to send out 60 field artillery weapons and 20 old anti-aircraft guns.

But MacArthur's optimism was undimmed. Soon after the outbreak of war in Europe he had made a public statement on 'the possibility of successful defense of the Philippines in case of a foreign invasion by Japan, if independence of the Commonwealth is encompassed in 1946 as now provided by law'. Presumably he was speaking of what the possibilities would be in seven years' time. Even so, his estimate of the naval and military power of Japan was still as much at fault as his estimate of the military potential of the 'Commonwealth'. He said that if the defence plan was carried through 'it would be a matter of serious doubt as to whether an enemy could concentrate superior forces at any vital Philippine area'. The maximum force that Japan could deploy 'could be more than matched by the Philippine nation'. It would cost the enemy, in his opinion 'at least a half-million of men as casualties and upwards of five billions of dollars in money to pursue such an adventure with any hope of success. . . . A Japanese blockade would be practically unfeasible without the tacit agreement of the other nations surrounding the Pacific.' And possession of the islands 'would introduce an element of extraordinary weakness in the Japanese empire', which would be split into two parts with its 'present military enemy' in between.[1]

In February 1941 MacArthur wrote Marshall a letter which 'may be regarded as the real reopening of General MacArthur's wholehearted relationship with the US Army, as distinguished from that with his immediate employer of the previous three years, the Philippine Government'.[2] MacArthur said that his mission was not only to prepare an independent defence of the Philippines by 1946 but also the task given him by the President of coordinating the Philippine forces so that they would be

[1] Waldrop, pp. 309-10.
[2] Mark S. Watson, *Chief of Staff: Prewar Plans and Preparations* (Washington, 1950), a volume in the official series *United States Army in World War II*, p. 426.

'utilizable to the maximum possible during the transitory period while the United States has the obligations of sovereignty'. He added that the planned army of 250,000 would be 50 per cent complete in 1941. It, plus a balanced air force and from 30 to 50 motor torpedo boats, was to provide 'an adequate defense at the beach against a landing operation by an expeditionary force of 100,000 which is estimated to be the maximum initial effort of the most powerful potential enemy'. He was contemplating the defence not only of Manila Bay but of all Luzon and the Visayas (the central islands of the archipelago) by blocking the straits leading to its inland seas. To achieve this he would need seven 12-inch guns, 25 155-mm guns and 32 mobile search-lights. He was informed that the heavy guns would not be available before 1943 and the medium guns and searchlights not before 1942. When Grunert was asked to comment he replied that the proposed defence of the inland seas was a step in the right direction; but repeated in effect his earlier comments on the state of readiness of the Philippine Army. It had had 'practically no field training nor target practice'.[1] There were only two torpedo boats and 42 aircraft in the Philippine defence force.

Staff talks between British, American and Dutch officers were held at Singapore in April 1941. The discussions were based on the assumption that, in a war against Japan with the United States involved, the Allies would concentrate first on the defeat of Hitler, maintaining a defensive policy towards Japan until the principal enemy had been defeated. The conference recommended that the defences of Luzon be strengthened and a bomber force be built up there and in China whence a bombing offensive could be conducted against Japanese communications and territories. When passing these recommendations on to Washington General Grunert noted that 'our present mission and restrictions as to means are not in accord therewith'.[2]

In July the American Chief of Naval Operations, Admiral Harold R. Stark, and General Marshall rejected the report; the United States was not planning to reinforce the Philippines. 'Because of the greater needs of other strategic areas', they said, 'the United States is not now able to provide any considerable additional reinforcements to the Philippines. Under present world conditions, it is not considered possible to hope to launch a strong offensive from the Philippines.'

Meanwhile tension between the United States and Japan increased and there were moves in Washington and the Philippines to reinforce the islands and establish a new overall command of all Filipino and American Army

[1] Watson, p. 431.
[2] M. Matloff and E. M. Snell, *The War Department. Strategic Planning for Coalition Warfare* (Washington, 1953), a volume in the official series *United States Army in World War II*.

forces. MacArthur himself told Washington in June 1941 that he proposed to close the office of Military Adviser since he anticipated that the Philippine Army would soon be absorbed in the United States Army, and suggested that he be appointed commander of all army forces in the Far East. In July the War Department did what they might well have done nine months earlier and drew up a plan which embraced and enlarged MacArthur's proposals: the Philippine forces would be called into the service of the United States; MacArthur would be recalled to active duty and appointed to command the combined army and army air force; money should be provided to enable the mobilization and training of the Philippine Army for perhaps a year; and 425 reserve officers would be sent out to the colony from the United States. The Secretary of War, Henry L. Stimson, and the President approved, and on 26 July MacArthur was given the command. On the same day Roosevelt ordered the freezing of Japanese assets in the United States.

MacArthur was reappointed in the rank of major-general, which had been his permanent rank on the active list from the time of his retirement as chief of staff until his retirement with the rank of general on the retired list in December 1937. Next day he was promoted lieutenant-general, and five months later he regained the rank of general.

As commander of United States Army Forces in the Far East (USAFFE) MacArthur supplemented his staff by drawing officers from the Philippine Department. Sutherland remained his chief of staff with Richard J. Marshall as deputy. His senior Intelligence officer was Lieutenant-Colonel Charles A. Willoughby. At the upper levels the staff thus assembled, recruited from a relatively small field of choice considering the extent of its new responsibilities, was to remain little changed during the rest of the war. Willoughby, who was destined to head MacArthur's intelligence staff thenceforward, was a German by birth and had become naturalized in 1910. After active service on the Mexican border in 1916–17 and in France in the 1st Division he had made a name as a writer on military affairs.

For years the general policy governing plans for the defence of the Philippines had been that the available forces should be concentrated for the defence of Manila Bay, which should be held until reinforcements arrived. In a similar way Britain was maintaining a heavily fortified base at Singapore ready to receive a fleet which would be sent there to the Far East if the Japanese attacked. Both plans had their critics. Thus, in 1933 Brigadier-General Stanley Embick, then commanding the harbour defences of Manila Bay, wrote to the commander of the Philippine Department that

> the Philippine Islands have become a military liability of a constantly increasing gravity. To carry out the present Orange Plan [the plan for a war with Japan] —with its provisions for the early dispatch of our fleet to Philippine waters—

would be literally an act of madness. . . . In the event of an Orange War the best that could be hoped for would be that wise counsels would prevail, that our people would acquiesce in the temporary loss of the Philippines, and that the dispatch of our battle fleet to the Far East would be delayed for the two or three years needed for its augmentation.[1]

On the British side critics, particularly Australians, were warning that if the Japanese attacked it would be at a time when the British Navy was preoccupied with war in the West, and that in any event the enemy would seize the Singapore base by attack from the landward side.

In War Plan Orange-3, the version current when MacArthur was recalled, it was assumed that the Japanese, with a force of some 100,000 men, would attack with little or no warning in the dry months of December or January, the main body being concentrated against Luzon, with its first objectives Manila and the naval base. In the American plan efforts would be made to prevent the enemy from landing, but if these failed the defending army was to be withdrawn into the Bataan Peninsula. 'Bataan was recognized as the key to the control of Manila Bay, and it was to be defended to the "last extremity".'[2]

It was a vital part of the plan that the Japanese invaders be delayed long enough to enable supplies for 180 days to be moved into Bataan. Presumably at the end of six months when the supplies there were exhausted the garrison would be compelled to surrender, since no possibility was seen of a successful naval counter-offensive reaching the beleaguered island within that time.

MacArthur spurned War Plan Orange and also a new plan, Rainbow 5, which 'called for a defensive strategy in the Pacific and Far East and recognized Germany as the main enemy in the event of a war with the Axis'; and 'accepted implicitly the loss of the Philippines, Wake and Guam'. He worked on a plan of his own for the defence of all the islands of the Philippines. And on 18 October Marshall from Washington informed MacArthur that new plans were being drafted there too. On 3 November when Major-General Brereton arrived in Manila to take command of MacArthur's air force, he bore a letter from Marshall to MacArthur. After reading it Mac-Arthur was delighted. 'Lewis, you are just as welcome as the flowers in May', he declared to Brereton, and to Sutherland: 'Dick, they are going to give us everything we have asked for.'[3] The letter authorized MacArthur to defend the whole archipelago.

MacArthur's advocacy of the new plan was emotional rather than rational, but he was a man of sentiment. And he seems to have held himself aloof from

[1] Watson, p. 415.
[2] Morton, p. 62.
[3] Brereton, p. 19.

everyday staff problems and to have relied on hunches rather than on study and reflection to guide his decisions at this time and later. Despite his hard experience as an infantry leader in France and his reiteration when he was Chief of Staff of the necessity for stern training and indoctrination of officer and NCO cadres and the effectiveness of relatively small, highly-trained forces, he remained oblivious to the rigorous training, iron discipline and relentless drive of his Japanese opponents.[1] And his staff seem to have been no more aware of these circumstances, though they were common knowledge among interested readers of books and periodicals.

An Australian Minister, Earle Page, visited MacArthur on his way to London in September and was assured by the American commander that the war in China had overextended Japan, who would need 'a long period of recuperation before she could undertake another major struggle. She had gone to the limit of her southward expansion if she wished to avoid it, and under present conditions further expansion could be successfully resisted.'[2] Page listened to equally comforting words in Washington, where Marshall assured him that by early 1942 the American forces would 'constitute such a serious menace to Japan that she would be forced out of the Axis'.

For the change of outlook in Washington, Stimson wrote afterwards that there were two leading causes. 'One was the contagious optimism of General Douglas MacArthur', who 'knew the current situation in the Philippines better than any other American officer, and was surprisingly hopeful about the capabilities of his forces. The second reason . . . was the sudden and startling success of American Flying Fortresses in operations from the British Isles. Stimson found his military advisers swinging to the belief that with an adequate force of these heavy bombers the Philippines could become a self-sustaining fortress capable of blockading the China Sea by air power. . . . Both the optimism of General MacArthur and the establishment of an effective force of B-17s were conditional upon time. . . .' On 6 October Stimson told the Secretary of State, Cordell Hull, that three months were needed 'to secure our position'.[3]

Thus the radical change of policy was based on one man's optimism, an unproven estimate of the effectiveness of the B-17 high-level bomber, which, in fact, had not then been in action over Europe in force, and a calamitous underestimate of the numbers of aircraft and equipped airfields needed to

---

[1] In his report as Chief of Staff in 1935 MacArthur had written that 'relatively small forces exploiting the possibilities of modern weapons and mechanisms will afford in future emergencies a more dependable assurance of defense than will huge, unwieldy, poorly equipped and hastily trained masses'.

[2] L. Wigmore, *The Japanese Thrust* (Canberra, 1957), a volume in the official series *Australia in the War of 1939–45*, pp. 93–4.

[3] H. L. Stimson and McG. Bundy, *On Active Service in Peace and War* (New York, 1948), p. 193.

even impede a well-armed and resolute enemy.[1] Two months after Stimson spoke there would be only 61 of these heavy bombers at American bases outside the mainland of the United States and not many more at home. When MacArthur took command there were 22,000 officers and men of the United States Army including 12,000 Philippine Scouts, the main infantry formations being the Philippine Division (one American and two Philippine Scout regiments). This was a small force by comparison, for example, with the one which Britain had assembled in Malaya—eight Indian or Malay brigades (including five British battalions) and two Australian brigades. In the Philippines were 210 aircraft, but the only reasonably modern machines were 31 P-40 fighters. In Malaya were some 150 aircraft, but the fighters were all Buffaloes, poor performers compared with the P-40, and the bombers mainly Hudsons, slow medium bombers.

It was decided that the Philippine Army could not be mobilized immediately because there were not enough quarters to accommodate the 75,000 men called up to form the ten reserve divisions. So MacArthur ordered that the Filipinos be called up in contingents from 1 September until 15 December, when mobilization would be complete. On 1 September one regiment from each division and cadres of divisional units were assembled. Thus a conviction that troops could be assembled in peacetime only in cosy quarters was allowed not only to delay the assembly of the army as a whole but would produce formations in which some units within each division had been given far more training than others. And in 1936 MacArthur had enunciated as a basic principle 'simplicity in supply, messing and camping arrangements, and the development of the utmost endurance and hardihood'. Competent officers and NCOs would be only thinly spread among the divisions. 'To each division were assigned about 40 US Army officers and 20 American or Philippine Scout non-commissioned officers who served as instructors. The officers were usually attached to division and regimental staffs; the enlisted men served in battalions or companies.'[2]

Indeed, particularly in view of the sort of warfare the army might expect if the Japanese did attack, training in improvised camps and bivouacs would have been more effective, and a larger allocation of officers to fighting units would have been appropriate. MacArthur organized his forces into four commands: North Luzon Force (Major-General Jonathan M. Wainwright) of

[1] In the spring of 1941 20 B-17s were sent to Britain. By September they had between them made 39 sorties; only about half of the aircraft had reached their objectives and eight had been lost. On 6 December the Commander-in-Chief of Bomber Command said that they were 'not suitable as day bombers'. But the Americans considered that the B-17s had been flown too high and not 'in formations large enough to ensure a proper bomb pattern'. W. F. Craven and J. L. Cate *Plans and Early Operations January 1939 to August 1942* (1948), Vol. I in the US Official series, *The Army Air Forces in World War II*, pp. 600–4.

[2] Morton, p. 26.

four Philippine divisions was deployed in that part of Luzon north of the Manila area; South Luzon Force (Brigadier-General George M. Parker Jr) with two Philippine divisions was deployed in the remainder of the island; Visayan-Mindanao Force (Brigadier-General William F. Sharp) with three divisions was allotted the defence of practically all the remainder of the archipelago; Major-General George F. Moore commanded the harbour defences in Manila and Subic Bays. In an area round Manila was a general reserve including the Philippine Division of the US Army and the remaining Philippine division of the Philippine Army.[1] Thus Wainwright, with four raw divisions and a few other units had the task of defending the area, about 300 miles from north to south, in which the main enemy attacks were expected. MacArthur instructed him that there was to be 'no withdrawal from the beach positions', which were to be held 'at all costs'.

Last-minute efforts were made to improve the training of officers and NCOs. The defence scheme had been in operation for four years and a half but at this stage 'many of the officers and non-commissioned officers were untrained and unqualified for their assignments. There were some first sergeants and company clerks who could neither read nor write.' Morton illustrated the problems of mobilizing and training the army by describing the experiences of one division, Colonel Clifford Bluemel's 31st. Its 31st Regiment had been mobilized on 1 September, and its 32nd Regiment on 1 November (but did not join the division until 6 December). The division itself was formed on 18 November when mobilization of the ancillary units was begun. The third regiment, the 33rd, began to arrive on 25 November. The artillery regiment, whose mobilization had not begun on 7 December, was equipped with eight World War I 75-mm guns, and thus the division's artillery support was at about one-ninth of the strength usual in an infantry division in those days and one-third of the strength established for a Philippine division. There were few motor vehicles; even personal equipment 'left much to be desired'.[2] Indeed it now transpired that the training during the past years had been of little value. Not only were its basic concepts faulty but the modest objective at which it aimed—the elementary training of private soldiers—had evidently not been achieved. There had been time in four years and more to go far towards producing cadres of competent junior leaders, to equip and exercise units and formations, and to build up regimental spirit. For the inadequacy of the plan and the lassitude with which it was carried out MacArthur and his staff must be reckoned mainly responsible. It was their task to be constantly in the field overcoming inertia, giving guidance and assessing results. The optimism of MacArthur con-

[1] The ten reserve divisions were numbered the 11th, 21st and so on up to the 101st.
[2] Morton, p. 28.

cerning the potentialities of the Filipino troops leads to the inescapable conclusion that neither he nor his staff knew what was going on, or that the staff knew and chose not to inform the commander.

From August onwards the War Department agreed to all MacArthur's requests for reinforcements and strained to provide them. Indeed it offered MacArthur more than he sought: early in September he was offered a National Guard division but declined it. By early December he had received an anti-aircraft regiment, two tank battalions and altogether some 8,500 officers and men, mostly for air and depot units. By 1 December he had 35 of the B–17 heavy bombers of which so much was hoped, and 107 good P-40 fighters. The 4th Marine Regiment had arrived from China.

The War Plans Division at Washington had recommended that MacArthur be given overall command of the naval forces in the Far East. On the other hand Admiral Thomas C. Hart, commanding the United States Asiatic Fleet (comprising two cruisers, plus destroyers and submarines) maintained that the navy should have tactical command of army aircraft when they were operating against enemy ships in areas where American ships were present. This proposal MacArthur regarded as 'entirely objectionable'[1]; MacArthur's relations with Hart deteriorated, and Marshall in Washington was disturbed about this development.

Japanese intelligence had a fairly accurate knowledge of the size and quality of MacArthur's forces. In the plan Lieutenant-General Masaharu Homma of the Japanese Fourteenth Army was allotted only two divisions, one brigade and a regimental group to compass the conquest of the Philippines. Homma would have powerful naval cover and the support of some 500 naval and army aircraft. He was under instructions to complete the occupation of the archipelago in 50 days, whereupon part of his army would be needed for operations in Java.

[1] Watson, p. 451.

V

Defeat in the Philippines

1941–42

On 24 November 1941 a signal reached Admiral Hart from Washington stating that there were only slight prospects of an agreement being reached with Japan and that Japanese troop movements indicated the likelihood of attack 'in any direction'. Hart passed the message on to General MacArthur, who three days later received a warning from General Marshall that attacks by Japan were possible at any moment. The message added that the United States Government wished that Japan should 'commit the first overt act' but that this should not be construed as restricting MacArthur to a course that might jeopardize his defence. That day the Navy Department sent the commanders of the Pacific and Asiatic Fleets a 'war warning'—'An aggressive move by Japan is expected within the next few days.'[1]

MacArthur, Hart and Francis B. Sayre, the High Commissioner, conferred on the 27th and next day MacArthur signalled Marshall that reconnaissance had been intensified and everything was in readiness. In the next few days aircraft reported Japanese shipping movements towards Malaya, and unidentified aircraft were detected over Luzon. On the 5th, Admiral Sir Tom Phillips, the newly-appointed Commander of the British Far Eastern Fleet, arrived in Manila to confer with Hart and MacArthur. Next day a Japanese convoy was sighted steaming westward from Indo-China. Phillips promptly flew back to Singapore and MacArthur ordered Wainwright to get ready to deploy his forces against an invader.

About 3 a.m. on the 8th (Philippine time) Hart learnt that half an hour earlier a signal from Pearl Harbor had been picked up announcing that it was being attacked from the air. General Sutherland heard of the raid from a news broadcast at 3.30 and telephoned MacArthur. It was not until two hours later that MacArthur learnt from Marshall that war with Japan had begun.

[1] Morton, p. 71.

As mentioned, there were in the archipelago only two airfields that could handle the big B-17s—Clark Field, north of Manila, and Del Monte, 800 miles away in Mindanao. Some days earlier two of the four squadrons of B-17s had been flown to Del Monte to be out of harm's way. Sutherland said afterwards that he had ordered that all the B-17s be removed to Mindanao, but Brereton had not done this because he was expecting the second group of B-17s to arrive soon and there would not be room for this group as well as the four squadrons from Clark Field. The fighters, including four squadrons each with 18 P-40s, and one squadron with old P-35s, remained on four fields in Luzon. One response to the situation in Luzon early on the morning of 8 December would have been to have sent the B-17s straightaway against the Japanese airfields in Formosa. Brereton has recorded that he proposed this course at 5 a.m. and again at 7.15 and 10, but in vain. From 8 a.m. onwards the B-17s were in the air but without bombs. About 10 a.m. a reconnaissance of Formosa was authorized. Soon afterwards, according to Brereton, MacArthur ordered an attack on Formosa that afternoon, and by 11.30 the B-17s were back on Clark Field being armed.

Meanwhile Japanese bombers had been over Luzon but had turned north after attacking the summer capital of Baguio and other targets. The main force of 108 bombers and 84 Zeros, whose task was to raid the airfields in southern Luzon, had been delayed by fog over Formosa and did not set off until 10.15. An hour and a half later they were above Clark and the Iba fighter field. When these and later attacks were over the raiders had destroyed 18 of the 35 B-17s in the Philippines, 53 fighters and 25 to 30 other aircraft. They lost seven fighters.

The disadvantages of the plan to send the heavy bombers against the Formosan fields were that reconnaissance had been very limited, the bombers would not have escorts, the P-40s having only about half the range of the Japanese Zeros; and in any event there were not enough of them to do decisive damage. MacArthur later denied that he had authorized an attack on the Formosan fields. He wrote that 'an attack on Formosa, with its heavy air concentrations, by our small bomber force without fighter cover . . . would have been suicidal'.[1] Another course, and a wiser one, would have been to have flown the remaining B-17s immediately to Del Monte with at least part of the fighter force. Thence, using Clark as an advanced base, they might have done some damage to the Japanese convoys later on.

The air raids were followed by Japanese landings on Luzon at points remote from Manila: Aparri and Vigan in the north on the 10th and Legaspi in the south on the 12th. MacArthur believed that these landings were made

[1] *Reminiscences*, p. 120. When this was written in 1964 MacArthur evidently still believed that the Japanese fighters that were over Luzon had been flown from carriers.

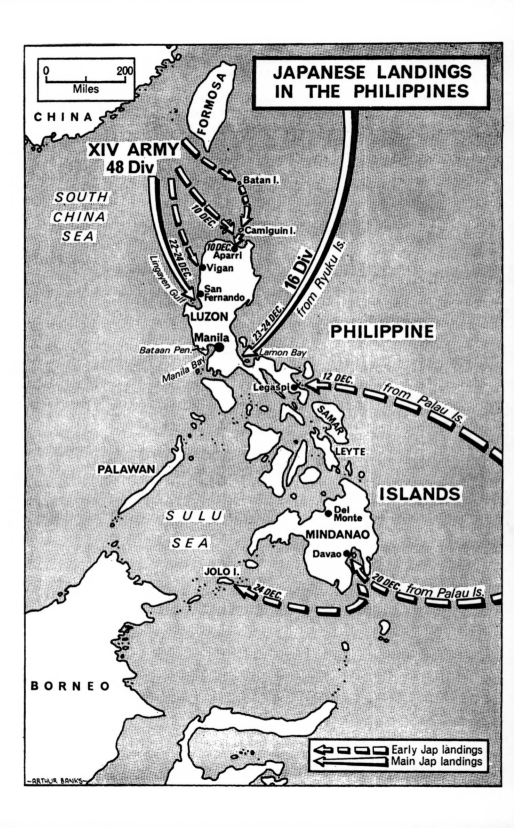

JAPANESE LANDINGS IN THE PHILIPPINES

CHINA

FORMOSA

XIV ARMY 48 Div

SOUTH CHINA SEA

Batan I.

10 DEC.

Camiguin I.

10 DEC.
Aparri

Vigan

22-24 DEC.

Lingayen Gulf

San Fernando

LUZON

Manila

Bataan Pen.

Manila Bay

Lamon Bay

23-24 DEC.

16 Div

from Ryuku Is.

PHILIPPINE

Legaspi

12 DEC.

from Palau Is.

SAMAR

LEYTE

ISLANDS

PALAWAN

SULU SEA

Del Monte

MINDANAO

Davao

20 DEC. from Palau Is.

JOLO I.

24 DEC.

BORNEO

0 — 200
Miles

~ARTHUR BANKS~

Early Jap landings
Main Jap landings

with the object of establishing airfields from which to cover major landings later.

When this new war broke out a convoy of seven vessels escorted by the cruiser *Pensacola* was on its way to Manila, carrying a field artillery brigade with 20 75-mm guns, ground staff for the second group of B-17s, 18 P-40s, 52 A-24 dive bombers and considerable stocks of ammunition. On the 12th the convoy was ordered to go to Brisbane instead and the commander of the troops, Brigadier-General Julian F. Barnes, was placed under MacArthur's command and ordered to get the troops, aircraft and supplies to the Philippines as soon as he could. MacArthur urged Hart to arrange for the escort of the convoy to Manila, with the help of Australian and Dutch naval and air forces, but Hart had to point out that this was not feasible; 'he seemed to be of the opinion that the islands were ultimately doomed', MacArthur said to Marshall.[1] About the same time MacArthur asked Washington for 300 fighters and 250 dive bombers; they could be flown in from aircraft carriers, he said. On the 15th Marshall assured MacArthur that aircraft would be rushed to the Philippines, and three days later he reported that early in January two more ships would unload aircraft in Australia, bringing the total to 230.

After Pearl Harbor, wrote the Secretary of War, Henry L. Stimson, 'the naval high command as a whole was shaken and nervous'.[2] They were indeed in no mood to send their carriers and cruisers on expeditions that must culminate in battles against superior enemy forces 3,000 or 4,000 miles from their own forward base. But MacArthur remained convinced that the navy could and should deliver a decisive counter-offensive that would halt the Japanese drive to the south and incidentally save the Philippines. As early as 10 December he had urged a foray by carriers against Japan itself so as to compel the enemy to withdraw the air forces that were covering the southern expeditions. Such a raid, undertaken in December, would have caused consternation in Tokyo and elation in Allied countries, but whether it would have persuaded the Japanese leaders to alter their timetable is doubtful.

By 13 December MacArthur was urging Marshall that the long-standing Allied decision to concentrate first on the defeat of Germany should be reversed and all available reinforcements used against Japan, which was 'completely susceptible to concentrated action'.[3] Alas, this proposal, like earlier ones, was evidence of the same lack of appreciation of Japanese sea power and the limited potential of the air forces then available in the United States as was his plan to defend the seas round the Philippine archipelago

[1] Quoted in Morton, p. 147.
[2] Stimson and Bundy, p. 199.
[3] Morton, p. 152.

with motor torpedo boats and counter a Japanese offensive with bomber raids from Philippine bases.

In the event, none of the men or equipment in the *Pensacola* convoy reached the Philippines. The ships arrived at Brisbane on 22 December and on the 28th the two fastest vessels sailed for Manila, but it was soon evident that they were not likely to get through safely. Artillery units on board were disembarked at Darwin or in Java.

MacArthur continued to press for naval action against the Japanese round the Philippines and the reinforcement of his air strength by planes flown from carriers. In December Marshall sent Brigadier-General Patrick J. Hurley, the former Secretary for War, and an admiring friend of MacArthur, to Australia to organize the running of supplies to the Philippines, but on the 23rd Marshall had to tell MacArthur that all he could expect would be aircraft flown from Australia or freighters from Australia, the ships presumably slipping through unescorted. In the event three supply ships reached the archipelago and by the 20th all the remaining B-17s had been flown to Batchelor Field near Darwin.

On 8 December mobilization of the Philippine Army had been almost complete. In the breathing space before the main landings a 1st Regular Division of the Philippine Army, mainly built round the training cadres, had been concentrated and allotted to the South Luzon Force; early in January a 2nd Regular Division would be formed from the Constabulary. After 8 December some Filipino formations were over-strength and surplus men were drafted into new units, including two regiments and two battalions of artillery armed with a total of about 80 guns hitherto lying idle. This belated organization of units that would need specially thorough and technical training was an odd commentary on the urgent requests during the previous months for more guns.

Soon after the Japanese onslaught opened MacArthur evidently decided that it had come too early for him to pursue his policy of defending the whole archipelago. On the 12th he informed President Quezon that if the Japanese landed in strength he would concentrate the army in the Bataan Peninsula, withdraw his headquarters and the government to Corregidor, and declare Manila an open city: in short, he would revert to the plan (War Plan Orange) that had been the accepted one up to the time of his appointment about four months earlier. Since MacArthur believed that the initial landings had been made with the object of providing air cover for a large-scale invasion—on 13 December Willoughby predicted that this would come in 15 days—MacArthur now faced three main tasks: first to transport great quantities of ammunition and food into Bataan; second to prepare for a series of rearguard actions to cover the withdrawal of his two Luzon forces into the peninsula;

and third to establish a defensive position across the neck of Bataan. The sooner the first task was begun the better, but MacArthur delayed a definite decision to withdraw into Bataan until the day after the main Japanese landings, and it was only then that the transfer of supplies began. This indecision and the loss of time it entailed was to exact heavy penalties. Throughout this period MacArthur behaved like an old-time fighter, recalled from retirement and suddenly thrust into the ring against a young and hard-hitting opponent whose lightning reflexes left him dazzled.

The task of conquering the Philippines, Thailand, Burma, Malaya and the Indies had been allotted by Japanese Imperial Headquarters to General Count Terauchi's Southern Army, which would have lavish naval and air support. It comprised four armies: the Fourteenth (two divisions, one brigade and one regimental group) aimed at the Philippines; the Fifteenth (two divisions) for Thailand and Burma; the Twenty-fifth (four divisions) for Malaya; and the Sixteenth (three divisions of which two would not be available until they had finished other tasks) for the Indies. Expeditions against Guam, Wake and New Guinea were tasks for a strong combined naval and army force controlled directly from Tokyo.

Lieutenant-General Homma's Fourteenth Army included the 48th Division, two of whose regiments were Formosan, and the 16th Division. One of the Formosan regiments had made the preliminary landings in north Luzon, and two battalions of the 16th Division, plus a battalion of marines, had made the preliminary landing in south Luzon. Homma then had only four infantry regiments left. He deployed three of these plus two regiments of tanks under the 48th Division at Lingayen Gulf and the other plus supporting units under the 16th Division in the south. On paper this was a flimsy force to fling against a defending army numbering nine divisions.

The choice of Lingayen Gulf for the main landings was not unexpected at MacArthur's headquarters. General Willoughby later recalled that in 1909 the American author Homer Lea in *The Valor of Ignorance* had predicted that the Japanese would land at Lingayen Gulf or Polillo Bight on the east coast or both, and converge on Manila. Willoughby said that 'the Lea forecast . . . formed the basis of plan and counter-plan in military and naval circles'.[1] Two Philippine divisions, the 11th and 71st, and the 26th Cavalry Regiment, a unit of the Philippine Scouts, were deployed round the shores of the gulf or close inland.

The main Japanese force was to land from 5 a.m. onwards at four points along a front of about 20 miles. Some 200 landing craft were used, ranging in size from small sampans to 50-foot craft carrying more than 100 men. The

[1] C. A. Willoughby and J. Chamberlain, *MacArthur 1941-51* (New York, 1954), p. 1.

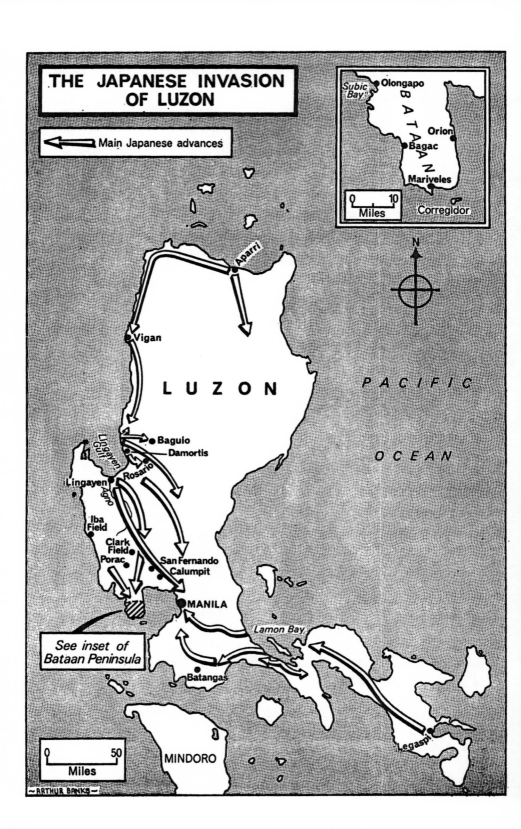

THE JAPANESE INVASION OF LUZON

← Main Japanese advances

BATAAN

Subic Bay
Olongapo
Orion
Bagac
Mariveles
Corregidor

0   10
Miles

N

Aparri

Vigan

L U Z O N

PACIFIC

OCEAN

Lingayen Gulf
Baguio
Damortis
Rosario
Lingayen
Agno
Iba Field
Clark Field
Porac
San Fernando
Calumpit
MANILA

See inset of Bataan Peninsula

Lamon Bay

Batangas

Legaspi

0   50
Miles

MINDORO

~ARTHUR BANKS~

first wave of troops was to fan out north (to link with the force that had landed in north Luzon ten days before) east and south and then concentrate on a thrust towards Manila. In stormy weather the transports dropped anchor in the gulf before dawn on the 22nd and between 5 a.m. and 8.30 the landing craft ploughed their way ashore through heavy seas and a surf which overturned many craft on the beach, stranding some of them and ruining signal gear. The landing of the second wave was delayed, but that day the tireless watermen got some artillery and tanks ashore. Once on land the infantry soon overcame the half-trained Filipino troops. An American submarine braved the shallow water of the gulf and sank a 5,000-ton minelayer, but that was all. Four Flying Fortresses from Darwin, having bombed the enemy base at Davao in Mindanao, flew on to Lingayen but made no hits.

General Homma was anxious. As a result of the loss of signal equipment he had had no reports from the troops ashore, and it was evident that the heavy surf had caused confusion; only one regiment of artillery had landed. Some of the staff urged a cautious policy of consolidating the beach-head and postponing the advance, but Homma decided to press on.

To stem the Japanese advance the 26th United States Cavalry and later the tank group were ordered to hold at Damortis, astride the coast road leading south, but only five tanks could be fuelled and sent forward in time and these were all hit by anti-tank guns. By evening the Japanese were in Damortis and American resistance was centring on the Rosario road junction towards which the fast-moving Japanese riflemen were then advancing along both the inland and the coast roads. Before the day was over the Japanese had thrust the cavalry regiment from Rosario, and next morning they held all their first objectives and were moving south through the central plain to Manila. The hopes that MacArthur had cherished about the Filipino Army had so far proved illusory. 'Only the Scouts of the 26th Cavalry had offered any serious opposition. . . . The untrained and poorly equipped Philippine Army troops had broken at the first appearance of the enemy and fled to the rear in a disorganized stream.'[1]

Next day was much the same. The 71st Division, astride the road south of Rosario, attacked by two Japanese battalions, which were reinforced in the afternoon by a tank and a reconnaissance regiment, and strafed from the air, was put to flight. New rearguard positions were taken up five to ten miles to the rear but that night the Japanese penetrated these, dispersing a regiment of the 91st Division, thrown into the battle from the Force reserve.

In the afternoon Wainwright had obtained MacArthur's permission to withdraw behind the Agno River, which flowed from the mountains to the head of Lingayen Gulf and which all roads to the south had to cross. The

[1] Morton, p. 136.

problem now was to hold astride these roads while the Bataan fortress was stocked and both the North and South Luzon Forces contrived what Mac-Arthur's staff described as a 'side slip' into the mountainous peninsula. On the 24th General Parker of South Luzon Force was appointed to organize the defence of Bataan with two Filipino divisions, one drawn from the North Luzon Force, the other from the South Luzon Force, and command in South Luzon passed to General Jones of the 51st Division. Already Mac-Arthur had prudently sent most of the well-trained Philippine Division into Bataan; but thus this regular formation would not be available to help in the critical task of covering the withdrawal.

On the 22nd MacArthur had told Marshall that he might have to with-draw into Bataan, and next day he gave Wainwright and the other com-manders definite instructions to this effect. In the message to Marshall, MacArthur had reported the proposals he had divulged to Quezon ten days before: that if he had to withdraw to Bataan he would declare Manila an open city and move his headquarters, the Philippine Government and office of the High Commissioner to Corregidor. Marshall promptly signalled his approval.

On the 25th Admiral Hart left Manila by submarine to join his main force, which had left Manila on the 14th and was already in the Indies. He did not pay a final call on MacArthur but sent him a message. The naval forces remaining comprised some submarines, soon to depart, and a few small vessels including six motor torpedo boats. Brereton had already joined his bomber force in Darwin. A small force of fighter aircraft remained on Luzon.

In South Luzon the Japanese had been no less successful. Here their reduced 16th Division had landed on 24 December at three points. Units of the South Luzon Force in the area—the 51st Division and the 1st Regular Regiment—were on the move at the time, as a result of orders from Manila, complicated by measures to halt the advance of the Japanese regiment that had landed at Legaspi on the 12th. By the end of the first day the Japanese were across the isthmus joining the main part of Luzon to its eastern lobe and poised to advance on Manila from the south and east.

The transfer of three divisions into Bataan left only three and the rem-nants of a fourth to carry out the withdrawal from the north, and one division plus a regiment in the south. Wainwright planned four successive rearguard positions from about the Agno River line southward down the valley through which ran the two main roads to Manila. The 91st Division was on the right, the 11th in the centre, and the 21st on the left. The Japanese attacked at the outset in two columns, a Formosan regiment plus a tank regi-ment on the right and the remainder of the division on the left. By 25

December the defenders had been pushed back to the Agno. Thence they were to withdraw each night in stages that could be covered by one night's march, until they were on a line about 15 miles north of the east–west road into Bataan; and there they were to hold until the South Luzon Force had moved through into the peninsula.

The Japanese were held on the Agno River line on the 25th and 26th, and then they halted to await the arrival of more artillery. By the 28th the defenders had made two strides southwards from the Agno and were on the last line but one. Here their role was to cause the Japanese to deploy for an attack and then move back to the final position before the attack got under way. That day MacArthur reported to Washington that his men were 'tired but well in hand'. He faced three Japanese divisions, he reported—actually only one. He planned to hold in the north until the South Luzon Force was in Bataan and then to 'pivot' North Luzon Force into the peninsula.

Now was Homma's opportunity to upset the American withdrawal by concentrating on cutting the road into Bataan. He knew of MacArthur's own withdrawal to Corregidor and the transfer of some troops to Bataan. But he had been set the task of taking Manila, and he obediently used his main force astride the eastern road leading to the capital and only a regimental group along the western route towards Bataan. Nevertheless on the night of the 29th the Japanese broke into the final rearguard position and next day were pursuing the 91st Division south of it. The withdrawal of South Luzon Force was endangered.

Meanwhile, under constant Japanese pressure, the two main components of South Luzon Force, the 51st Division and the 1st Philippine Regiment, had succeeded in extricating themselves through the isthmus south of Manila and were hastening north. On the 31st the 51st Division was moving through Calumpit, and the Philippine Regiment was preparing to follow that night. The South Luzon Force had got through, after a well-managed seven-day withdrawal of 140 miles, much of it through rugged country. It remained to pull back the rearguard that had been holding astride the roads leading into the peninsula. On the morning of the 31st Sutherland told Jones that he was in command of the medley of troops composing the rearguard, but failed to inform Wainwright of this. The consequent misconceptions were sorted out by the commanders concerned.

That afternoon Jones ordered a counter-attack by a company of tanks supported by artillery against a Japanese force, including their two tank regiments, that was evidently preparing a decisive breakthrough. The American tanks knocked out eight Japanese tanks and withdrew; after this the Japanese advanced more cautiously and by 1 January 1942 most of the organized troops on Luzon were either in Bataan or about San Fernando, on the western, less-threatened road, and the main body of Homma's army was pushing on towards undefended Manila, which he entered on 2 January.

A fighting withdrawal in the face of a mobile and aggressive enemy is a severe test of the discipline and skill of the best-trained troops. It demands uncommon coolness, careful timing, close coordination of all arms and exact obedience. That the two Luzon forces managed so well was evidence of good planning by MacArthur, Wainwright and Jones, fine leadership by the sprinkling of competent regimental officers, American and Filipino, increasing confidence here and there throughout the force, and the high quality of the few regular troops employed.

A more orthodox plan on MacArthur's part would have placed regular formations—including the Philippine Division, for instance—in the final rearguard position, and let the tattered Filipino divisions withdraw through fresh troops well dug in and ready to bring the Japanese drive to a sharp halt. But after ten days the Philippine Division had not been engaged.

From 2 to 6 January the final rearguards withdrew the last 15 miles or so into Bataan along the roads from San Fernando and Porac, pressed by a Japanese regiment on each route. Before dawn on the 6th the 26th Cavalry and the tanks crossed the last big river north of the neck of Bataan and the bridge was blown. Just south of the river astride the main road, at the suggestion of Colonel Casey, MacArthur's chief engineer, a final rearguard position had been established by a regiment of the Philippine Division, the object being to delay the enemy while the main body of the defending army continued to dig in along the main line of resistance farther south. The 26th Cavalry and two regiments of the weary 71st Division were also halted here but the Japanese allowed no respite. On the 6th one of the Formosan regiments attacked with strong artillery support, and next day the American delaying force withdrew.

In the complex withdrawal at least the skeleton of each formation had remained intact, but about 13,000 men had been lost, mainly as a result of the desertion of dispirited Filipinos from Wainwright's force.

The building up of supplies in Bataan had been only moderately successful. War Plan Orange required that supplies for 43,000 men for six months should be on the peninsula. But as a result of MacArthur's unwillingness to begin moving stocks before the main Japanese invasion opened, this was not achieved. Corregidor had rations for 10,000 men for six months, but Bataan only rations for 100,000 men for 30 days, and its military population was not the 43,000 contemplated in the plan but 80,000, and there were about 26,000 civilian refugees. Before the last troops were within the fortress MacArthur had placed the troops and civilians on Bataan and Corregidor on half rations—about 2,000 calories. On Bataan immediate steps were taken to secure local produce: cattle, fish and the still unharvested rice.

MacArthur now had on Bataan the Philippine Division, two regular Philippine Army divisions and seven Philippine Army reserve divisions, a formidable-sounding force with which to oppose Homma's army corps. And on 2 January the Japanese commander had been informed by Tokyo that the timetable for the invasion of Java had been advanced and his best formation, the 48th Division, which under the original plan he was to retain to the end of January, would be transferred to the Sixteenth Army straightaway. In return he was to receive the 65th Brigade (six battalions).

The Bataan Peninsula is 25 miles long and 20 miles wide at its neck. Along its spine jungle-clad mountains rise to 4,700 feet. On the eastern side the coastal plain is wide in the north but narrows to the south. On the west the mountains reach almost to the sea. There was a road along each coast and one east–west road linking them about halfway down the peninsula. The main line of resistance had a ten-mile sector on the east and a five-mile sector on the west, the two being separated by mountains rising to over 4,000 feet. MacArthur deployed his II Corps (General Parker) including four Philippine Army divisions and the Philippine Division on the right, and I Corps (General Wainwright) with one Philippine regular division, two Philippine Army divisions and other units and part of another one on the left. The southern end of the peninsula was named the Service Command Area, and there Brigadier-General Allan C. McBride had part of the depleted 71st Division and the 2nd Regular Division. Eight to ten miles south of the main line of resistance the troops in reserve were preparing a rear battle position on which a last stand would be made if the enemy broke through.

During the 15 days of the Japanese offensive in Luzon the Japanese had been gaining ground far and wide. Hong Kong had fallen on Christmas Day, Japanese forces had established bases on Jolo Island and in north Borneo. In Malaya in the four weeks since the first landings the Japanese Twenty-Fifth Army had advanced half way down the peninsula. On 27 December MacArthur had correctly predicted that the Japanese would extend their conquests into the Indies and complete the isolation of the Philippines. He urged that air forces be hurried to the south-west Pacific, that a sea route to Mindanao be kept open and troops landed there. Presumably he contemplated Mindanao playing the part he had intended that Luzon should play in his original plan: a base for a bomber offensive across the Japanese line of advance. Two days later the British general Wavell was placed in command of the American-British-Dutch-Australian area (ABDA), which embraced

Burma, Malaya, the Indies, the Philippines and part of northern Australia. One of Wavell's tasks was to hold the Malay Barrier, another to lend help to Luzon.

On 1 January MacArthur was again urging Marshall that the Allies should send sea, land and air forces through the Indies to Mindanao. On 7 January he elaborated his plan for reinforcing Mindanao, where, he said, 'an army corps should be landed at the earliest possible date ... time is ripe for a brilliant thrust with air carriers'.[1]

The previous day it had been decided to send an army corps from the Middle East to the Far East—the I Australian Corps from Syria—but its destination was Malaya, and towards Malaya was sailing also the 18th British Division, originally intended for Egypt. Apart from two Indian brigades and a British armoured brigade these were the only formations of Allied troops allotted to the Far Eastern theatre east of Burma before the fall of Java, and only the 18th Division arrived in time to be landed where originally intended.

Marshall gently encouraged MacArthur's expectations: aircraft were on the way; he hoped that the development of 'overwhelming air power' would permit 'an assault in the southern Philippines'. These comforting words left unanswered the question where the necessary air power and infantry were to come from, not to mention the naval forces needed to cover their movements.

The American leaders in Washington had not yet learnt that propaganda if deceitful either directly or by implication does more harm than good. Thus when President Roosevelt on 28 December had broadcast to the Filipinos that 'the United States Navy is following an intensive and well-planned campaign against Japanese forces which will result in positive assistance to the defense of the Philippine Islands', his hearers accepted this assurance without the mental reservations with which the politician must have justified his statement. The final result of this and similar propaganda from Washington was to deepen the final disillusionment and resentment of the people the messages were intended to encourage.[2]

The truth was that the American leaders had long ago reached the conclusion that there was nothing they could do to save the Philippines. Thus on 14 December Brigadier-General Eisenhower of Marshall's planning staff had reported to his chief:

General, it will be a long time before major reinforcements can go to the Philippines, longer than the garrison can hold out with any driblet assistance, if the

[1] Quoted in Morton, p. 239.
[2] R. E. Sherwood in *The White House Papers of Harry L. Hopkins* (London, 1949), p. 467, says that this message was sent in response to a request by MacArthur for something to offset the Japanese propaganda.

enemy commits major forces to their destruction. But we must do everything for them that is humanly possible. . . . Our base must be Australia, and we must start at once to expand it and to secure our communications to it. . . .[1]

Marshall had replied: 'I agree with you.' Nothing was gained by the weakness that Marshall displayed in continuing to encourage MacArthur's expectations and those of the people he led.

When the next phase opened both MacArthur and Homma were vastly ill-informed about the forces opposing them. MacArthur believed, and therefore so did Washington, that there were six Japanese divisions on Luzon; in fact there were two, one of which would soon depart and be replaced by a far smaller formation. Homma's staff told him that only 25,000 troops in poor shape were on Bataan—in fact there were three times as many. Homma decided that the reduction of Bataan would be easy and allotted this task to the new and inexperienced 65th Brigade (Major-General Akira Nara) plus a regiment from the 16th Division, nine battalions in all, supported by a tank regiment and a fairly powerful array of artillery. One column would break through the defenders' line in the east and another on the west, and then the main force would advance along the eastern coastal plain to Mariveles at the tip of the peninsula.

There was no delay. On the afternoon of 9 January Nara's artillery opened fire and the infantry advanced. The attack got away to a bad start. The Japanese believed the American line to be several miles north of its actual position, and attacked into thin air; worse still, the defenders' artillery fire was unexpectedly heavy. As a result there was little contact between the opposing forces in the eastern sector that day. And on the west the Japanese force was still moving south through undefended and unexplored territory and would not find itself poised to attack the main line until the 19th.

On the morning of the 10th MacArthur and Sutherland crossed over from Corregidor and visited the two corps commanders. Afterwards Sutherland expressed the opinion that the Japanese would move through the difficult country on the left of the eastern sector and not along the road, and advised both corps commanders to strengthen their inland flanks. Next day the corps commanders were expressly ordered to extend their front lines so as to cover the hitherto undefended mountains between them.

On the 11th the Japanese astride the east coast road were beaten back by a regiment of the Philippine Scouts, and elsewhere along the line their units lost their way on the jungle tracks and became disorganized. It was now evident to Nara that he had to cope with greater problems and stronger resistance than he had expected. He put his third regiment into the battle and, as Sutherland had predicted, began to make his main effort through the hills

[1] D. D. Eisenhower, *Crusade in Europe* (London, 1948), p. 25.

against Parker's inland flank. Here the Japanese met with such success that by the 15th Parker's reserves had been committed and the main line was in peril.

On the 15th MacArthur issued a rousing message to be read to all troops. It read in part: 'Help is on the way from the United States. Thousands of troops and hundreds of planes are being dispatched. The exact time of arrival of reinforcements is unknown as they will have to fight their way through Japanese attempts against them. It is imperative that our troops hold until these reinforcements arrive. No further retreat is possible.'

But having foreseen the danger of the open flank MacArthur's staff were not surprised when Parker that day asked for reinforcements from the Force reserve and promptly sent him the main body of the Philippine Division (one United States and one Philippine Scouts regiment) and a division from Wainwright's corps, which was still not under heavy attack. On the 16th a Filipino division on Parker's left gave way. He ordered the Philippine Division to counter-attack next morning with its two regiments forward, but only one of them found its way to its jumping-off position in time. At 8.15 a.m. on the 17th it advanced but was soon held. For the four days from the 18th to the 21st the two regiments attacked repeatedly but made few gains. The Japanese steadily drove back the left flank of Parker's corps while the 9th Japanese Regiment was advancing deep through the mountains still farther west and threatening to envelop the American line.

The Japanese were now executing a somewhat similar manœuvre against Wainwright's inland flank and by the 21st a battalion, advancing through the foothills of the central range, had established a block on the main road, thus severing the communications of most of the I Corps. Counter-attacks against the block failed and on the 25th the defenders began to trickle back on foot along the coast. Twenty-five field and mountain guns were abandoned and the corps was left with only six.

MacArthur did not visit Bataan again. On the 22nd he had sent forward Sutherland, who decided that the main line of resistance would have to be abandoned, and warned both Parker and Wainwright that they would receive written orders that night to pull back to the reserve line. MacArthur approved Sutherland's decision and signed the order. Next day he signalled Marshall that his heavy losses would force him soon to withdraw to a new line where he intended 'to fight it out to complete destruction'. He added gloomily that if he died Sutherland should succeed him.[1]

Covered by a rearguard force drawn from the Philippine Division and two Filipino divisions, and supported by the tank group, the weary men of the II Corps fell back under heavy pressure to the reserve line on the 24th and 26th, and by that time I Corps also was in the new position.

[1] Morton, pp. 291, 295.

The Japanese success had been won by three regiments each about 2,000 strong and they had lost 1,400 men in the 16-day battle. They now faced a shorter and more formidable line, from Bagac to Orion, along which were deployed in I Corps three divisions plus other units and in II Corps four depleted divisions. MacArthur's staff initially planned to withdraw the three regiments in the Philippine Division into force reserve, but Sutherland soon cancelled this arrangement and the two corps commanders retained their Philippine Scout regiments. This reversal of orders led to some confusion.

Before the American withdrawal was over Nara had embarked on a series of amphibious attacks on the south-west coast of the peninsula aimed at cutting the coast road far to the rear of I Corps. And on the 26th he renewed his offensives against both sectors of the main line. The seaborne attacks were made by two battalions of the 20th Regiment (from the 16th Division). On the night of 22–23 January one battalion was landed at two widely separated points on the coast. Such a move was not unexpected and the area was defended by a motley force of Philippine Constabulary and Filipino, naval and air force troops. The Japanese, put ashore at a place well south of the intended spot and in some confusion, were contained by a hastily assembled force and shelled by guns on Corregidor, but were resisting doggedly when on the night of the 26th a fresh company was sent in to reinforce them. It was landed well north of the right place and it too was contained. Then, on the moonlit night of 1 January, yet another procession of barges was seen moving south. As they approached the shore they were bombed and strafed by the four surviving P-40s of the defending air force and shelled by artillery, but about half the force, initially a reduced battalion, got ashore and joined the company already established at the northern landing place. Not until 8 February were the two raiding battalions finally wiped out except for 34 men who were removed by barges which made an otherwise unsuccessful attempt to take off the whole force.

Meanwhile the Orion–Bagac line had been under intermittent attack. The Japanese now deployed the weak 65th Brigade and the 9th Regiment on the east, and a force of some 5,000 men on the west. On the east a series of Japanese thrusts were held and on the night of 2 February Nara abandoned the attack and pulled his men back to the north bank of the Pilar River. On the west the Japanese broke through the American line and established three small pockets up to 1,000 yards behind it, but these were pushed back by 15 February and the American line remained intact.

Corregidor, which had been under intermittent air attack since 24 December, was now being shelled by heavy artillery from across the bay. When he moved to Corregidor MacArthur first established his headquarters in barracks on the summit of the island. This conspicuous target was soon destroyed by bombs and eventually the commander's offices and quarters were moved to the wide Malinta tunnels beneath whose arched roofs were crowded offices, hospital wards, storerooms and sleeping quarters. In and round the tunnel area MacArthur was a conspicuous figure, striding calmly about carrying a walking stick, smoking his corncob pipe, and dressed simply except for his gold-braided field-marshal's cap.

The Japanese force had now spent its strength. Already on 8 February Homma had ordered that the battle be broken off and the troops withdrawn for rest and reorganization well north of the American line. This manœuvre was completed a week later under cover of a mock attack. Meanwhile Homma had been asking Tokyo for reinforcements; but seven weeks were to pass before these arrived and the offensive was renewed. Four years later Homma declared at his trial for 'war crimes' that if MacArthur had attacked in mid-February he could have regained Manila 'without encountering much resistance on our part'. The defenders were now in good heart and generally in better shape than ever before. The forward units were patrolling aggressively. Some commanders favoured a counter-offensive aimed at least at regaining the original line. Such sentiments were understandable but nothing of substance would have been achieved by re-forming in the longer and more vulnerable position.

Before the lull began on Bataan the leaders in Washington had been considering the problem of extricating MacArthur from the Philippines. If he remained he would eventually have to take part in the inevitable surrender, and the capture of so eminent a leader was something to be avoided at all costs. The rations of the defenders of Bataan would last for only a few months more and, on past performances, as soon as the Japanese chose to concentrate, say, two fresh and full-strength divisions against Bataan, they would swiftly overcome the defenders; the reduction of Corregidor might take longer. On 4 February Marshall had sent a message to MacArthur saying that if only Corregidor remained 'the need for your services there might well be less pressing than at other points in the Far East'.[1] He added that there were two possible alternatives: transfer to Mindanao, where the defending forces—one Filipino division and some Constabulary—were intact, the Del Monte airfield was in American hands, and the Japanese had left only one battalion, concentrated round Davao; or transfer to Australia whence he could command all United States forces in the Far East. If MacArthur was withdrawn it would be on the direct order of the President.

Since the attack on the reserve line on Bataan had opened the Japanese had made spectacular gains on other fronts. On 31 January the British forces had withdrawn on to Singapore Island, against which the Japanese

[1] Quoted in Morton, pp. 353-4.

Twenty-Fifth Army launched an attack on 8 February. Singapore was surrendered on the 15th. Seaborne forces spread across a front of some 3,200 miles had seized Rabaul in New Guinea and Balikpapan on Borneo on 23 January, Kendari in Celebes on the 24th, Ambon on the 31st, Macassar on 9 February, Palembang in Sumatra on 14 February, Bali on 18 February. Now not only the Philippines were encircled but also Java.

Meanwhile on 8 February Quezon, with the approval of his Ministers, had sent a message through Marshall to Roosevelt proposing that the United States immediately grant the Philippines independence, that the islands be neutralized, the American and Japanese forces withdrawn, and the Philippine Army disbanded. In an accompanying message the High Commissioner, Sayre, said that if help could not arrive in time he supported these proposals. And MacArthur added a long dispatch warning Marshall that his forces were 'near done' and their 'complete destruction' might come at any time. 'So far as the military angle is concerned', he added, 'the problem presents itself as to whether the plan of President Quezon might offer the best possible solution of what is about to be a disastrous *débâcle*.'[1] The messages shocked Roosevelt, Marshall and Stimson, who wrote in his diary that Quezon's message was 'wholly unreal' and took no account of 'what the war was for or what the well known characteristics of Japan towards conquered people were'.[2] Marshall drafted a reply to MacArthur for the President's signature. In it Roosevelt authorized MacArthur to arrange for a capitulation of the Filipino elements of his forces if necessary, but added:

> American forces will continue to keep our flag flying in the Philippines so long as there remains any possibility of resistance. I have made these decisions in complete understanding of your military estimate that accompanied President Quezon's message to me. The duty and the necessity of resisting Japanese aggression to the last transcends in importance any other obligation now facing us in the Philippines.
>
> There has been gradually welded into a common front a globe-encircling opposition to the predatory powers that are seeking the destruction of individual liberty and freedom of government. We cannot afford to have this line broken in any particular theatre. As the most powerful member of this coalition we cannot display weakness in fact or in spirit anywhere. It is mandatory that there be established once and for all in the minds of all peoples complete evidence that the American determination and indomitable will to win carries on down to the last unit.

If the evacuation of Quezon and his Ministers appeared reasonably safe, the President added, they should go to America via Australia. He sent a

---

[1] Quoted in Stimson and Bundy, p. 201.
[2] Stimson and Bundy, p. 201.

stirring message to Quezon, assuring him that the United States and its 26 allies would fight on until 'the entire Axis system and the governments which maintain it' had been overcome.

MacArthur replied that they would fight on to the end; he had no intention of surrendering his Filipino troops. And on the 16th he was again urging an attack on the Japanese lines of communication. Five days later Marshall told him that the President was considering ordering him to transfer his headquarters to Mindanao, and on the 22nd MacArthur was informed that arrangements were in hand to appoint him to command of the Allied forces in the south-west Pacific, with headquarters in Australia, and that he was not to remain in Mindanao for more than a week.

MacArthur's 'first reaction was to try and avoid the latter part of the order, even to the extent of resigning my commission and joining the Bataan force as a simple volunteer', but Sutherland and the rest of the staff 'felt that the concentration of men, arms and transport which they believed was being massed in Australia would enable me almost at once to return at the head of an effective rescue operation'. MacArthur did not reply until 24 February when he sought leave to delay his departure.

> Unless the right moment is chosen for so delicate an operation a sudden collapse might result. These people are depending on me now; any idea that might develop in their minds that I was being withdrawn for any other reason than to bring them immediate relief could not be explained.[1]

In the last week of February first Quezon and then Sayre left Corregidor in submarines for Australia. On the 25th MacArthur was informed that he could decide the time of his departure and he replied that it would be about 15 March. Major-General George H. Brett, commanding United States Army Forces in Australia, was instructed to send three B-17s to Mindanao, and the navy to send a submarine to Corregidor. The communiqué of 8 March said that reports from reliable sources were that Homma had committed *harakiri*; and next day's communiqué announced that General Yamashita, whose Twenty-Fifth Army had taken Singapore, had been appointed to succeed Homma. There was no truth in these reports but they may have encouraged the weary and hungry defenders of Bataan and Corregidor. By 10 March the lull on Bataan had lasted for more than three weeks and MacArthur decided that 'the right moment' had arrived. Instead of awaiting the submarine, not due from Australia until the 15th, he resolved to embark part of his staff and his family for Mindanao in four motor torpedo boats. He took with him his wife, his small son and a Chinese nurse, 16 officers and his secretary. The officers included Sutherland, Marshall, Willoughby, and his

[1] *Reminiscences*, pp. 140-1.

senior signals, engineer, anti-aircraft and air officers. The boats left Corregidor at 9.15 p.m. on the 12th and reached northern Mindanao at dawn on the 14th. Major-General William F. Sharp, the commander of troops in the southern islands, took the party to Del Monte airfield. Only one of the four B-17s flown from Darwin had arrived, and it was so decrepit that Sharp had sent it back empty. Other aircraft arrived on the 16th and MacArthur and his party took off in two of them soon after midnight on the 17th, reaching Batchelor Field at 9 a.m. that day.[1]

Soon after his arrival MacArthur told newspaper reporters that he understood he had been ordered to Australia to organize an offensive the principal object of which was to relieve the Philippines. 'I came through', he said, 'and I shall return.'

When he learned of MacArthur's arrival Brett telephoned the Australian Prime Minister, John Curtin, and in accordance with instructions from the President informed Curtin that MacArthur had arrived and had assumed command of United States Army Forces in Australia. He added that it would be 'highly acceptable' to the President and 'pleasing to the American people' if the Australian Government nominated MacArthur as Supreme Commander of all Allied forces in the south-west Pacific. That day the Australian War Cabinet agreed to this proposal and Curtin informed Washington and London accordingly.

Meanwhile in the fortnight before MacArthur's departure for Australia the Japanese had conquered the Indies. Wavell's ABDA Command had been dissolved on 25 February. By 1 March, in a series of encounters disastrous to the Allies, almost all the vessels of the combined American-British-Dutch-Australian cruiser and destroyer force had been sunk. On the day of MacArthur's embarkation the army in Java had been surrendered.

Resistance would henceforth be controlled from three widely separated bases: India, where Wavell was in command of the land forces; Australia, where MacArthur was to become supreme commander; and Hawaii, whence Admiral Nimitz directed his Pacific Fleet, the most powerful single threat to the new Japanese Greater East Asia Co-prosperity Sphere.

MacArthur's leadership in the Philippines had fallen short of what might have been expected from a soldier of such wide experience and one held in such high esteem. In the training of the Philippine Army he and his staff had achieved far less than they might have done in the six years up to December

---

[1] In his *Reminiscences* MacArthur describes how the aircraft were pursued from Timor onwards by Japanese dive bombers and fighters, which attacked Batchelor ten minutes after he had left in another plane for Alice Springs in the south; but there is no record of a raid on a Darwin airfield on either the 17th or 18th.

1941, but MacArthur does not seem to have been aware how unready the Filipino troops were. In his strategical counsels, dispatched week after week to Washington, he failed to comprehend the limitations of American sea power or the extent of the ground organization needed by a big bomber force. The relief of the Philippines was primarily a naval problem and the depleted Pacific Fleet lacked the means of mounting a successful expedition into distant waters commanded by the navy that, by January 1942, was the most powerful in the world, and had demonstrated its skill in sea–air warfare and night operations, and the deadly effectiveness of its torpedoes. When coping with his local task, his failure on 9 December or thereabouts to order prompt transfer of supplies into Bataan seems to have been based on sentiment rather than reason. And when the battle for Bataan was being fought he seems not to have realized the importance of the front-line troops seeing their commander. This was strange in view of his record as a front-line leader in France in 1918. 'The commander', wrote General Alexander, then MacArthur's opposite number in Burma, 'should ensure that his troops shall see him.' It was particularly desirable that 'the battling bastards of Bataan' should see their leader.

> *No mama, no papa, no Uncle Sam;*
> *No aunts, no uncles, no cousins, no nieces;*
> *No pills, no planes, no artillery pieces.*
> *... And nobody gives a damn.*

Another Bataan ballad that began:

> *Dugout Doug MacArthur lies ashaking on the Rock*
> *Safe from all the bombers and from any sudden shock*

was unjust, but it is part of the business of the good general to make sure that the opportunity to perpetrate such libels does not occur to anyone.

And Willoughby has described how the men on Corregidor were impressed and encouraged by MacArthur's coolness under the devastating air and artillery bombardment to which the fortress was subjected. 'His quixotic defiance of the enemy was not an exhibition of Renaissance Italian bravado, but the subtle application of psychology. It was intended as a deliberate act of leadership. To dare the bombs in a sally to the open is a commander's bitter privilege. *Noblesse oblige!* The men liked it. The subtle corrosion of panic or fatigue, or the feeling of just being fed-up, can only be arrested by the intervention of a true commander....'[1]

The continued resistance of the force on Bataan after Singapore and the Indies had fallen made heartening news among the Allied peoples. But, as we have seen, this extension of time was very largely a result of the transfer of the

---

[1] Willoughby and Chamberlain, pp. 37, 43.

48th Division from Homma's army at a critical time, and the exhaustion of the weakened force that remained. It cost a far stronger Japanese army as many days of actual combat to take Malaya and Singapore Island as it cost Homma to take Bataan and Corregidor. Willoughby's assertion after the war that the 'epic operation in Bataan and Corregidor became a decisive factor in the ultimate winning of the war', that it disrupted the Japanese timetable 'in a way that was to prove crucial', and that, 'because of Bataan the Japanese never managed to detach enough men, planes, ships, and material to nail down Guadalcanal' are contradicted by simple facts of history, geography and arithmetic. So far from allowing the operations on Luzon to upset their general timetable, the Japanese took steps that resulted in prolonging the resistance of Luzon in order to speed up their conquest of the Indies. And between the time of their advance into the Solomons and the American counter-landing on Guadalcanal in August, three months after the fall of Corregidor, they had ample troops available to build up their strength in the South Seas.

By mid-March two main tasks lay immediately ahead of the Japanese and they did not expect them to be hard ones: to complete the conquest of Burma and cut the Burma Road, and to reduce Bataan and the island fortress of Corregidor in the Philippines.

The reason why the Japanese had achieved their objectives so swiftly and at such small cost in blood and equipment was simply that at every level and in almost every department they surpassed their enemies. Their strategy and their higher tactics had been superior to their opponents'. In the western Pacific and round the Indies their naval forces were not only overwhelming in size but more efficient than those of the Allies. Their fighter aircraft in particular and their pilots were far better than had been expected. Their troops were for the most part battle-hardened, well trained for the tasks they were given, and capable of rare feats of endurance. Their landings of whole armies on surf beaches were of a magnitude then only dreamt of in the West. The Allied naval forces in the Far East were ill-balanced and uncoordinated, and so weak in numbers that if each ship had gone to the bottom taking a Japanese ship with it the loss to the Japanese would not have been crippling. Their air forces were weak in fighters; their bombers achieved some notable successes, but by the end of February the Japanese had lost from all causes only 38 merchant ships despite the great size of their many convoys, the distances they had to cover and their slow speed.

On land the strongest resistance had come from Western troops or well-indoctrinated Asian regulars. If the defending armies had mainly comprised trained European troops the invaders would have undoubtedly suffered some serious setbacks, but in Malaya, the Philippines and Java the defending troops were mainly Asians, many of whom had not much stomach for a war against troops who were not only Asians too but soon proved to be deadly opponents.

In every area some Asian troops as well as civilian leaders soon changed over to the Japanese side. It was ironical that the Japanese forces whose destruction of Western power in East Asia had the effect finally of releasing the East Asian people from Western government were by temperament and training so ill-equipped to win friends on the Asian continent and in the Indies. Soon they were to prove far harsher overlords than the Europeans had been.

VI

Securing Papua

1942–43

MacArthur with his family and his aides travelled from Alice Springs in central Australia by rail, while the others of the staff flew to Melbourne, the site of the headquarters of the Australian Navy, Army and Air Force and of General Brett. At Alice Springs he was met by Patrick J. Hurley. Hurley spoke encouraging words: the Americans had always had a hero; in their life-time there had been Dewey, Pershing, Lindbergh; the people had now taken MacArthur to their hearts. 'You are the hero.'[1]

Among the officers who had flown to Melbourne was Brigadier-General R. J. Marshall, who returned to meet MacArthur in Adelaide (where the 7th Australian Division was then arriving from the Middle East) with at last some detailed information about the forces assembling in Australia.

It appears that Marshall reported that there were only 25,000 American troops in the country, and most of these were in air corps, anti-aircraft and base units. There were some 260 American aircraft, many of them un-serviceable. A message had arrived from General Marshall in Washington describing the command arrangements and informing MacArthur that the American air units in his command—nine groups including two of heavy bombers—would be brought up to full strength, and the 41st and the 32nd Divisions would be sent to Australia. For the time being shortage of ships and 'critical situations elsewhere' would limit army forces in the south-west Pacific to these divisions.

One of MacArthur's biographers implies that MacArthur was informed that the Australians were 'in a state of near panic' and planned to withdraw to a 'Brisbane Line', 'leaving all the northern ports open to the Japanese'.

This news literally stunned MacArthur. He turned deathly white, his knees buckled, his lips twitched.... After a long silence, MacArthur whispered

[1] Lee and Henschel, p. 160.

miserably 'God have mercy on us'. Unable to sleep he spent the whole night pacing the train.[1]

At Spencer Street railway station in Melbourne MacArthur was welcomed by service leaders, a guard of honour and some thousands of onlookers. He was wearing his field-marshal's cap, shirt with no medal ribbons and well-creased trousers. His short speech into the microphone ended with the words: 'My success or failure will depend primarily upon the resources which our respective governments place at my disposal. My faith in them is complete. In any event I shall do my best. I shall keep the soldier's faith.'

A few days later he drove to Canberra to meet the Australian Prime Minister (and leader of the Labour Party) John Curtin, a sensitive, dedicated and resolute leader with whom MacArthur 'came to a sense of mutual trust, cooperation, and regard that was never once breached by word, thought or deed'. Their relations were not to prove quite as smooth as that; but it is true that in the next three years Curtin gave him unqualified support, sometimes against the counsel of his own senior commanders. 'Mr Prime Minister', said MacArthur, 'we two, you and I, will see this thing through together. . . . You take care of the rear and I will handle the front.'[2]

In Canberra the American Ambassador, on behalf of the American President and Congress, at a brilliant ceremony, presented MacArthur with the Medal of Honour, the high decoration for which he had twice before been recommended. The citation read:

> For conspicuous leadership in preparing the Philippine Islands to resist conquest, for gallantry and intrepidity above and beyond the call of duty in action against invading Japanese forces, and for the heroic conduct of defensive and offensive operations on the Bataan Peninsula. He mobilized, trained and led an army which has received world acclaim for its gallant defense against a tremendous superiority of enemy forces in men and arms. His utter disregard of personal danger and under heavy fire and aerial bombardment, his calm judgment in each crisis, inspired his troops, galvanized the spirit of resistance of the Filipino people and confirmed the faith of the American people in their armed forces.

The circumstances leading up to this award tend to contradict the gossip that General Marshall was not personally as well disposed as could be expected towards MacArthur. On 30 January Marshall had asked Sutherland to report any act for which MacArthur might be awarded the medal. There was no reply. In February two Congressmen introduced a Bill to award the medal. Marshall again asked MacArthur's staff to write a citation but they said they preferred Marshall to do so, and he did. Later in the year Mac-

[1] Lee and Henschel, p. 161.
[2] *Reminiscences*, p. 151.

Arthur refused Marshall's suggestion that he should recommend Wainwright for the same honour. 'His animosity towards Wainwright was tremendous', Marshall said later.[1]

In Canberra on 26 March MacArthur, accompanied by Sutherland and Brigadier-General Marshall, attended a meeting of the Advisory War Council, which comprised members of the Ministry and representatives of the Opposition parties. He told this body that he doubted that the Japanese would invade Australia, where 'the spoils were not sufficient to warrant the risk'. They might make raids and try to secure air bases on the continent. The Japanese had over-extended themselves and were gambling on gaining quick and decisive results while the democracies were unprepared. The Allies should concentrate sufficient forces in the Pacific to strike a decisive blow in one place, and should take a chance in other theatres. The Allies were not able to send much help to Russia and could not yet invade Europe. In the meantime they should concentrate against Japan. He favoured a concentration of a United States–United Kingdom fleet for an offensive against this enemy. He urged his hearers to maintain the view that the Pacific was the predominant theatre.

Views of this kind, which MacArthur would put forward with increasing emphasis in later months, ran counter to the accepted Allied policy of beating Hitler first, meanwhile maintaining an active defensive attitude towards Japan.

In Washington Admiral King was not opposing the general policy of concentrating against Germany, but was strenuously arguing that the needs of the Pacific theatres were being dangerously neglected. Thus, three days after MacArthur's statement to the Australian political leaders, King was arguing that the movement of army units and particularly air units to the Pacific be given priority because the needs of the Pacific were 'more urgent in point of time'. Thus, as an American historian has written, to carry out the policy of building up forces in Britain 'would require the President to overrule the two senior American officers that were preoccupied with strategy in the Pacific'.[2]

For a while Roosevelt was inclined towards yielding to King, and on 29 April told the Pacific War Council that he wished to increase the aircraft assigned to MacArthur to 1,000 (as MacArthur had sought) and the American combat troops there to 100,000; but ten days later he was persuaded that this was inadvisable and the build-up in the British Isles must not be slowed down. In the meantime a Japanese setback in the south-west Pacific had temporarily reduced the dangers King had underlined.

[1] F. C. Pogue, *Ordeal and Hope 1939-42* (New York, 1966).
[2] Matloff and Snell, pp. 211, 216.

Of MacArthur in the first few months after his arrival in Australia there are two pictures, one often in contradiction of the other. To the public he was presented, as in the citation for the Medal of Honour, as a dynamic and resolute leader whose troops in the Philippines were still resisting, though Singapore and Java had fallen. His public announcements were eloquent and stirring. His words and demeanour immensely impressed the Australian political leaders and people. One of Roosevelt's reasons for transferring MacArthur to Australia had been that he was disturbed about the morale of the Australians.[1] His arrival certainly had an invigorating effect, but whether the morale of the cool and enthusiastic Australian people was in urgent need of stimulus is doubtful, though there is evidence that the spirit of some political leaders needed to be calmed. The other picture shows a tired commander, bitterly disappointed to find that his dream of leading a ready-made force promptly back to Luzon was not to be realized, resentful of the failure of Washington to give him the forces he wanted, and fearful lest his new base should suffer the same fate as the old one.

It was perhaps not unreasonable of MacArthur to imagine that the United States and their allies might have concentrated in Australia in the past four months a big force of trained and equipped troops supported by a powerful air force. The expanded American Army had been in being since 1940. By mid-1941 it included 33 divisions, including eight of regular infantry and four armoured, and there were 160,000 men in the air corps. How different from 1917!

But the Japanese had put the equivalent of five divisions on the sea in the first fortnight of war. In four months only four American divisions, two of them incomplete, had been embarked, one for New Ireland, one for New Caledonia, one for Hawaii and one for Australia.

On the other hand MacArthur's estimates had left out of account the time needed by a nation on a peacetime footing to assemble shipping, the length of the haul across the Pacific, the size of the necessary overseas base organizations and the unreadiness of the American staffs to cope with immense new problems. Already the inadequacy of the training of officers and men in both their land and air forces was being revealed.

Meanwhile, before command arrangements in his new area could be completed, MacArthur's status vis-à-vis his generals in the Philippines had to be sorted out. Before he left the Philippines he had reorganized the commands there into four, each of which would be directly responsible to him from his new base in Australia. He placed General Wainwright in command of all troops on Bataan, General Moore of the harbour defences of Manila Bay, Brigadier-General Bradford G. Chynoweth of the forces in the Visayas (the

[1] Sherwood, p. 514.

central islands of the archipelago), and General Sharp of those on Mindanao. He left Colonel Lewis C. Beebe, a senior administrative officer of his staff, on Corregidor in charge of an advanced headquarters of USAFFE, but Beebe would be responsible only for supply; operations would be controlled from the headquarters in Australia.

In his last instructions to Wainwright he told him that he was determined to come back as soon as he could with as much as he could, and urged him to organize the defence in depth and 'give them everything you've got with your artillery. That's the best arm you have.'[1] He urged Moore to hold Corregidor until he should return, and instructed him to reserve half rations for 20,000 men until 30 June to feed the Philippine Division, which was to be transferred to Corregidor if Bataan could not be held.

Inexplicably MacArthur omitted to inform his superior, Marshall, of these command arrangements, and the War Department assumed that after 12 March Wainwright was in general command in the Philippines, addressed him as such, and promoted him lieutenant-general. It was not until 21 March that MacArthur explained the set-up to Marshall, who pointed out to the President that it was 'unsatisfactory'—an understatement—and, in any event, under his instructions MacArthur, as Supreme Commander, might not directly command any national force. MacArthur then agreed that Wainwright should be in command of all forces in the Philippines. Wainwright moved his headquarters to Corregidor and appointed General King to the Bataan force.

To understand the situation that faced MacArthur in Australia it is necessary to trace decisions made in the previous three months. As mentioned, soon after the outbreak of war with Japan the American leaders had decided to establish a military base in Australia. On 17 December, Marshall had agreed to Eisenhower's proposals that initially only an air base be established. It was appropriate that eventually a senior air corps officer, General Brett, should be appointed to command it.

In the last week of December and the first part of January Roosevelt, Churchill and the British and American chiefs of staff had thrashed out a common strategic policy. The basic principle was still to concentrate first against Hitler's Germany. So far as the south-west Pacific was concerned a chain of bases across the Pacific was to be garrisoned with small forces; and some 30,000 troops, mainly air, anti-aircraft and base personnel, were to be sent to Australia.

On 14 February, when the fall of Singapore was imminent, General Wavell had raised the question of diverting one or both of the divisions of I Australian Corps, then allotted to the Far East, to Burma or Australia. And

[1] J. M. Wainwright, *General Wainwright's Story* (New York, 1946), p. 4.

in this crisis American policy of restricting the American force in Australia more or less to air, artillery and depot troops was suddenly changed, and the 41st American Division was ordered there. Already, early in March, Churchill had asked Roosevelt to send two more United States divisions to the south-west Pacific so that Australia and New Zealand could be persuaded to leave the 9th Australian and the New Zealand Divisions in the Middle East. Roosevelt replied that the 41st Division would soon sail for Australia, where most of it would arrive in April, and that another division would sail in April and May. This would be the 32nd.

By this time American infantry units that would eventually be augmented and formed into the 'Americal Division' had gone to New Caledonia by way of Australia, and the Australian Government had insisted on the diversion of I Australian Corps to Australia, though at its suggestion two brigades of the 6th Division were to be left temporarily in Ceylon.

Indeed, in spite of the basic strategy, far more American troops were sent to the south-west Pacific in the first four months of 1942 than to the Western theatre: 79,000, of whom 57,000 were to land in Australia (though some 5,000 of these soon went on to Java and India).

Thus in the five weeks between MacArthur's departure from Corregidor and his formal assumption of command in Melbourne the forces available to him had been notably reinforced: in March and April the veteran 7th Australian Division and the 6th less two brigades, and early in April most of the United States 41st Division.

General Sir Thomas Blamey, who had commanded the Australian Imperial Force in the Middle East and latterly had been also Deputy Commander-in-Chief there, arrived home on 23 March and on the 26th was appointed Commander-in-Chief of the Australian Army. By 9 April Blamey had reorganized the army in Australia so that it comprised: First Army (Lieutenant-General J. D. Lavarack, who had commanded the Australian Corps in the Syrian operations), Second Army (Lieutenant-General Sir Iven Mackay, who had commanded the 6th Division in North Africa and Greece and later the home forces in Australia), III Corps (Lieutenant-General H. G. Bennett, who had commanded the 8th Australian Division in Malaya), Northern Territory Force (Major-General E. F. Herring, commander of the 6th Division), New Guinea Force (Major-General B. M. Morris). These formations included one armoured, two motorized and seven infantry divisions.

MacArthur's appointment was part of a world-wide reorganization of Allied commands that had been agreed upon a few days before he reached Australia. There would henceforth be three main theatres: Pacific, directed by the United States Joint Chiefs of Staff; Indian Ocean and Middle East, directed by the British Chiefs of Staff; and European-Atlantic, a joint responsibility of the American and British Chiefs of Staff. The Pacific theatre was divided into two main areas: Pacific Ocean, including a south, a central and a north Pacific area; and the south-west Pacific, including Australia, New Guinea, and northern Solomons, the Philippines and most of the Indies.

On 1 April MacArthur was presented with a directive approved by the combined British and United States Chiefs of Staff, which instructed him to hold the 'key military bases of Australia as bases for future offensive action', to check the enemy advance across Australia and Australia's essential lines of communication, to maintain the position in the Philippines, to destroy enemy vessels carrying raw materials from the conquered areas to Japan, and so on. All instructions to MacArthur would come through the United States Chief of Staff.

It was not until 18 April, a month after his arrival, that agreement to his directive had been reached by the participating governments and they had allotted their combat forces to his command. On that day he assumed his new command and circulated General Order No. 1, which announced that his immediate subordinates would be:

Commander Allied Land Forces, General Sir Thomas Blamey
Commander Allied Air Forces, Major-General George H. Brett
Commander Allied Naval Forces, Vice-Admiral Herbert F. Leary
Commander United States Forces in the Philippines, Lieutenant-General Jonathan M. Wainwright
Commander United States Forces in Australia, Major-General Julian F. Barnes.

Next day MacArthur named his senior staff. All except three were drawn from those who had come with him from the Philippines. On 9 April Marshall had suggested to MacArthur that a number of the higher positions on his staff should be given to Dutch and Australian officers. When he learned of MacArthur's appointments, Marshall again urged him to appoint Australian and Dutch officers, but MacArthur declined to do so, finally stating that there was no prospect of obtaining qualified senior staff officers from among the Australians, who did not have enough to meet their own needs. On the other hand an Australian official historian has written:

There is no record of MacArthur having asked Blamey to provide senior staff officers; yet there were in the Australian Army many senior specialists in each branch of staff work who were at least the equals of the Americans in military education and had the advantage of experience in recent operations in Africa, Europe and Asia.[1]

[1] D. McCarthy, *South-West Pacific Area First Year: Kokoda to Wau* (Canberra, 1959), p. 29.

Rather than form a general headquarters on which all three services were represented, MacArthur chose to direct operations through a staff that, at its upper layers, was drawn entirely from the United States Army. The naval, land and air headquarters was each housed either in close proximity to or in the same building as GHQ. One result of this arrangement, according to Brett, was that MacArthur, who 'did not have a full appreciation of air operations', also did not have a senior air officer on his immediate staff, that 'lack of command and staff meetings resulted in directives difficult to interpret. Orders were issued without discussing them with those who had to carry them through.' Brett 'found the same reaction' from Leary and Blamey.[1]

Within his own command Brett himself followed a very different policy. He created an Allied staff on which, for example, his chief of staff was an Australian but his deputy chief of staff American, his director of operations American but director of Intelligence an Australian, and so on.

Blamey's staff as Commander Allied Land Headquarters was an amalgam of the staff of Australian Army Headquarters as it had been on his return to Australia, and the former staff of the Australian Imperial Force in the Middle East. He seems to have taken no steps to create the sort of Allied staff that Brett had set up, but it is difficult to see whence at that stage an American component for such a staff would have been drawn.

When Blamey was appointed Commander Allied Land Forces he retained his appointment as Commander-in-Chief of the Australian Army, and thus, according to one of his critics, 'attempted to wear two pretty big hats at the same time, a feat rendered all the more difficult by the geography of the theatre'.[2] As Commander-in-Chief Blamey was the Australian Government's senior military adviser and responsible for the supply, training and other rearward echelons of the Australian Army that had not been allotted to MacArthur. As MacArthur's commander of land forces he controlled all the fighting formations of MacArthur's army, whether Australian or American. It was as though in Western Europe General Brooke had been at the same time Chief of the British General Staff and Commander of the Allied army group invading the Continent.

In theory this assumption of two roles was all wrong and Blamey should have chosen one appointment or the other. In practice it had solid advantages. It resulted in the Australian Government having one senior military adviser who was also the commander of all the Australian troops. With the Australian air force a different policy was eventually followed. The authority of the Australian Chief of the Air Staff was restricted to administration, supply and training, and he was responsible to the Minister for Air; an independent

[1] G. H. Brett (with Jack Kofoed), 'The MacArthur I Knew', *True*, October 1947.
[2] E. G. Keogh, *South-West Pacific 1941-45* (Melbourne, 1965), p. 143.

RAAF Command was established which contained most of the fighting part of the force and whose commander was responsible to Brett. In the upshot there were constant disputes between the two Australian officers concerned, and to solve this problem the Australian Government sought the appointment of a senior RAF officer, Australian-born preferred, who would have occupied a dual role similar to Blamey's in the army, but this solution was not acceptable to MacArthur.

In retaining both commands Blamey may have been looking ahead. It was likely that eventually Americans would outnumber Australians. When this happened, or earlier, the continuance of an Australian as commander of Allied Land Forces would not have been politically acceptable in the United States or militarily desirable in the south-west Pacific, and some arrangement would need to be made whereby American forces operated entirely under their own commanders. It will be seen that soon after the arrival of an American army commander and staff such a situation was brought about.[1]

Incidentally, according to American Army doctrine as of 1921, the Chief of Staff probably would himself serve as commanding general of the field force and move into the field in a major theatre of operations, presumably overseas or at least outside the boundaries of the United States. The assumption in the 1920s was that, once there, he would follow General Pershing's practice of directing operations in virtual independence of the War Department, which in turn would devote all energies to the zone of interior functions of mobilizing men and material resources. Since it was to be hoped that he would either retain his position as Chief of Staff or be succeeded in that position by the incumbent Deputy Chief of Staff, friction between the army in Washington and at general headquarters overseas could be controlled and minimized.[2]

Thus MacArthur, with his feeling of isolation and neglect, drew closely about him the small and devoted staff that had served him so long, and was disinclined to dilute it with outsiders; the outgiving Brett had organized a truly Allied staff; but Blamey's headquarters was almost entirely Australian. A few months later, when General Eichelberger was being briefed before leaving Washington to command a corps in Australia, he was told that MacArthur had been asking for American officers to help the Australians with their staff work. Evidently MacArthur's intention in asking for these officers was to establish a substantial—and appropriate—quota of Americans within Blamey's headquarters. When Eichelberger arrived in Australia he

---

[1] Later in the year MacArthur's air commander also assumed two hats: he became commander of a new Fifth Air Force while commander of AAF, and thus was in a situation similar to Blamey's.

[2] Ray S. Cline, *Washington Command Post: the Operations Division* (Washington, 1951), a volume of the official series *United States Army in World War II*.

discovered that: 'The Australians didn't think they needed much help from anyone. Many of the commanders I met had already been in combat . . . in North Africa and, though they were usually too polite to say so, considered the Americans to be—at best—inexperienced theorists.'[1]

MacArthur's naval force comprised, in April, a few cruisers—one American, three Australian and two New Zealand—a modest number of destroyers, a few submarines and a considerable number of smaller vessels of the Australian Navy. His air forces were fairly imposing on paper but many of the planes in the American component were unserviceable and comparatively few of the Australian squadrons had first-class aircraft. Two Australian combat squadrons were operating from Darwin and three from New Guinea bases, and a group of American B-17s from Townsville in north Queensland. Altogether on 18 March only 12 heavy bombers, 27 dive bombers and 177 fighters were operational in American units. The strongest component of his forces was the army, which in numbers and equipment was comparable with the one the Japanese would soon face in India. How would he deploy it?

One biographer and colleague has MacArthur, as soon as he assumed command, making a decision 'bold almost to the point of desperation . . . to move forward more than a thousand miles into . . . Papua. He planned to stop the Japanese advance on the Owen Stanley mountain range of New Guinea. Thence he would take the offensive. . . . History has shown that this was one of the world's greatest decisions of military strategy.'[2]

Another colleague-biographer described the decision as 'in ultimate effect one of the greatest in world strategy' and one which 'changed the national morale from despair and defeatism to confidence and victory'.[3]

There is no contemporary record of such a decision, except to the extent that the construction and improvement of airfields in north Queensland and Papua were accelerated. The first reference to the decision occurs in a statement made to newspaper correspondents at GHQ on 18 March 1943, the anniversary of the nomination of MacArthur as Supreme Commander. The correspondents were told that

> when General MacArthur came to Australia, the defence plan . . . involved north Australia being taken by the enemy. This was based on the conception of the 'Brisbane Line' of defence. It had been drawn up on the fundamental that the littoral of islands to the north of Australia would be overrun by the Japanese. It was the intention of Australia to defend along a line somewhere near the Tropic of Capricorn, which would be known as the Brisbane Line. At that time the role of Port Moresby was to 'hold the enemy to enable mainland defences to be

[1] R. L. Eichelberger, *Jungle Road to Tokyo* (London, 1951), p. 29.
[2] C. Whitney, *MacArthur: His Rendezvous With History* (New York, 1956), pp. 64-5.
[3] Willoughby and Chamberlain, pp. 67, 78.

brought into action'. It was General MacArthur who abandoned the 'Brisbane Line' concept and decided that the battle for Australia should be fought in New Guinea.

If such an intention was in MacArthur's mind it should have been expressed by orders to move, for example, additional infantry forces northward in Australia and into New Guinea. The stages by which the garrison on the New Guinea mainland was reinforced will be described later in this chapter. Suffice to look forward here and say that its infantry component had been increased to a brigade in January 1942 and was not added to until 19 May when, solely on Blamey's orders, a second brigade was sent in. There were then in Australia 12 divisions, including the two veteran Australian divisions (one of them two brigades short) and two American divisions.

The concept of a 'Brisbane Line' had developed in February when the then commander of the home forces, the sage and dour Iven Mackay, had informed the Australian War Cabinet that, in accordance with principles long accepted in Australian military planning, he had concentrated his main force so as to cover the area from Brisbane to Melbourne and did not propose to reinforce Tasmania or north Queensland, although the troops then in north Queensland should remain there for reasons of 'morale and psychology'.[1] He asked that the Government either confirm his policy or give 'further direction regarding such defence'. The Cabinet was still warmly debating the matter late in February—the Army Minister's electorate was in north Queensland—when news of the imminent return of I Australian Corps rendered the discussion out of date. By the time of MacArthur's arrival in Australia the plan of the Australian Chiefs of Staff was to increase the force at Darwin from two brigades to a division, in Western Australia from one brigade to a division, at Townsville (north Queensland) from one brigade to a division. The consequent movement of troops had begun in March.

MacArthur's first directive relating to a general plan was issued on 25 April and gave Allied land forces the task of preventing any landing in the north-east of Australia and on the south-west coast of New Guinea, and added:

> The Allied Land Commander responsible for the areas in the vicinity of Port Moresby and along the north-east coast of Australia to include Brisbane will immediately perfect plans for the coordination of all the defensive forces in their respective areas and will implement the necessary machinery for assuming command when the necessity requires.

The meaning of this part of the directive is obscure, but it could hardly be interpreted as announcing an immediate decision to fight the battle for

[1] Though in a vastly larger area this deployment was similar to the one MacArthur had adopted on Luzon, where few troops had been left in the northern part of the island, and the main force concentrated in defence of Lingayen Gulf, Manila Bay, Bataan and points south.

Australia in New Guinea. Indeed the directive was based on an appreciation presented the previous day by Brigadier-General Chamberlain, his senior operations officer, warning that Intelligence reports suggested the possibility of a carrier strike against north-east Australia between Brisbane and Townsville between 28 April and 3 May.

When MacArthur arrived in Australia he was still surrounded by a cloud of resentment not only against the leaders in Washington but against the navy and the air corps wherever they might be—Hart had deserted him, and the air corps was inefficient. Brett, his air commander, and predecessor as senior United States army officer in Australia, was made to bear some of the brunt of these hard feelings. Eight days passed before MacArthur agreed to see Brett at all, and he devoted this first meeting largely to a tirade against the air corps and its ways. At the middle and lower points of contact, however, such problems were eventually solved in this command as in others by people eager to make the coalition forces work smoothly together.

MacArthur had been in Australia about a fortnight when the six weeks' lull on Bataan ended. During March General Homma's depleted 16th Division and 65th Brigade were given 7,000 replacements, and by mid-March the veteran but under-strength 4th Division had arrived from Shanghai and an augmented regiment of the 21st Division from south China. Homma deployed all four formations for an offensive to open on 3 April. The main thrust was to be made by the 4th Division and 65th Brigade against the inland flank of the II Philippine Corps (General Parker). After a five-hour bombardment by about 150 guns and mortars and a big force of aircraft, the Japanese infantry advanced and soon scattered one Filipino division and part of another. By the end of the second day the Japanese had seized a wide sector of the main line of resistance. General King sent forward the greater part of the Philippine Division to make a counter-attack. This move failed, and by the end of the 6th the wedge the Japanese had driven through the main line of resistance was 7,000 yards deep and they were still advancing. In the next two days the II Corps was in confusion.

> Stragglers poured through the rear in increasingly large numbers until they clogged all roads and stopped all movement forward. Units disappeared into the jungle never to be heard from again. In two days an army evaporated into thin air.[1]

On the 7th two Japanese regiments attacked the east coast sector and by the end of the next day had advanced eight miles and were nearing King's headquarters and the crowded hospitals near the tip of the peninsula. That night Wainwright ordered King to attack on the western sector towards

[1] Morton, p. 442.

the Japanese base at Olongapo on Subic Bay. This plan was inspired by MacArthur who on the 4th—the second day of the offensive—had instructed Wainwright to prepare such an attack, in which finally both corps were to envelop the Japanese base, seize the supplies there and break out into central Luzon; even if these objectives were not attained many of the troops were to make their way out of Bataan and fight as guerillas. It was too late, and Wainwright, although he obediently issued the order, knew it. Already on the 7th King had indicated to Wainwright that he might have to surrender. But Wainwright was under orders from both the President (in his message of 9 February) and MacArthur (as recently as 4 April) not to surrender Bataan. King therefore faced the choice of obeying orders which would result in the massacre of thousands of his men or taking his own decision to surrender contrary to orders. At midnight on the 8th–9th he informed his staff that he would surrender; he had not told Wainwright because he did not wish him to have to share the responsibility, nor did he seek advice from his staff. That night explosions thundered and huge fires lit up the area round Mariveles as the destruction of ammunition, heavy equipment and the naval installations was carried out. In the confusion about 2,000 soldiers, sailors, nurses and others were ferried to Corregidor. King surrendered some 78,000 men. On Corregidor 14,700 remained; the three smaller fortified islands in Manila Bay and three Filipino divisions in the southern islands were still in being.

Farther south in MacArthur's command there was in April little contact with the Japanese. Between late January and early March the Japanese commanders at Rabaul awaited orders. Then on 8 March they put about 3,000 army and navy troops ashore at Lae and Salamaua on the north-east coast of New Guinea. The small detachments of the New Guinea Rifles at these ports fell back into the mountains and, operating from bases in the air-supplied goldfield towns of Wau and Bulolo in the highlands, parties of intrepid scouts, helped by loyal New Guineans, kept the Japanese garrisons under observation. It was not until late in April that Japanese patrols began to probe inland. Round Port Moresby, on the other side of the lofty mountain spine, General Morris commanded a force including a brigade of militia and a small battalion of Papuan troops. Japanese aircraft had been bombing the Port Moresby airfields from February onwards and Australian flying-boats and medium bombers, and American B-17s from north Queensland retaliated against Rabaul. Late in March an Australian fighter squadron, armed with P-40s (Kittyhawks) provided by the Americans arrived at Port Moresby, where hitherto the only defence against Japanese raiders had been given by a few anti-aircraft guns. This squadron in a single attack destroyed 14 enemy aircraft on the ground or in the air at Lae. In April five airfields were in use or nearing completion round Port Moresby.

Blamey had at his disposal several Independent Companies, rigorously trained in guerilla warfare, and he decided early in April to send one of them to New Guinea to operate against the Japanese round Lae and Salamaua. In the last week in April the formation of Kanga Force built round this company was begun.

At Darwin, the other forward base, General Herring commanded about 15,000 troops, soon including three infantry brigades. A group of three United States fighter squadrons armed with P-40s was being built up and there were two Australian bomber squadrons. Late in April Herring's head-quarters had picked up wireless signals from Timor and learnt for the first time that an Australian-Dutch force there, including one of the Independent Companies, had survived the Japanese invasion in February and was firmly established in the mountains overlooking the enemy base at Dili.

This was the situation when the Japanese made their next major move in the south-west Pacific: a seaborne expedition mounted at Rabaul and aimed at Port Moresby. Covered by a naval force including three aircraft carriers, a convoy carrying an infantry regiment and a battalion of marines sailed from Rabaul for Port Moresby on 4 May; earlier a small force had set out for Tulagi in the Solomons. Warned by decoded Japanese signals and other intelligence, the Americans had concentrated in the Solomon Sea a formidable force including two carriers. In a series of engagements from 5 to 8 May in which the opposing surface craft never fired on each other, the Americans lost the aircraft carrier *Lexington* and two other vessels and the Japanese the small carrier *Shoho*. But the invading force was turned back.

It was a major strategical success for the Allies, because it was doubtful that the garrison round Port Moresby could have successfully resisted the intended invasion; and possession of all the eastern New Guinea mainland by the Japanese would have greatly delayed a successful Allied counter-offensive. But at the time there was little rejoicing in high places. There were now only two undamaged American carriers in the Pacific, and intercepted Japanese signals suggested that a large Japanese expedition would set out later in May perhaps against Hawaii. On the 12th MacArthur told the Australian Prime Minister that there were in the SWPA 'all the elements that have produced disaster in the western Pacific since the beginning of the war'; he had asked Marshall a few days earlier for two aircraft carriers, a corps of three divisions and, again, an increase in his air force to a first-line strength of 1,000.[1]

---

[1] A few days before the Coral Sea battle, Curtin at MacArthur's request had sought Churchill's aid in providing reinforcements, including two British divisions destined for India. Churchill asked Roosevelt whether MacArthur had 'any authority from the United States for taking such a line', and MacArthur was rebuked for using this unorthodox channel of communication.

Meanwhile, just before the surrender on Bataan, the President had been prevailed upon to modify his instruction 'to fight on as long as there remains any possibility of resistance', and had sent a message through MacArthur to Wainwright setting Wainwright free to make his own decisions. By the time the message reached MacArthur, Bataan had been surrendered and MacArthur decided that there was no need to pass on the President's instruction. Soon afterwards Roosevelt sent a comforting signal to Wainwright expressing hope that he could hold Corregidor but again giving him freedom of action. Wainwright, who informed MacArthur of this, now knew that the President's earlier instruction had been sent to MacArthur for approval, and on the 13th told MacArthur that, as he had not been informed to the contrary, he assumed that MacArthur did not agree with it. MacArthur then replied that the President's message left Wainwright free to decide.

While the Coral Sea battle was being fought news reached MacArthur that Corregidor had fallen. From 4 April onwards Japanese guns in increasing numbers bombarded the rocky island which was only a mile and a half across at its widest part and three miles and a half long. In the next four weeks the defending batteries, which included 56 coast and 76 anti-aircraft guns, were silenced, the vegetation all shot away and the whole surface of the island cratered by shells and bombs. The men were on half rations and during the long ordeal became increasingly weak and jaded. An increase in the weight of the bombardment at the beginning of May and the concentration of fire on the flat, narrow tail of the island suggested that an assault in that area was imminent.

Homma's plan was to land one regiment at the eastern end on the night of 5–6 May and four battalions at the western end on the following night. As darkness fell on the 5th the assaulting troops embarked and the landing craft set out across the four-mile-wide channel. The tide swept the craft eastward and they reached the shore in scattered formation about 1,000 yards from the intended spot, under heavy fire from the defenders' artillery and small arms. Perhaps half the troops in the first wave of 2,000 were killed or drowned and more than half the craft were wrecked, but the survivors pressed on with their usual gallantry, and by 1 a.m. some had reached the southern shore and some had pressed about the same distance towards the Malinta tunnels in the centre of the island. There on a narrow front they held on and repulsed counter-attacks but were soon running short of ammunition. But by midmorning the defenders had lost about 1,800 killed and wounded and Wainwright decided that the enemy would soon seize the tunnels and the hospitals, and that he should surrender. He broadcast a message to Homma, but there was no reply. At length an American envoy crossed to the Japanese line and later Wainwright went forward. He was taken to Homma's headquarters where he tried in vain to persuade the Japanese general that he was not empowered to surrender the troops in the southern islands. He was sent back to Corregidor where he first had to surrender to the local Japanese commander and then signed the capitulation of all troops in the archipelago. On Corregidor and the other island fortresses in Manila Bay some 12,000 prisoners were taken, including about 8,700 Americans. Throughout the whole archipelago about 140,000 troops became prisoners of the Japanese.

MacArthur's weakness for sumptuous prose and his tolerance, perhaps encouragement, of exaggeration by his subordinates often laid him bare to biting criticism by his detractors. Thus when Corregidor fell his statement to the press ran: 'Corregidor needs no comment from me. It has sounded its own story at the mouth of its guns. It has scrolled its own epitaph on enemy tablets, but through the bloody haze of its last reverberating shots, I shall always seem to see the vision of its grim, gaunt and ghostly men, still unafraid.'

On 25 May MacArthur informed his four subordinate commanders that the Japanese would probably repeat their attack on Port Moresby some time after 10 June, and that he had decided to bring the air force squadrons at Port Moresby to full strength, to prepare the dive bomber (A-24) squadrons for operations from Papuan fields, to reinforce the anti-aircraft artillery in north Queensland, and to move a battalion northward to Cairns. Already, as mentioned, Blamey had moved a brigade to Port Moresby.

However, the Japanese expedition which had been predicted soon after the Coral Sea battle turned out to be aimed at Midway Island and the western Aleutians, and it resulted in the crippling defeat of the Japanese carrier force in the great battle of 4 June. The magnitude of the calamity was concealed from the Japanese government and people, but to their naval leaders it was now evident that little hope of final victory remained.

Heartened by the success at Midway, MacArthur on 8 June, when the Japanese fleet was still withdrawing to its home bases, sent Marshall proposals for an offensive aimed at capturing Rabaul and thus forcing the enemy back on his base at Truk, 700 miles to the north, and creating a situation that could be 'further exploited at once'. To do this he required an amphibious division and a naval force including two carriers. Marshall, hitherto, off and on, a determined opponent of reinforcing the Pacific at the expense of the build-up against Germany, now proposed to King that the attack on Rabaul be mounted early in July, using a marine division followed up by three army divisions (presumably the 32nd and 41st American and 7th Australian) and, going one better than MacArthur, supported by three carriers. King rightly objected to this plan: his carriers would be exposed to attack by land-based aircraft in seas where they would have no protection by

Allied land-based aircraft; and he was insistent that 'primarily naval and amphibious operations' should be under naval command.

It was now clear, as the allocation of areas between MacArthur and Nimitz had foreshadowed, that the counter-offensive, as far ahead as could be foreseen, would be conducted by two separate commanders and from two directions: by MacArthur's mainly army force from the south and by Nimitz' mainly naval force, eventually moving along an east-west axis. The alternative of concentrating on a drive from the South-West Pacific Area, whose advanced bases were far nearer to Tokyo than was Hawaii, might lead to a degree of subordination of naval forces to an army commander that was unacceptable to the navy for reasons partly doctrinal and partly emotional.

About this time Stimson in Washington was complaining of the uncooperative attitude of 'the admirals', whom he found 'uncontrolled by either their Secretary or the President' and whose differences with the army were too frequent and sometimes petty. 'General MacArthur was a constant bone of contention', he wrote. 'Stimson was bound to admit that the extraordinary brilliance of that officer was not always matched by his tact, but the Navy's astonishing bitterness against him seemed childish.'[1]

After further argument the Joint Chiefs agreed on a plan that was expressed in a directive on 2 July—their first governing strategy of the war against Japan. It announced that the objective was to seize the New Britain–New Ireland–New Guinea area. There would be three phases: first, a commander designated by Admiral Nimitz and under his command would take Santa Cruz, Tulagi (off Guadalcanal) and adjacent islands; second, MacArthur's forces would take the remainder of the Solomons plus the northeast New Guinea coast; third, MacArthur would seize Rabaul and adjacent positions in and round New Guinea and New Ireland. King proposed that the first task should be begun on 1 August, and 'arrangements for the second and third phases' made not later than 20 July—18 days ahead.

MacArthur and Ghormley on 8 July jointly recommended that the Tulagi–Santa Cruz operation be postponed until they had been provided with the means to follow up at once with the second and third tasks. King insisted on pressing on with task one, and acidly commented that three weeks earlier MacArthur had said that with amphibious forces and two carriers he could advance on Rabaul, but 'confronted with the concrete aspects of the task, he now feels that he not only cannot undertake this extended operation but not even the Tulagi operation'. This was fair comment on MacArthur's overoptimistic Rabaul plan; but his afterthoughts had been justified. He lacked the means, sea, land and air, of starting an offensive aimed at promptly driving the enemy out of New Guinea and the Solomons.

[1] Stimson and Bundy, pp. 280–1.

On 17 June at his second meeting with the Australian Advisory War Council MacArthur had enlarged upon the arguments he had advanced to the council in March. Since then, he said, the situation of Australia had been transformed. There had been great progress in expanding training and arming the services, and Coral Sea and Midway had assured the defence of Australia. All the Japanese victories had been won through air superiority, their advance having been covered by land-based aircraft. The cause of Allied defeats had been failure to challenge Japanese sea power. The reason for the Japanese seizure of a base in the Aleutians was to cut communications between the United States and Siberia preliminary to an attack on Russia against whom she had concentrated 30 divisions. He was opposed to the policy of defeating Germany first and considered it not possible to form a second front in Europe. To do so would require 50 divisions. Britain could not find more than 18 or 20, and to find ships to send the remainder from the United States would require four to five years. In any event he was very doubtful that an army could get through the defences of France and the Low Countries. The best way to help Russia would be to establish a second front in the Pacific by an offensive aimed at recovering New Guinea followed by a thrust to the Philippines or through the Indies to Malaya. He needed aircraft carriers, additional aircraft, and an amphibious division. These, with the support of the 7th Australian and 32nd and 41st American Divisions would capture Rabaul and the remainder of New Guinea.

If MacArthur overestimated the difficulty of opening a second front in western Europe the American leaders underestimated it. In May Roosevelt had proposed August 1942 as the latest date for a landing there. And MacArthur's prognostication about a Japanese attack on Russia was shared by Churchill, who told the Pacific War Council on 25 June that movement of Japanese troops and aircraft seemed to point to an imminent Japanese attack on Russia. (The Japanese were in fact withdrawing troops and aircraft from the southern area to the north, but as a defensive move against Russia.)

Meanwhile modest steps had been taken to strengthen the defensive position in New Guinea. From February onwards the possibility of the Japanese landing on the north coast and advancing across the mountains towards Port Moresby had been canvassed. But little had been done to meet this threat by early June when MacArthur's staff received intelligence from those who were monitoring Japanese radio traffic, suggesting that the Japanese might land round Buna and advance over the mountains through Kokoda. (The eavesdropping was efficient, for it was not until the middle of June that General Hyakutake, commanding the Seventeenth Army, received definite orders to prepare an overland attack on Port Moresby if he found it feasible.)

On the Allied side a force built round a battalion was sent across the Owen

Stanleys to Kokoda and in the first half of July there was a widespread north-ward movement of troops and much forward planning in anticipation of the expected arrival of Japanese on the Papuan coast. From 25 June onwards a force, eventually including two Australian brigades, had been established at Milne Bay to build and protect an airfield at this eastern extremity of the island. The 41st and 32nd Divisions had been moved to Queensland from their remote camps at Melbourne and Adelaide. On 20 July MacArthur moved his own headquarters from Melbourne to Brisbane. Five days earlier, as a first step towards the achievement of the objectives set out in the 2 July directive, he had issued an outline plan to establish a base at Buna where he planned to have a garrison of 3,200 men early in August and to develop fields from which aircraft could attack Rabaul without having to fly over the for-bidding Owen Stanley Range.

But the Japanese got there first. On the night of 21 July and next day an advance-guard of about 2,000 troops of Major-General Tomitaro Horii's South Seas Force (144th and 41st Regiments plus technical troops, the total strength to be about 14,000) landed round Buna and Gona under the guns of a small naval squadron. By the 29th leading Japanese troops were in Kokoda which the small Australian force in the mountains arrogantly regained briefly on 8 August. By the third week in August the Japanese had thrust two Australian militia battalions back to Isurava and were meeting the veteran 21st Brigade which had been hurried to New Guinea from 12 August onwards. That day Lieutenant-General S. F. Rowell of I Australian Corps had taken command of Port Moresby and soon afterwards Major-General A. S. Allen of the 7th Division was in control of the forward troops.

It was at this stage that the second prong of the Japanese advance towards Port Moresby was inserted. On the night of 25 August a Japanese force comprising about 2,000 marines began landing a few miles east of the Milne Bay airstrip; more were to follow. The Japanese expected to encounter two or three companies. They found two brigades, the 7th Australian that had formed the original garrison and the veteran 18th Australian (7th Division) which had arrived between 12 and 21 August, the whole Milne Force, commanded by Major-General C. A. Clowes, numbering some 8,800 men. Clowes, his brigadiers and many of his 4,500 infantry had seen hard fighting in the Middle East.

In the next ten days the Australians, vigorously supported by two Australian fighter squadrons which destroyed the invaders' barges, sank a transport and caused heavy casualties, halted the Japanese and finally drove them back. Japanese naval vessels rescued about 600 men and others escaped overland to Buna; the rest—perhaps 2,000—were lost. The Australians had

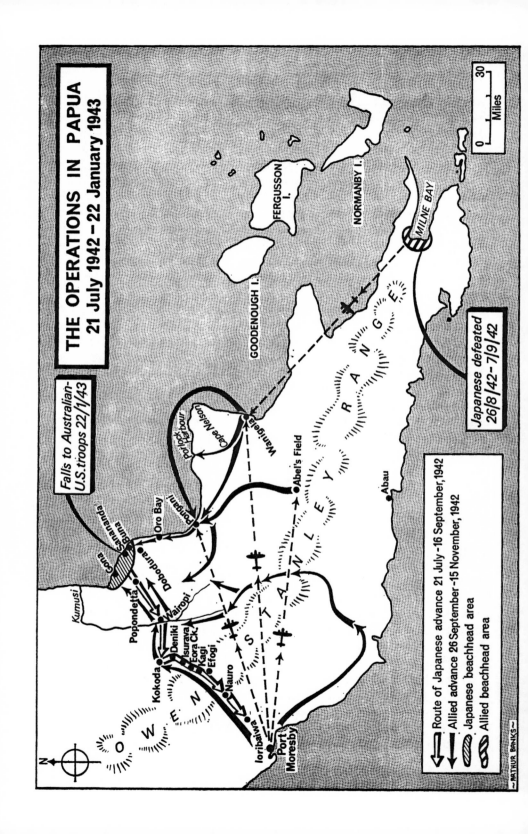

THE OPERATIONS IN PAPUA
21 July 1942 – 22 January 1943

Falls to Australian–
U.S. troops 22/1/43

Japanese defeated
26/8/42–7/9/42

Route of Japanese advance 21 July–16 September, 1942
Allied advance 26 September–15 November, 1942
Japanese beachhead area
Allied beachhead area

N

0   30
Miles

MILNE BAY

NORMANBY I.

FERGUSSON I.

GOODENOUGH I.

OWEN STANLEY RANGE

Port Moresby
Ioribaiwa
Nauro
Efogi
Kagi
Eora Ck.
Isurava
Deniki
Kokoda
Popondetta
Wairopi
Dobodura
Kumusi
Buna
Sanananda
Gona
Oro Bay
Popndri
Abel's Field
Wanigela
Cape Nelson
Pollock Harbour
Abau

~ARTHUR BANKS~

373 battle casualties. For the first time a Japanese amphibious force had been decisively defeated.

The threat to Milne Bay, combined with the continued Japanese advance through the Owen Stanleys, had caused MacArthur much anxiety. In mid-July he had been planning a great offensive that would drive the enemy back to Truk. Six weeks later his troops were fighting to retain two forward bases and had been forestalled at a third. At Milne Bay Clowes' handling of his troops had been cautious, and rightly so because the invader had command of the sea and might land anywhere. But MacArthur complained of the brevity of the reports from Milne Bay. (Major-General Vasey, attached to MacArthur's headquarters, wrote to Rowell about these messages: 'I am more convinced than ever that our reports need to be written in Americanese; they don't understand our Australian English.') On the 30th, in a signal to Washington, MacArthur said that he was not yet convinced of the efficiency of the Australian units. That day Rowell, who knew that his force was under criticism, wrote to Vasey: 'I am sorry that GHQ take a poor view of the Australians. In some cases that is all too true, but I wish [MacArthur's general staff officers] could visit the jungle and see what the conditions are instead of sitting back and criticizing.'

MacArthur's own name might with justice have been included in this comment. Since his arrival in his new command he had exhibited the same failure to inspect the troops in training and to examine the battlefields as he had done in the Philippines. And, as Rowell was pointing out, his staff had largely followed his example, and were insufficiently informed about the New Guinea terrain and conditions. On 13 August Sutherland, on the advice of Casey, his chief engineer, had proposed that preparations be made to block 'the pass' through the Owen Stanleys by demolitions. In the course of a tart reply Rowell wrote that:

> The amount of explosive which could be carried by native porters for the five days' trip at present needed to reach the top of the Owen Stanley Range would hardly increase the present difficulties of the track. Some parts of the track have to be negotiated on hands and knees, and the use of some tons of explosives would not increase these difficulties.

MacArthur and his entourage still had much to learn about the facts of warfare in the mountains of East Asia. As will be seen, it was not until October that MacArthur paid his first brief visit to New Guinea. He moved to Port Moresby with an advanced headquarters on 6 November.[1]

[1] The reference to this move in Willoughby and Chamberlain's *MacArthur: 1941-51* makes it appear that it happened in July and at the same time reveals a remarkable lack of knowledge or forgetfulness on the part of MacArthur's senior Intelligence officer of New Guinea conditions and the deployment there. Willoughby wrote that when reports made it plain that the Japanese planned to cross the Owen Stanleys MacArthur 'moved into Port Moresby personally, along with his staff,

As in the Philippines MacArthur failed also to inform himself adequately about the state of training of his troops. In his proposals for an early offensive against Rabaul he assumed that his two American divisions were ready to take part in exacting large-scale operations in July. But when General Eichelberger arrived from America in August to command I Corps, which included those divisions, he found them 'in no sense ready for jungle warfare' and told MacArthur that he thought the 32nd Division (which had been in training for nearly two years) 'was not sufficiently trained to meet Japanese veterans on equal terms'.

An Australian historian wrote of these troops at this time:

> To Australian eyes there was some lack of realism in the outlook of the newly-arrived formations, staff work seemed defective and training methods somewhat unpractical. The Australian soldier lived hard during training; in battle he was in many respects no more uncomfortable than he had often been before. The American formations on the other hand tended, in Australian opinion, to clutter themselves up with inessential paraphernalia, and thus to increase the difference between camp life and battle conditions to such an extent that contact with the latter was bound to produce a rude shock, even to the most high-spirited.[1]

New men of Eichelberger's calibre were badly needed in the higher layers of MacArthur's command, and earlier in August one had arrived who soon had an electrifying effect. MacArthur's dissatisfaction with Brett as his air commander had not diminished. He sought in Brett's place Lieutenant-General Frank M. Andrews, a very senior officer, but Marshall, who had been distressed by MacArthur's criticisms of Brett, offered Major-General George C. Kenney or Brigadier-General Doolittle, who had led a bombing raid on Tokyo in April. MacArthur chose Kenney as he considered Doolittle's lack of seniority would make him unacceptable to the senior Australian air officers.

Kenney was an exuberant and confident commander who swiftly won the confidence of MacArthur, whom at the outset he found 'a little tired, drawn and nervous'. Kenney persuaded MacArthur that his air force, as run by Kenney, would make up for his lack of naval power, soon gave Sutherland, who had been dictating to Brett, his comeuppance, and blew through the torpid and discontented American Army Air Force organization like a cleansing

---

to join a handful of Australians and local Europeans who had come to New Guinea to prospect for gold and who remained to fight'. At that time, if July is intended, there were two brigades of Australian troops in Papua and more on the way. And the handful of Australians and local Europeans had numbered in fact about 7,000, employing some 50,000 local labourers. The rich Bulolo Valley goldfields, with about 1,000 Europeans and 10,000 native workers, were maintained by some 40 aircraft, carrying 12,000 passengers and 9,000 tons of cargo a year.

[1] McCarthy, pp. 32-3.

breeze. Brett had been able to see MacArthur eight times in four months. The ebullient Kenney saw to it that he was constantly in and out of the commander-in-chief's office, and was at his elbow when he went abroad. Their admiration was reciprocal. To Kenney MacArthur was 'the best general this country has ever produced'.[1] In MacArthur's view: 'Of all the brilliant air commanders of the war, none surpassed [Kenney] in those three great essentials of combat leadership: aggressive vision, mastery of air tactics and strategy, and the ability to exact the maximum in fighting qualities from both men and equipment.'[2]

'MacArthur's restoration to full health and activity', wrote one of his biographers, 'might well be dated from the day that Kenney walked into his headquarters in Brisbane, sat quietly through a long tongue-lashing on the subject of airplanes and pilots, gave an unusual promise of "personal loyalty" which MacArthur demanded from all "outsiders" in those days, and set about helping his new commander win the war. The importance of Kenney to MacArthur in the following years cannot be overestimated.'[3]

So far, except at Milne Bay, the opposing land-based air forces had not played a decisive part in the struggle for New Guinea. Rabaul and Port Moresby had exchanged raids. The convoys that had carried the invaders to Buna had been attacked but without great effect. But at Milne Bay air action had been, in Rowell's opinion, 'the decisive factor' and thenceforward under Kenney's vigorous direction the role of his Fifth Air Force, as it was soon named, would prove a dominant one.

In September MacArthur received also a new and more congenial commander of his naval forces, Vice-Admiral A. S. Carpender.

Meanwhile, phase one of the Joint Chiefs' three-phase offensive had opened on 8 August when the reinforced 1st Marine Division had been put ashore on Guadalcanal and Tulagi, and on sea and land and in the air a long battle of attrition had begun. By the middle of September one American carrier had been sunk and two damaged, and four cruisers (one Australian) and other smaller ships sunk. The Japanese had lost one carrier. But the Americans had some 20,000 men ashore. Two Japanese regiments sent in as reinforcements had been cut to pieces. One of these regiments had been intended for the Milne Bay operation and, as we have seen, had hastily to be replaced by a force of marines.

MacArthur was now taking steps towards organizing from his slender resources a flotilla of small vessels to carry troops and supplies along the New Guinea coast. On 6 August he had issued an operation instruction for the

[1] G. C. Kenney, *The MacArthur I Know* (New York, 1951), p. 9.
[2] *Reminiscences*, p. 157.
[3] Lee and Henschel, p. 167.

establishment at Milne Bay of an amphibious force equipped with small vessels aimed at securing the coast as far as Cape Nelson. And on 28 August, when the issue at Milne Bay still seemed in doubt, he warned Marshall that the Japanese might strike at New Guinea under cover of the Guadalcanal operation and that he was powerless to prevent this because of the absence of a great part of his naval forces which had been sent into the struggle round Guadalcanal. On the 31st the War Department informed him that these naval units—Rear-Admiral Crutchley's cruisers and destroyers—were returning to his command and that he was authorized to deal directly with Nimitz and Ghormley to arrange mutual support between the two commands. Thereupon MacArthur sent Sutherland and Kenney to Noumea, where Nimitz announced that he could not spare MacArthur any ships, air cover or amphibious troops. MacArthur was not satisfied and on 6 September told Marshall that because of lack of 'maritime resources' he could not increase his land forces in New Guinea. It was imperative that his shipping and his naval forces be increased so that he could send strong reinforcements to New Guinea and make 'creeping advances' along the north coast. His appeal was of no avail. He would have to make the best of what he had, and soon was doing this to some effect, as will be seen.

The seeming deadlock on Guadalcanal and the continued advance across the Owen Stanleys had caused alarm at Brisbane and in Washington. On 30 August MacArthur sent a message to the Joint Chiefs that:

> unless the strategic situation is constantly reviewed in the light of current enemy potentialities in the Pacific and unless moves are made to meet the changing conditions, a disastrous outcome is bound to result shortly; it is no longer a question here of preparing a projected offensive; without additional naval forces, either British or American, and unless steps are taken to match the heavy air and ground forces the enemy is assembling, I predict the development shortly of a situation similar to those that have successfully overwhelmed our forces in the Pacific since the beginning of the war.

MacArthur could not know that next day in Tokyo Imperial General Headquarters would order Horii to go on the defensive on the southern slopes of the Owen Stanleys.

The Japanese advance towards Port Moresby was halted in mid-September about 30 air miles from the coast; five Australian battalions were then securely in position astride the Japanese line of advance. But MacArthur was restless. His Australians had taken too long to drive the Japanese out of Milne Bay and, though in stronger numbers than the Japanese in the Owen Stanleys, had been pushed back. On 6 September he told Marshall that 'aggressive leadership' was lacking in the Australian Army. On 12 September Kenney, on his return from a brief visit to New Guinea, had convinced Mac-

Arthur that a defensive attitude permeated the Australian force and (wrongly) that Rowell was planning a withdrawal that would put most of the airfields into Japanese hands; 12,000 white men, said the animated Kenney, were being chased by two or three thousand Japanese. He urged MacArthur to let him fly an American regiment to New Guinea for propaganda reasons, and let Blamey put them into the fighting.

Four days later when Blamey also returned from New Guinea he reported to the Government in very different terms: the Allies had some 30,000 troops in New Guinea, the Japanese about 10,000, but the enemy was stronger in the forward area because of Allied supply difficulties. Two fresh brigades (25th and 16th) with three artillery regiments had arrived or were on the way, and an American regiment was to be sent in to gain experience. The commanders were confident that Port Moresby would not be taken by land and so was he.

But later that day MacArthur telephoned Curtin and told him that the reason for the unsatisfactory position was the inefficiency of the Australian troops. He proposed to send American troops in to stem the attack. Within a week he would have 40,000 troops in New Guinea. Blamey should at once take personal command there. Curtin promptly instructed Blamey to do so.

It was a proposal that was not only unorthodox but unwise, though not without precedent. Indeed a very recent precedent had been provided by General Auchinleck, the commander-in-chief in the Middle East, who three months earlier had gone forward and taken personal command of the Eighth Army in North Africa, but had first removed the former army commander, a step which Blamey had no intention of taking. But Blamey could not refuse an order from his Prime Minister acting on advice from the commander-in-chief. Probably with the intention of treating the arrangement as an *ad hoc* one soon to be terminated he took with him to New Guinea not even a skeleton staff. He arrived on the 23rd. There was a clash of temperament and opinion between him and Rowell, who naturally resented the arrangement, and on the 28th Blamey relieved him of his command. It was ironical that at that time the Japanese were beginning to withdraw. That day the Australians who had been probing forward against little resistance since the day of Blamey's arrival attacked into thin air and advanced upon empty positions strewn with abandoned equipment. The Japanese advancing on Moresby had run out of supplies and their commanders had decided that the force could not be maintained at the end of a primitive track through a tangled jungle-clad range rising to 6,500 feet. On 18 September headquarters in Tokyo had ordered that the South Seas Force should withdraw to a beach-head on the north coast and that Hyakutake should concentrate on regaining

Guadalcanal. When this had been done he was to resume the two-pronged advance on Port Moresby, both through the mountains and by way of Milne Bay.

The setbacks in Papua had been largely the result of the failure of MacArthur and Blamey to send some of their best troops to the threatened area soon enough and promptly to organize air supply on a maximum scale. Until mid-August the infantry deployed in Papua had been drawn from the militia and contained some fine units, as the fighting round Kokoda and Milne Bay had shown, but some that were below average in training and morale. It was not until mid-August when the Japanese were nearing the summit of the range that a corps commander and staff were sent in and the movement of the 7th Division to Papua began.

In the first week of August the two brigades of the 6th Division that had been garrisoning Ceylon had reached Melbourne. By 21 September one of these was at Moresby. Thus by the end of September a formidable force was assembled in Papua: the 7th Division (Major-General A. S. Allen) with two AIF and one militia brigades, the 6th Division (Major-General G. A. Vasey) including two Australian brigades and the 128th US Regiment, and at Milne Bay two brigades to which a third would soon be added. More than half the infantry battalions now forward had served in the Middle East, and most of the others had been in the recent severe fighting in Papua.

On 1 October MacArthur issued orders for the offensive. The immediate objective was to drive the Japanese north of the Kumusi River. There would be two lines of advance: through Kokoda (by Australians) and over tracks farther south (by Americans). At the same time a small force would occupy Goodenough Island and the Papuan coast from Milne Bay to Cape Nelson. The paramount problem was the supply of forces advancing through the mountains. Blamey pointed out to MacArthur in a detailed study on 5 October that in this phase about 7,000 troops and 3,900 native carriers would have to be supplied by dropping from the air. The problem would be eased by the capture of the Kokoda airfield, and every effort would be made to run small craft from Milne Bay to Wanigela to supply the coastwise advance, but in view of Japanese naval and air strength this would be a precarious route. Kenney assured Blamey that he could provide for all the air transport and air dropping needed. The organization of the coastwise maritime force continued. In October a safe channel through the reef-strewn waters from Milne Bay to Cape Nelson was charted and MacArthur ordered the movement of men and supplies to the Buna area in transports escorted by 650-ton Australian corvettes which would later be used also as troop transports. Thus on 11 December a transport would unload tanks on Oro

Bay and a few days later three corvettes would land a battalion in the area. Between 11 and 29 December 2,076 troops would be landed at Oro Bay.

It was the day after he issued his operation instruction that MacArthur, visiting New Guinea for the first time, was driven forward to the roadhead and was able to see from a distance the tangle of jungle-clad ranges into which the troops were advancing. To the commander of the fresh 16th Brigade then moving forward to take over the advance he said: 'Lloyd, by some act of God, your brigade has been chosen for this job. The eyes of the Western World are upon you and your men. Good luck and don't stop.'

In the background of the promising opening of the Papuan offensive was the problematical situation on Guadalcanal where, Marshall told MacArthur on 16 October, the position was 'most critical'. MacArthur replied: 'It is now necessary to prepare for possible disaster in the Solomons; if we are defeated in the Solomons as we must be unless the Navy accepts successfully the challenge of the enemy surface fleet, the entire SWPA will be in the gravest danger.'

On the 21st Roosevelt gave the Pacific War Council a hint that Guadalcanal might not be permanently tenable. And so great were MacArthur's misgivings that on 31 October he prepared a plan for withdrawal from the north coast and perhaps from all Papua in the event of the Japanese securing Guadalcanal and concentrating against New Guinea.

Despite Kenney's assurances the air supply to the troops in the Owen Stanleys remained a serious problem. As early as 7 October General Allen informed General Herring, who had now replaced General Rowell at Port Moresby, that it appeared that the air force could not ensure the dropping of 50,000 pounds daily—this figure provided for 30 per cent wastage. If supply could not be assured a large proportion of the forward troops would have to be withdrawn. But through October air supply improved, the troops pressed on, and on the 28th smashed the Japanese rearguard at Eora Creek. MacArthur had been dissatisfied with the rate of advance and had sent forward sharply critical signals: Kokoda airfield must be secured promptly; the tactical handling of the troops was faulty, and so on. Blamey supported the criticism, and on the day of the decisive success at Eora Creek Allen was required to hand over the 7th Division to General Vasey.

The broken Japanese rearguard was pursued to Kokoda, which was entered on 2 November and where the first supply plane landed two days later. Beyond Kokoda Vasey carried out an enveloping attack and virtually destroyed the Japanese force in the mountains. About 600 Japanese dead were counted and many of the survivors, including General Horii, were drowned trying to cross the flooded Kumusi. The Japanese dead in this last fight in the mountains outnumbered the Australian battle casualties in the Owen Stanleys from July to November—625. And the Australian infantry had now gained a tactical superiority over the Japanese in bush warfare that was to steadily increase in the next three years.

MacArthur's pincers were now closing in on the Japanese beachhead round Buna. On the right the 128th American Regiment had been flown to Wanigela where it joined the 2/10th Battalion flown in from Milne Bay early in October. In the centre the 126th Regiment was assembling about Pongani having moved partly by air and partly on foot. On the left the two Australian brigades that had advanced through the mountains were pressing on towards Gona and Sanananda. Meanwhile, Goodenough Island had been seized from some 300 Japanese marines who had been stranded there during the Milne Bay operation.

On 2 November MacArthur ordered that the attack on the Japanese beachhead should open on the 15th. That day saw the end of a naval battle off Guadalcanal in which the Japanese lost two battleships, a carrier, three destroyers, and 11 transports carrying the greater part of their 38th Division; the Americans lost three cruisers and seven destroyers. MacArthur did not know that at that stage the enemy, his reserves practically exhausted, abandoned efforts to reinforce Guadalcanal but decided to continue to keep the troops on the island supplied. Thus about the same day the operations on both islands entered a similar and final phase: the destruction by the Allies of outnumbered but resolute enemy forces.

In Papua this situation had been made possible by air transport of troops and supplies on a scale foreshadowed in the German seizure of Crete the year before. Kenney's assurance that MacArthur's air power (still not much greater than the Japanese) would compensate for his lack of sea power had been justified. And increasing air transport was now being supplemented by the small vessels ferrying troops and supplies along the coast.

In accordance with MacArthur's directions, Herring ordered a four-pronged attack on the Buna beachhead by the 32nd US Division (Major-General Edwin F. Harding) on the right, 7th Australian Division (Vasey) on the left. In Harding's area the 128th Regiment was to advance along the coast on Buna, the southern bastion of the Japanese stronghold, with the 126th Regiment moving on its left. In Vasey's area the 16th Brigade was to advance through Soputa to Sanananda, the 25th to Gona. GHQ estimated the Japanese strength at about 4,000; Vasey's staff estimated them at 1,500 to 2,000; Harding's staff placed not more than a battalion at Buna. The Americans advancing towards Buna believed that it would be a walkover. In fact there were some 8,000 Japanese troops in the stronghold, the forward units being dug in along a front of about 11 miles in a series of positions mainly composed of low bunkers built of coconut logs and earth, reinforced with oil drums filled with sand and with steel sheets. They were in three main groups—round Buna, Sanananda and Gona—and along the road to Sanananda was a series of outlying positions. The country surrounding the fortress was mostly swampy and malarial, humidity was high and the heat intense.

Throughout MacArthur's area the Japanese command had now been reorganized. On 16 November Lieutenant-General Hitoshi Imamura, with the headquarters of a new Eighth Area Army, took command of all troops in New Guinea and the Solomons. Hyakutake's Seventeenth Army was now responsible only for the Solomons and the Eighteenth Army under Lieutenant-General Hatazo Adachi was made responsible for operations on the New Guinea mainland. The battle in Papua soon resolved itself into three separate struggles that were to continue at Gona until 9 December, Buna until 2 January and Sanananda until 22 January. By 19 November, when the 25th Brigade began to attack the Gona fortress after two days of marching through jungle and swamp, it had been reduced by casualties in the earlier fighting, malaria and heat exhaustion to fewer than 1,000 men, about the same number as the still invisible enemy facing them in positions whose great strength the Australians soon discovered. After several ineffective thrusts the 25th Brigade was replaced by the 21st plus a militia battalion. A series of costly attacks led to the final clearing of the Gona area on 9 December.

It was the reduction of the larger and more strongly manned Buna beachhead that caused MacArthur his greatest concern. The 128th Regiment advanced to the attack on 16 November. That day a convoy of luggers and a barge carrying vital supplies forward, and also General Harding himself and other senior officers, was destroyed by Japanese fighters. Harding and others swam ashore, but this setback delayed the advance until the 19th. And on the 17th Harding's 126th Regiment was detached to the 7th Division. Advancing in drenching rain, the regiment on Harding's right was soon halted by fire from well-hidden Japanese positions and by seemingly ubiquitous snipers. The inexperienced American troops were dazed and disheartened by the strength of the defences and the discovery that the enemy were not half-starved survivors of the Owen Stanleys but fresh and well nourished. The Americans attacked again and again but with little effect. Harding's left column was halted in appalling swamp land covered by enemy fire. On 30 November a full-scale attack was sent in but it wilted. After two weeks the Japanese line had not been dented.

The 32nd Division had lost 492 men killed or wounded and many others were sick with malaria and dysentery. They were on short rations, their clothes were wet and tattered, their feet swollen. They had no flame-throwers or tanks and the Japanese bunkers seemed to be proof against bombardment by artillery and aircraft.

Harding's requests for reinforcements had met little success. He had asked the Australian Corps commander, Herring, to send him his third regiment—the 127th—then at Port Moresby, but Herring told him that he appeared to have 'ample reserves'. He had asked for tanks, and was promised some lightly protected machine-gun carriers; for ten more field guns, and was promised four, some time in December.

Meanwhile at Port Moresby on the 25th Blamey and Herring had visited MacArthur at Government House and, when MacArthur suggested bringing his second American division from Australia, Blamey said bluntly that he would rather have more Australians at the front because he knew they would fight. This, wrote Kenney later, was 'a bitter pill for MacArthur to swallow'; but he agreed to fly an Australian brigade from Port Moresby to the battle zone. MacArthur was greatly upset by this devastating criticism of his infantry. His well-conceived plan to wipe out the Japanese force in Papua, despite his lack of sea power, by trickling troops along the coast to the Buna area in small craft and by supplying his two divisions there mainly by air had bogged down; the cause, he was convinced, was lack of resolute leadership.

On the 27th he sent a staff officer to the front; he returned with a gloomy account of the morale and general condition of the American troops. Thereupon MacArthur sent Sutherland over the ranges to Dobodura.

Herring, who had now moved his headquarters to Popondetta, landed on the 30th at the Dobodura airfield, where Harding's headquarters were established. Harding again asked for his 127th Regiment, arguing that he had no reserves. Herring 'seemed to take an almost detached view of the trials and tribulations of my all-American contingent', Harding wrote later. Then Sutherland arrived at the airfield. He too would not agree to send in a fresh regiment, arguing that the air force could not maintain additional troops in the Buna area until more supplies were forward at the Dobodura base. Sutherland said that adverse reports about the 32nd Division had been reaching MacArthur and because of them MacArthur had ordered Eichelberger forward to New Guinea and would probably send him to the front. Sutherland then asked Harding if he intended to make any changes among his senior commanders. Harding said that he did not. Sutherland flew back to MacArthur and advised that he should relieve Harding on the ground that he insisted on retaining regimental officers and commanders of doubtful competence. Later that day Eichelberger arrived at Port Moresby with seven staff officers. He and his chief of staff were ordered to report to MacArthur at once. They found him striding up and down the verandah at Government House.

American troops, he told the officers, had dropped their weapons and run from the enemy. He had never been so humiliated in his life, and it was the kind of thing that he would not stand for. Harding, he said, had failed and the blame for what had happened was his. What was needed at Buna . . . was aggressive leadership. . . . 'Go out there, Bob, and take Buna or don't come back alive.' Then pointing to General Byers he added 'and that goes for your chief of staff, Clovis, too.'[1]

Next day he said to Eichelberger that if he took Buna he would give him a DSC, recommend him for a high British decoration and release his name for newspaper publication.[2]

Eichelberger was appalled at the condition of his troops and decided that 'inspired leadership' was lacking. 'I stopped all fighting', he wrote later, 'and it took two days to effect the unscrambling of units and an orderly chain of command.' He replaced Harding with Major-General Waldron, hitherto commanding the American artillery, and placed officers of his own staff in command of each wing of the division. By the 14th, having been reinforced by his division's third regiment and a few more guns, and after attacks in which high-spirited leaders emerged, the 127th Regiment entered Buna village, but it was evident that the men were in no shape to complete the capture of the rest of the Buna stronghold.

Already on 6 December Blamey had proposed to MacArthur that the reduction of the Buna position would demand tanks and at least one fresh battalion from Milne Bay. It was at this stage that corvettes ferried a squadron of Australian tanks and a battalion of the 18th Brigade forward; two more soon followed. On the 14th MacArthur urged Eichelberger to hasten the attack. But it was 2 January before the Americans and the fresh Australian brigade (which lost about 45 per cent of its strength in the battle) destroyed the last Japanese posts.

Meanwhile Vasey's division had been pressing on towards Sanananda. The weary and depleted 16th Brigade, now only about 1,000 strong, was held at Soputa. Herring reinforced them with the greater part of the 126th Regiment and then with two militia battalions, but these made little progress. In mid-December Herring put in his last reserves—two Australian units. All AIF brigades except one at Milne Bay and one in the Northern Territory, where effective garrisons were essential, had now been used up or were committed. The performance of MacArthur's American troops had been disappointing and he knew that he would receive no fresh American infantry reinforcements at least until Guadalcanal had been secured. His thoughts turned again to the 9th Australian Division in Egypt. In May and early June

[1] John Miller Junior, *Guadalcanal: The First Offensive* (Washington, 1949), a volume in the official series *United States Army in World War II*, p. 204.
[2] Eichelberger, p. 22.

he had pressed the Australian Government to seek its return, but after the Midway battle and during the advance of Rommel in the Middle East he advised the Government not to press the matter. In October, however, he again advised Curtin to urge the division's return, and Curtin did so. But the division was then heavily engaged at El Alamein and the Australian Government was persuaded to let the matter rest.

Early in December Blamey reported to the Prime Minister that the American troops could not be classified as attack troops and operations had revealed 'a very alarming state of weakness in their staff system and their war psychology'. He considered that it would be many months before the Americans, including the 41st Division, attained a high standard. The 6th and 7th Australian Divisions needed a long rest. If the 9th Division was not returned the position in New Guinea would involve considerable danger, and they would have to go on the defensive. Curtin with MacArthur's support thereupon sought the return of the division early in the new year, and on 15 December Churchill announced that ships would be found to take it home at the end of January.

Meanwhile on the 17th, before he had heard this decision, MacArthur had written to Blamey suggesting an ingenious plan: that 'a heavy cadre involving the majority of the officers of the 9th Division detailed by name' be transferred to Australia so that a new AIF division could be formed there.

MacArthur now decided to draw on his 41st Division for reinforcements to break the deadlock at Sanananda, but the day its 163rd Regiment arrived at Port Moresby MacArthur ordered Blamey to send it to Buna instead. Blamey protested. Nothing, he wrote, could be 'more contrary to sound principles of command than that the Commander-in-Chief . . . should take over the direction of a portion of the battle'. The regiment went to the Sanananda sector, where with the doughty 18th Brigade, switched from Buna, the last Japanese was overcome on 22 January.

Probably 13,000 of the 20,000 Japanese who were landed in Papua were killed. The Australians lost 2,165 dead in battle, the Americans 913. Some 28,000 men in both forces were suffering from malaria. The cost in lives of all Allied troops in securing Papua had been almost twice as great as on Guadalcanal, where about 1,600 American marines and army troops died in battle.

The Australian historian of the campaign has argued that from 2 January onwards, when the only surviving Japanese stronghold was the one round Sanananda, MacArthur might well have ordered that the 6,000 Japanese (perhaps 1,800 of them hospital patients) be hemmed in and thus have spared his troops most of the 1,200 or so casualties suffered in the last three weeks of fighting. He had secured the needed airfields and the remaining Japanese offered no threat. Herring's chief of staff, Berryman, had advised a blockade of the Sanananda position. But, McCarthy concluded, 'with the desirability present of lifting the Allied morale as high as possible by finishing the operations in Papua decisively and completely—the decision to press the coastal fighting to the bitter end was probably inevitable'.[1]

We know now that on 4 January Imperial General Headquarters had decided to abandon both Papua and Guadalcanal. The few survivors west of Gona were to make their way to Salamaua as best they could. From Guadalcanal in the next few weeks destroyers by night embarked some 13,000 troops and took them to Bougainville and Rabaul. At the same time the Japanese commander decided to strengthen his position round Lae and Salamaua where the garrisons had been engaged in sporadic fighting with Australian Independent Companies and local volunteers for the last eight months.

When the fighting in the Owen Stanleys was still in a critical stage Blamey on 18 October had written to MacArthur that the seizure of Lae and Salamaua should be planned. It might be possible to land a force from the air at Nadzab in the valley of the wide Markham River and advance thence on Lae. But MacArthur was not yet ready for such a project. The Japanese commanded the sea, he replied, and could bring overwhelming force to bear on the north coast. Great caution was needed. Two brigades should remain at Milne Bay, Blamey proposed to leave only one.

But in January the reinforcement of Kanga Force in the highlands of southern New Guinea above Lae and Salamaua became a matter of urgency. In the second week of January the Japanese began shipping the 51st Division to Lae and Salamaua, when it was to seize the Bulolo valley and be poised to take part in the renewed attack on Port Moresby when the time came. It would later be joined in the area from Salamaua to Wewak by the 41st and 20th Divisions, the three forming the main part of Adachi's Eighteenth Army. To meet the new threat the 17th Australian Brigade was flown to Wau where its first troops arrived just in time to help check the Japanese and whence by early February the Japanese were in full retreat.

This achievement by Kenney's transport aircraft was followed by a resounding success on the part of his bombers and fighters. On 2 and 3 March these attacked a convoy of 16 ships including seven transports laden with 6,400 troops for Lae. All the transports and four destroyers were sunk. About 2,300 troops were killed. Only about 900 reached Lae. This was the end of Japanese attempts to carry troops in large transports to southern New Guinea. Henceforth they had to be sneaked in by barges. In MacArthur's

[1] McCarthy, pp. 532-3.

words: 'Control of the air and sea lanes had passed to the Allies, marking the end of the Japanese offensive in the Southwest Pacific.'[1]

As is usual in such conditions intelligence reports greatly exaggerated the Japanese losses and the communiqué based on those reports announced that 22 ships had been sunk and 12,000 troops destroyed. The unwillingness of MacArthur's staff to publish or even admit revised estimates was symptomatic of a publicity policy at GHQ that was increasingly irritating leaders and troops in the field and alienating the Press. Thus in May 1942 when some of Kenney's bombers had mistakenly dropped bombs in the direction of Admiral Crace's squadron during the Coral Sea battle, drastic measures were taken to expunge this information from even the historical record. Again and again from Buna onwards the communiqués would announce that an operation had been successfully concluded when it was fairly evident that weeks, even months, of costly fighting lay ahead. Australian troops were sardonic about the policy whereby 'Allied' troops were referred to in the communiqués when the Australians were doing the fighting, but American troops when Americans were concerned. That the ambiguous term Allied troops was taken by American newspapers' readers to mean Americans seemed to be demonstrated when Americans, arriving to take over from a base that Australians had captured, were astonished to find only Australians in occupation.

The exaggerations and sometimes mendacity of the communiqués were obviously aimed at the American public in general and Washington in particular, and apparently the intention was to give the impression that successes were being won more swiftly and at less cost and that enemy losses and sometimes enemy strengths were heavier than they were.

The communiqués could not deceive the forward troops and indeed demonstrated a degree of indifference on the part of the flatterers who surrounded MacArthur towards the feelings of the men who were doing the fighting. The regrettable publicity policy of GHQ was directly controlled by Colonel L. A. Diller, one of the little group who had escaped with MacArthur from Corregidor. It seems to have derived largely from the defensive and mistrustful attitude of this group towards Washington, MacArthur's own abnormal sensitiveness to criticism and appetite for favourable publicity. As mentioned, when he sent Eichelberger forward to command the Americans at Buna he told him that if he captured the village he would not only award him decorations but would release his name for newspaper publication, and apparently said this in all earnestness and not as a little joke.

While GHQ was in Brisbane the GHQ communiqués inspired some anonymous comic poet to produce a lampoon that busy typewriters circulated

[1] *Reminiscences*, p. 171.

far and wide throughout the continent and beyond. Some sample verses
ran:

> *Here, too, is told the saga bold,*
> *   of virile, deathless youth*
> *In stories seldom tarnished with*
> *   the plain unvarnished truth.*
> *It's quite a rag, it waves the flag,*
> *   Its motif is the fray,*
> *And modesty is plain to see in*
> *   Doug's Communiqué. . . .*
>
> *'My battleships bombard the Nips from*
> *   Maine to Singapore;*
> *My subs have sunk a million tons;*
> *   They'll sink a billion more.*
> *My aircraft bombed Berlin last night.'*
> *   In Italy they say*
> *'Our turn's tonight, because it's right in*
> *   Doug's Communiqué. . . .'*
>
> *And while possibly a rumour now,*
> *   someday it will be fact*
> *That the Lord will hear a deep voice say*
> *   'Move over God—it's Mac'.*
> *So bet your shoes that all the news*
> *   that last great Judgment Day*
> *Will go to press in nothing less than*
> *DOUG'S COMMUNIQUE!*

After the Bismarck Sea battle MacArthur received congratulatory messages
from Roosevelt, Churchill, Curtin and the veteran RAF commander
Trenchard. About this time he was awarded the DSM for the third time and
in May appointed to the Grand Cross of the British Order of the Bath, an
honour which specially gratified him.

Whether or not he was a hero to the American people as a whole, there
were influential citizens at home who regarded him as the outstanding
leader. Some of the President's friends were urging that he be given supreme
command of all the armed forces. And in February the Republican Senator
Vandenberg was considering the nomination of MacArthur at the next
presidential election.[1]

Throughout this phase the small Australian–Dutch force had been con-
ducting guerilla operations on Timor. Various proposals had been made from
one direction or another to withdraw the force, which was under increasing

[1] Pogue, *Ordeal and Hope 1939–42*, p. 374.

pressure, or alternatively to send an expedition to retake the island. On 25 January MacArthur wisely ruled out one ambitious plan for a counter-invasion and soon the main force was withdrawn.

So ended MacArthur's first year as an Allied commander-in-chief. On each land front—Milne Bay, central Papua and southern New Guinea—periods of frustration and anxiety had ended in decisive success. On each front air power had played a decisive part: the fighters at Milne Bay, the transports in the Owen Stanleys, on the Buna coast and at Wau. MacArthur's planning had been bold and imaginative. Once its execution was begun the issue on the ground was decided in soldiers' battles to which the commander-in-chief could contribute little except by way of reinforcements and exhortation.

The successes had been achieved with minimal local help from the US Navy, which had waged its own campaign in the Solomons, only 400 miles from MacArthur's battlefields. Round Guadalcanal during the critical half year there had been a maximum concentration of American naval strength and transports. Next door MacArthur had to make do with his small Australian–American cruiser and destroyer force in support and, directly serving the battle area, a valiant hotchpotch of Australian corvettes, merchant ships (mainly Dutch), luggers and captured landing craft.

The land fighting on Guadalcanal had been a successful defensive battle, at the end of which 13,000 Japanese troops were withdrawn. The victory in Papua was the first successful offensive against a Japanese army in the Pacific War. The invading force had been thrust back across the mountains, encircled and destroyed. MacArthur could now resume the planning of the larger offensive the enemy had interrupted six months earlier.

VII

Advance to Morotai

1943–44

By April 1943 the tide had turned in the Allies' favour on every land front. In January a German army had surrendered to the Russians at Stalingrad and the long siege of Leningrad had been broken. Soon 205,000 Axis troops would surrender in Tunisia. In the south Pacific the Japanese had abandoned Guadalcanal and their advance towards Wau in New Guinea had been repulsed.

But General MacArthur and Admiral Halsey considered that they lacked the means of promptly following up the Japanese defeats. In the South Pacific Area Halsey had a formidable fleet including six battleships, five carriers and 13 cruisers; and he had seven infantry divisions, three of which needed rest after Guadalcanal. His Thirteenth Air Force possessed some 500 aircraft. MacArthur had his Seventh Fleet, so named in March, built around two Australian cruisers and one American; Kenney's Fifth Air Force with 1,400 aircraft including many second-line machines; and 15 divisions (12 Australian,[1] two US Army and one US Marine) but nearly all the battle-tried formations were either in need of a long period of recuperation from tropical diseases or were still engaged in New Guinea. These included the 1st Marine Division, 32nd and 41st US Divisions, and the two veteran AIF divisions. Resumption of the offensive originally planned nine months before and aimed at Rabaul would demand amphibious forces, but so far Rear-Admiral Daniel E. Barbey's Seventh Amphibious Force, established in January, was only a skeletal training organization. By June it would be able to employ in operations only four destroyer-transports (old destroyers converted), six LSTs and about 30 landing craft.

Although his American combat troops included only three divisions with a

---

[1] Two of these were in Western Australia and one in the Northern Territory. Two were armoured divisions, for which no active role would be found in the SWPA although from time to time individual regiments had been and would be employed in the field.

corps headquarters, MacArthur in January had succeeded in enlarging the superstructure of his command by adding an American Army headquarters to the two Australian Army headquarters already in existence. He asked the War Department for and was given Lieutenant-General Walter Krueger, a very senior commander aged almost 62 and then commanding the Third Army in the United States. Krueger was a dour, studious, tenacious soldier who had come up from the ranks. The new army was named the Sixth. Thus there were now three Army headquarters and four corps headquarters (New Guinea Force merged with I Australian Corps, II Australian Corps, III Australian Corps—in Western Australia—and I United States Corps). As mentioned, MacArthur had not wanted an Australian as Commander of Allied Land Forces. The existence of an American Army headquarters would enable him to concentrate his American formations under a senior American commander, whom he soon made directly responsible to him and not to Blamey.

By this time Kenney's handling of his air force had caused MacArthur to change his views of ten years before on the desirability of an autonomous air arm. He told a delighted Kenney that his opposition when Chief of Staff to a separate air force was the greatest mistake of his career.[1]

Meanwhile planning had been going on at the highest levels. President Roosevelt, Mr Churchill and their staffs met at Casablanca in January to decide Allied strategy in the next phase of the war. When it came to deciding what resources would be deployed against the main enemy, Germany, and how much to the 'holding war' in the Pacific, General Marshall proposed that 70 per cent should be allotted to the Western theatre and 30 per cent to the Pacific, and Admiral King supported him, declaring that only 15 per cent of Allied resources were then employed against the Japanese. (Presumably he was including Russian as well as British and American resources in this estimate.) These percentages were nebulous notions of the kind that are advanced in committee as a starting point for discussion. At all times more than 30 per cent of American naval power had been in the Pacific. At this meeting the British Chiefs of Staff, to whom that part of the globe east of Singapore and west of the Americas was little known, urged that the Allies should go on the defensive in the Pacific. Admiral Pound, the senior British naval representative, thought it would be impossible to regain the Philippines until after the defeat of Germany.

The conference confirmed the policy, imposed on Washington by insoluble differences between the army and navy (the Japanese suffered from the same lack of control at the top), of pursuing two lines of advance in the Pacific: from Hawaii and from the south-west Pacific. It was accepted that if

[1] Kenney, *The MacArthur I Know*, p. 179.

there was no invasion of Europe in 1943 the Americans would press on in the Pacific. And on 24 January Roosevelt had announced to the Press his unfortunate decision to demand unconditional surrender of each of the Axis Powers. One by one the lessons of history were being forgotten.

The Combined Chiefs of Staff agreed at Casablanca that the first moves in the Pacific would be to take Rabaul, secure the Aleutians and then advance on Truk and the Marianas, not along the short route from Rabaul but by way of the Marshalls and Gilberts. Operations in the Pacific and the Burma-Chinese theatre were placed fifth in a list of priorities. First came the protection of sea communications, second aid to Russia, third operations in the Mediterranean, fourth the build-up of forces in England.

Thenceforward the general design of Allied strategy in the Pacific was unchanged, though there were important adjustments of timing and intermediate objectives. The unity of command which both MacArthur and King advocated, but from different angles, would not be achieved, nor would the main forces be concentrated in a concerted advance along a single axis. As General Arnold wrote after the war:

> The Navy had been determined from the start to make and keep it a Navy war, under Navy control. . . . Another thing—the War Department, for many years, had seemed to have the attitude that we shouldn't try to obtain unification of command in the Pacific. We must not bring the facts out squarely. We must not get the Navy mad at us right now. We must accept things as they were, even though we thought a change might be for the better. . . . So we continued operating in our inefficient way, with first three, then two commands—MacArthur's and Nimitz'—both working towards the same end—the defeat of Japan, with overlapping lines of communication, overlapping air operations, overlapping sea operations, and, finally, overlapping land Army operations.[1]

Of King, Marshall's biographer wrote that 'although far more conciliatory than his bleakness of manner and rudeness in debate often indicated, he was less disposed than the Army chief to seek agreement and was extremely jealous of the interest of the Navy.'[2]

Towards the end of 1943 on his way home from the Cairo Conference Marshall spent the day at MacArthur's headquarters and there was frank discussion. As MacArthur recalled it later Marshall said:

> Admiral King claimed the Pacific as the rightful domain of the Navy; he seemed to regard the operations there as almost his own private war. . . . He was adamant in his refusal to allow any major fleet to be under other command than that of naval officers although maintaining that naval officers were competent to command ground or air forces; he resented the prominent part I had in the

[1] H. H. Arnold, *Global Mission* (London, 1951), p. 249.
[2] Pogue, *Ordeal and Hope 1939-42*, p. 373.

Pacific War; he was vehement in his personal criticism of me and encouraged Navy propaganda to that end; he had the complete support of the Secretary of the Navy, Knox, the support in general principle of President Roosevelt and his Chief of Staff, Admiral Leahy, and in many cases of General Arnold, the Head of the Air Force.[1]

MacArthur said that he felt that it was fantastic that interservice rivalry or personal ambitions should interfere with the winning of the war: he had publicly stated that to secure unity of command he would accept a subordinate assignment.

On 6 January, before Casablanca opened, King proposed to MacArthur that until the capture of Rabaul the forces in the Solomons and those in the south-west Pacific should be under separate commanders—MacArthur and Halsey—and that after the fall of Rabaul MacArthur should direct the offensive but under Nimitz' command. Marshall instructed MacArthur to consult Nimitz and Halsey about plans for taking Rabaul. Before this conference was held MacArthur replied that Rabaul could not be captured without long preparation and greater resources than he then possessed. King still needled MacArthur to state his detailed plans for task two of the July directive: Lae, Salamaua and north-east New Guinea. MacArthur asked permission to send staff officers to Washington for talks. As a result representatives of the SWPA, South Pacific and Central Pacific Areas met in mid-March. Meanwhile the sinking of the Japanese convoy in the Bismarck Sea had transformed the situation. Kenney, Sutherland and Chamberlain represented the SWPA at this conference, which was to prove of more significance to MacArthur's future operations than the remote discussions at Casablanca had been.

Sutherland presented a plan dated 28 February and code-named *Elkton*. He estimated that 79,000 to 94,000 Japanese were in New Guinea and the Solomons, where they were mainly concentrated in defence of naval and air bases, with areas in between mostly unoccupied. They had an estimated 383 land-based aircraft and a fleet including four battleships, two aircraft carriers and 14 cruisers. If attacked they could be promptly reinforced by up to 12,000 troops, 250 aircraft and a great part of the Combined Fleet. Task one of the Joint Chiefs' directive of July 1942 had been completed, he added. To achieve tasks two and three would require advances by south Pacific forces along the Solomons and by SWPA forces in New Guinea and New Britain. The *Elkton* plan proposed five operations: first, seizure of airfields on the Huon Peninsula from which to support landings on New Britain; second, seizure of airfields on New Georgia; third, seizure of airfields on New Britain and Bougainville; fourth, capture of Kavieng, thus isolating Rabaul

[1] *Reminiscences*, p. 183.

(but possibly Kavieng might be taken after Rabaul); fifth, capture of Rabaul. To achieve this MacArthur and Halsey wanted five more divisions, 45 more air groups, plus additional naval forces, transports and landing craft.

On the first day of the conference Sutherland radioed MacArthur that the Washington delegates had promptly told the Pacific delegates that they could not have these reinforcements. Only two or three more divisions and a limited number of aircraft could be transported to the south-west Pacific and maintained there.

The Pacific delegates were asked what they could do in 1943 with the forces allotted. They replied that they would advance to south-east Bougainville, Woodlark and Kiriwina Islands, Cape Gloucester and Madang—that is, task two of the July directive.

Later the Joint Chiefs sought a timetable for these operations. The south Pacific leaders wanted to land on New Georgia about 10 April. MacArthur, consulted by radio, opposed concurrent action in the SWPA and south Pacific and wanted New Georgia postponed until he had secured the Huon Peninsula and could support Halsey by heavy bombing of Rabaul. After that New Georgia could be taken and Rabaul attacked from west and south simultaneously.

Finally on 28 March the Joint Chiefs cancelled the July 1942 directive and issued a new one that followed the lines of *Elkton*. The operations in the Solomons would be conducted by Halsey, but subject to 'general directives' from MacArthur, who was asked to submit detailed plans.

Halsey had come to Brisbane to discuss the *Elkton* plan with MacArthur and each was favourably impressed with the other. The bluff and friendly Halsey was not possessed by the prejudice against MacArthur that worked strongly in other naval commanders. Afterwards Halsey described MacArthur at this their first meeting:

> Pacing his office, almost wearing a groove between his large spare desk and the portrait of George Washington that faced him; his corncob pipe in his hand (I rarely saw him smoke it); . . . making his points in a diction I have never heard surpassed.[1]

For his part MacArthur found Halsey 'blunt, outspoken, dynamic' and 'a strong advocate of unity of command in the Pacific'; but 'there seemed always to be an undercurrent opposed to him in the Navy Department. . . . The bugaboo of many sailors, the fear of losing ships, was completely alien to his conception of sea action. I liked him from the moment we met. He was about my age.'[2]

[1] W. F. Halsey and J. Bryan, *Admiral Halsey's Story* (New York, 1947), p. 155.
[2] *Reminiscences*, p. 117.

At this meeting Halsey persuaded MacArthur that the invasion of New Georgia and the landings in the Trobriands should be simultaneous, and thus the New Georgia operation would come before the one against the Huon Peninsula. As a result MacArthur's detailed plan provided that the offensive (originally planned for 1 June) would open on 30 June with the operations against Kiriwina, Woodlark and New Georgia. Lae would be seized two months later, Salamaua and Finschhafen six weeks after that, and then, two weeks later, Madang. In mid-December Halsey would take Buin-Faisi (south Bougainville) and in January Buka (north Bougainville). Meanwhile in December SWPA forces would occupy western New Britain. From New Britain and Bougainville fighters and medium bombers would be able to attack Rabaul and Kavieng in preparation for the amphibious expedition against Rabaul.

On land and in the air the forces of MacArthur and Halsey were vastly stronger, on paper, than those of their opponents, and the commanders' requests for reinforcements amounting to five more divisions and a doubling of air strength to 3,700 planes was evidence of their conviction that against Japanese troops they needed overwhelming numbers and fire power. From Rabaul General Imamura and his Eighth Area Army controlled, in the Solomons, Lieutenant-General Haruyoshi Hyakutake's Seventeenth Army, which included one division, the 6th, and independent army and naval units equal to another; on the New Guinea mainland Lieutenant-General Adachi's Eighteenth Army, including the 20th, 41st and 51st Divisions; and at Rabaul under his direct command the 38th Division and independent brigades and regiments enough to form two more. The 17th Division would arrive at Rabaul in August, and the naval troops there were equivalent to another division.

There had been a difference of opinion between the Japanese Navy and Army about the policy to be followed in the Solomons: the army wished to fall back to Bougainville but the navy to hold New Georgia and Santa Isabel. As a compromise the Eighteenth Army was concentrated at Bougainville but naval troops and some army troops remained in the central Solomons under naval command.

In the five months from February to June the only fighting on land by troops under MacArthur's direction had been in the tangle of mountains between the Australian base at Wau and the Japanese base at Salamaua. There an Australian force, still air-supplied, eventually including the 3rd Australian Division headquarters and five battalions, gradually pushed the Japanese back along the ridges dominating Salamaua and patrolled deeply farther north.

MacArthur's plans for the opening of the offensive on 30 June had provided for a feint landing in the Salamaua area that day. But Blamey obtained MacArthur's agreement to substituting for the feint the actual seizure of Nassau Bay by seaborne forces. This would enable a junction to be made with the Australian force inland and seaborne supply of the combined force. At the same time it might draw enemy troops away from Lae, a main objective in the next phase.

Before the first moves in the proposed offensive began yet another high level strategic conference was held—*Trident*, which opened at Washington on 12 May. Here it was confirmed that there would be two lines of advance in the Pacific, and it was decided that seven additional army divisions would be needed for the capture of the Marshalls and Carolines and the remainder of New Guinea.

On 11 June Admiral King complained of the inactivity in the Pacific since the Papuan and Guadalcanal operations; advised an attack on the Marshalls about 1 November, and said that MacArthur should fix precise dates for the SWPA operations. MacArthur sensibly replied that to name any dates after 30 June would be guesswork. King continued to demand a definite timetable and to press that Nimitz be given authority to fix the dates of all amphibious operations in the Pacific—in effect to subordinate MacArthur to the Pacific naval command. Marshall wanted existing command arrangements preserved, with the Joint Chiefs timing both commanders' operations.

On 15 June the Joint Chiefs told MacArthur that, tentatively, operations against the Marshalls would open about mid-November and the 1st Marine Division would be withdrawn from Australia and the 2nd Marine Division with all landing craft and most of Halsey's naval ships from the south Pacific to take part in this offensive. Again MacArthur was asked for a timetable. He replied by stating a case for concentrating on an advance along his south-north axis. He was convinced, he wrote on 20 June, that the best course was an advance from Australia through New Guinea to Mindanao.

This movement can be supported by land-based aircraft which is utterly essential and will immediately cut the enemy lines from Japan to his conquered territory to the southward. By contrast a movement through the mandated islands will be a series of amphibious attacks with the support of carrier-based aircraft against objectives defended by naval units and ground troops supported by land-based aviation. Midway stands as an example of the hazards of such operations. Moreover no vital strategic objective is reached until the series of amphibious frontal attacks succeed in reaching Mindanao. The factors upon which the old Orange plan were based have been greatly altered by the hostile conquest of Malaya and the Netherlands East Indies and by the availability of Australia as a base.[1]

[1] M. Matloff, *Strategic Planning for Coalition Warfare, 1943-44* (Washington, 1959), a volume in the official series *United States Army in World War II*, p. 188.

The withdrawal of the two marine divisions, he added, would make the capture of Rabaul impossible and have 'profound political repercussions'—presumably in Australia, which was most improbable. At last he set out a timetable for operations planned for the remainder of the year, and listed the troops needed to carry them out: two regimental combat teams for the seizure of Kiriwina and Woodlark on 30 June, three Australian divisions and the 1st Cavalry Division to take the north-east New Guinea coast beginning on 1 September, the 1st Marine Division and 32nd Division with the 24th and 41st Divisions in reserve to attack western New Britain from 1 December. Halsey would take New Georgia with the 43rd Division and would begin the capture of Bougainville about 15 October.

In the event few of these predictions and allocations were realized, thus confirming MacArthur's earlier statement that they would be guesswork. But his arguments produced swift results: Marshall refused to withdraw the 1st Marine Division from MacArthur's command and confirmed the decision to move the 1st Cavalry and the 24th Division to Australia.

Also in June came a proposal to move two bomber groups from either MacArthur's or Halsey's command to the central Pacific about November or perhaps later. On 24 June MacArthur told Marshall that the withdrawal of the two groups would 'collapse the offensive effort' in the South-West Pacific Area, and reiterated that the offensive against Rabaul should be considered 'the main effort' and 'not be nullified or weakened by withdrawal to implement a secondary attack'. MacArthur not only retained these bomber groups but soon received two additional groups of fighters.

The only major operation in the first phase of the offensive was in Halsey's area where, on 21 June, the main body of a marine battalion occupied an area at the south end of New Georgia and began making a fighter strip there, and on the 30th landings were made on nearby islands. From 2 to 5 July the main body of the reinforced 43rd American Division began landing on each side of Munda on New Georgia, which initially was garrisoned by two Japanese infantry battalions and a marine unit. On Kolombangara Island, a few miles to the north-west, were four more battalions. In the New Georgia group a long and painful struggle developed into which a second American division—the 43rd—and, later, parts of the 25th American and 3rd New Zealand Divisions were drawn. Not until early October were the central Solomons secured, after fighting which an American historian has described as ranking with Guadalcanal and Buna 'for intensity of human tribulation'.[1] The Americans lost 1,136 dead but gained airfields from which their fighters could operate over Bougainville, the next stepping-stone towards Rabaul.

MacArthur's landings in the Trobriands were in the nature of an exercise

[1] S. E. Morison, *Breaking the Bismarck's Barrier*, p. 224.

and one which was much needed. The islands were not occupied by the Japanese. Indeed Australian coastwatchers had long been stationed there. A regiment of the 1st Cavalry Division was put ashore on Woodlark and an infantry regiment on Kiriwina.

Also on the 30th a force built round a battalion of the 41st Division landed at Nassau Bay, unopposed but in some confusion, and linked with parties of the 3rd Australian Division. During July and August the two Australian brigades and one American regiment thrust the Japanese back to their last line of defence round Salamaua.

MacArthur was now ready for the seizure of Lae and the Huon Peninsula as a step towards gaining control of western New Britain. The arduous advance on Salamaua had succeeded in its aim of drawing troops from Lae. In the last half-year Australian troops had secured and developed airfields on the plateau west of the peninsula. The plan was now to land the 9th Division east of Lae, to put American paratroops down at Nadzab (this was Blamey's idea) and thereafter to move troops of the 7th Australian Division to Nadzab, some by air and some on foot. These would advance along the Markham Valley and attack Lae from the west. The offensive would open on the 4th.

Blamey reorganized the command in New Guinea in preparation for an offensive which would be carried out mainly by Australians. He brought General Mackay forward to Port Moresby from the Second Australian Army as temporary commander of New Guinea Force. General Herring's I Corps comprised the 7th and 9th Divisions (the latter in its first operation since El Alamein), the 5th Division round Salamaua and the 11th Division. The 3rd Division, and outlying forces in the highlands were directly under Mackay. Never before in the Pacific war had so formidable a force been launched against the Japanese at the outset of an offensive.

Meanwhile Kenney's air force, growing in size and improving in skill and confidence, had been operating from its advanced airfields and had won a notable success. Reconnaissance had shown some 200 aircraft of the Japanese Fourth Air Army on the four fields round Wewak, headquarters of this air army and Adachi's Eighteenth Army. On 17 August Kenney's squadrons caught most of the enemy aircraft on the ground and destroyed about 100 of them. Thenceforward the Japanese land-based forces ceased to offer a serious threat to MacArthur's advance in New Guinea, though it made brave but sporadic efforts. During the landing of the 9th Division east of Lae on the morning of 4 September nine aircraft attacked a big convoy and damaged two LCIs. In the afternoon small numbers of aircraft including torpedo bombers crippled two LSTs, and finally a force of about 70 aircraft from Rabaul attacked; perhaps 23 were shot down by 48 of the new American long-range Lightning fighters. Altogether Japanese aircraft caused about 170 casualties to a force of which nearly 8,000 had been landed before midday with 6,200 to follow by the next day.

The airborne landing went equally well. Inspecting the 503rd Parachute Regiment, which was to descend on Nadzab, MacArthur found 'as was only natural, a sense of nervousness among the ranks' and decided he would fly with them. 'I did not want them to go through their first baptism of fire without such comfort as my presence might bring them. But they did not need me.' After this 'to my astonishment I was awarded the Air Medal. . . . I felt it did me too much credit.'[1]

The three battalions of the parachute regiment with a detachment of Australian gunners and eight guns had been embarked in 87 transport planes. Australian pioneers and engineers had made a forced march to the Nadzab area and the parachute landings were unopposed either on land or in the air. There was hard fighting along both lines of advance to Lae and for the 9th Division some difficult river crossings, but on the 16th leading troops of each division entered Lae. About 1,500 Japanese were killed; the Australians had 188 casualties. But some 6,000 Japanese of the reinforced 51st Division escaped north-west from Lae and began to struggle painfully over the forbidding ranges towards the north coast of the Huon Peninsula. The landing east of Lae marked an epoch in MacArthur's advance. He now possessed in Barbey's amphibious force of naval transports, landing craft and his supporting engineer troops the means and the procedures whereby he could place a division or more ashore, and an air force that could guarantee protection against major intrusion by enemy aircraft.

Adachi, having ordered withdrawal from Lae—he had little choice—determined to hold in the Ramu Valley and at Finschhafen. He ordered his 20th Division from Madang to Finschhafen and sent an additional regiment into the Ramu Valley. The main body of his 41st Division was still at Wewak.

As mentioned, MacArthur had planned to attack Finschhafen six weeks after Lae. But the speedy capture of Lae and Salamaua (entered on 11 September) and indications that the enemy was reinforcing Finschhafen caused him to reconsider his timetable. Already on 31 August Blamey had proposed to MacArthur that after the capture of Finschhafen by a seaborne force he should seize a base between Finschhafen and Bogadjim, 178 miles farther on, and then descend on Madang, the final objective, with seaborne and airborne forces and his air-supplied 7th Division from the Ramu Valley. At the same time he advised that Krueger should take Cape Gloucester before he attacked Madang which was much farther from Finschhafen than Cape Gloucester was.

---

[1] *Reminiscences*, p. 179.

MacArthur's staff agreed in general and chose Saidor as the intermediate objective. They advised MacArthur that Saidor might make Madang inessential. After much discussion MacArthur, on 15 September—the day before Lae fell—ordered Blamey to seize Kaiapit and Dumpu in the Ramu Valley and develop airfields there; on the 17th he ordered Blamey to advance on Finschhafen as soon as possible.

His orders were promptly executed. In a brilliant action an Australian Independent Company took Kaiapit on 19 September and by 6 October part of the airborne 7th Division had been flown to Dumpu. A brigade of the 9th Division landed north of Finschhafen on 22 September, five days after MacArthur's order was received. Despite the presence of some 5,000 Japanese round Finschhafen (not 350 as Willoughby had estimated) the Australian brigade had fought its way into Finschhafen by 2 October. After a period of hesitation MacArthur agreed to provide means of transporting a second brigade to Finschhafen to help meet an inevitable Japanese counter-offensive.

Meanwhile the higher staffs in Washington and Brisbane had been discussing future plans. On 21 July Marshall proposed to MacArthur that instead of assaulting Rabaul he might encircle and isolate that fortress by taking Kavieng, Manus and Wewak. MacArthur replied that it would be hazardous to attack Wewak, which was heavily garrisoned, before Rabaul. He would prefer to isolate and bomb Wewak during the advance on Rabaul. Possession of Rabaul was necessary to provide him with a naval base from which to support further operations. (In the event, however, Rabaul was not captured during the war.)

In August MacArthur sent to Washington his outline plan (*Reno*) for an advance to the Philippines. From Rabaul he proposed to move along western New Guinea and thence to Mindanao by way of Halmahera, Morotai and Menado in Celebes. He believed he could capture Rabaul and the Admiralties by mid-1944 but would not reach Mindanao before 1945, or perhaps later.

At this time the joint planners in Washington were drawing up a tentative timetable. They predicted that the central Pacific forces, having attacked Kiska on 15 August, would take the Gilberts on 15 November, the Marshalls on 1 January 1944, Ponape on 1 June, Truk on 1 September, Palau on 31 December; and MacArthur, having attacked on the Lae–Madang coast on 1 September, would take Buin on 15 October and New Britain and Kieta on 1 December, would neutralize Rabaul and take Wewak on 1 February, Kavieng on 1 May, Manus on 1 June, Hollandia on 1 August, and would reach Manokwari by 30 November. Thus they reasserted that Rabaul should be by-passed despite MacArthur's insistence that he needed it, and they pictured MacArthur's forces reaching the equator by nine stages while

Nimitz' forces in five stages reached Palau 500 miles to the north and somewhat nearer the Philippines. They also plainly stated that the advance through the central Pacific should be the main one and operations in MacArthur's area and Burma subsidiary. They considered that objectives for 1945 and 1946 would be the Philippines, Formosa, the Ryukyus and Malaya. Operations against the Japanese homeland would begin in 1947 and continue into 1948.

At the *Quadrant* conference at Quebec in August the British Chiefs of Staff questioned the desirability of advancing against Japan along two axes and suggested that MacArthur's forces should merely hold their gains while the main drive was made through the central Pacific. This would enable more strength to be added to the invasion of Europe in May 1944. But King now said that both operations were essential, and Marshall that the necessary troops and equipment were in MacArthur's command or on the way. The policy of isolating Rabaul instead of assaulting it was confirmed.

> The decision to neutralize Rabaul marked the first official pronouncement of a policy of by-passing strong centres of resistance and foreshadowed the gradual replacement of the earlier conservative step-by-step method of operations in the Pacific.[1]

MacArthur's recollection long afterwards that after Buna his policy was 'to by-pass Japanese strong points and neutralize them by cutting their lines of supply' was inaccurate. And so was his recollection that his 'primary goal in 1943 was to cut off the major Japanese staging area, the menacing airfields, and the bulging supply bases at Rabaul'.[2]

MacArthur was disappointed when the *Quadrant* conference laid down no programme for his forces, and he feared that the increasing weight being given to the central Pacific drive might mean that his advance was halted short of the Philippines. But the Joint Chiefs reassured him in October that the Japanese were to be pressed from every direction; planning for the capture of Mindanao should continue. Thereupon MacArthur sent the Joint Chiefs a revised *Reno* plan in which he proposed a compromise concerning Rabaul: it would be by-passed at first but captured later. The new plan provided for the isolation of Rabaul by the capture of Kavieng and the Admiralties about 1 February. For these operations he thought he would need seven divisions, two parachute regiments and 59 air groups, with ten divisions for garrison tasks. In later phases he would in June secure Humboldt Bay and positions in the Arafura Sea, in August the Vogelkop, and in October Geelvinck Bay. These operations would employ six divisions and one parachute regiment plus 13 divisions for garrisons. Menado would be

[1] Matloff, p. 235.
[2] *Reminiscences*, pp. 166-8.

attacked in December 1944 and Mindanao in February 1945. MacArthur sent Sutherland to Washington in November to discuss this revised plan with the Joint Chiefs before the *Sextant* conference to be held in Cairo later that month. Sutherland expounded the advantage of a major advance via the Philippines, but the joint planners decided that the forces MacArthur sought could not be provided.

However, in spite of the policy of defeating Hitler first, 13 American Army divisions and three marine divisions were now deployed against the Japanese, compared with 13 army divisions against Germany.[1] Seventy-five groups of the Army Air Force were deployed in the European theatre and 35 in the Pacific, but this was offset by the concentration of naval air forces in the Pacific.

A timetable for the operations against Japan in 1944 was presented at the *Sextant* conference. In MacArthur's area it predicted the seizure of western New Britain by 31 January and thereafter of Hansa Bay in February, Kavieng in March, Manus in April, Hollandia in June and the Vogelkop in August. During the year the central Pacific forces were to advance to the Marianas and thence begin bombing Japan in December. The general plan was to advance to the Formosa–Luzon area. The main decisions at Cairo concerned operations against Germany. There was final agreement to cross the Channel in the spring of 1944 and to subordinate operations in the Mediterranean to this main drive.

The incursion of New Guinea Force into the Huon Peninsula at Finschhafen and into the Ramu Valley led to a long struggle which lasted in the first area until early December and in the second until the end of January, and culminated in the total defeat of that part of Adachi's army that was forward of the Sepik River and the disastrous retreat of the survivors to Wewak. In mid-October the Japanese had launched a counter-attack which succeeded in reaching the coast north of Finschhafen and cutting the Australian force in two, but by 20 October this effort had been defeated. The 9th Division then took the offensive and, thrusting west to Sattelberg and north to cut the lines of communication from the coast, had defeated the enemy by the first week in December and were pursuing survivors along the coast towards Madang.

It will be recalled that MacArthur's plan provided that Buin-Faisi in south Bougainville would be taken in October, a month before the invasion of New Britain. But in July Halsey, impressed by the strength of Japanese resistance in New Georgia, proposed to by-pass Bougainville and seize bases

---

[1] By September 1943 there were five American Army divisions— 6th, 7th, 27th, 33rd, 40th—in the Central Pacific Area; four—25th, 37th, 43rd, Americal—in the south Pacific; four—24th, 32nd, 41st, 1st Cavalry—in the SWPA. At the end of 1943, 92 American LSTs, 110 LCIS and 10 attack transports were deployed in the European theatre, compared with 125 LSTs, 99 LCIS and 34 attack transports in the Pacific.

on Shortland Island, whence he would neutralize the Japanese bases at strongly defended Buin with artillery fire. MacArthur agreed. In September Halsey, now impressed by the ease with which he had secured Vella Lavella, proposed an even easier course: to occupy the Treasury Islands and a position on Choiseul, and thence advance to Kieta or Empress Augusta Bay. MacArthur opposed this cautious plan because he wished the south Pacific air force to be within fighter range of Rabaul when he invaded western New Britain in December or January. He agreed that Halsey should occupy bases in the Treasuries and Choiseul in October but insisted that he should seize a base on Empress Augusta Bay on 1 November. From 12 October Kenney's air force stepped up its bombing of Rabaul, sending over 300 to 400 aircraft at a time.

Thus on 27 October a New Zealand brigade seized the Treasuries from a small Japanese garrison and marines made a diversionary raid on Choiseul. And on 1 November troops of the 3rd Marine Division landed at Torokina in Empress Augusta Bay, which was defended by only about 270 troops, and soon had formed a perimeter about 15 miles long and five deep around the airfield sites. By 9 December American fighters were based on Torokina, 250 miles from Rabaul.

So far in New Guinea the fighting had been done mainly by MacArthur's Australians. Henceforward in MacArthur's plan his Americans would lead the advance and under American command. He solved the problem presented by the existence of an Australian as commander of Allied Land Forces in February 1943 by naming Krueger's Sixth Army 'Alamo Force' and giving it the status of a task force directly under his command. It was a roundabout manœuvre to attain a desirable end which could have been achieved more straightforwardly. It was evident that when American troops took over the main task it would be politically unacceptable, and indeed militarily inadvisable, for them to be directed by an Australian commander and staff. After February MacArthur in effect had two task forces: Blamey's Australian Army Group and Krueger's Sixth Army, now poised to undertake the next phase of the offensive, the invasion of New Britain.

After much discussion at MacArthur's headquarters as to the exact objectives in New Britain MacArthur agreed to the requests of his naval commanders, Carpender and Barbey, that a PT boat base be established on the south coast. Arawe was chosen and a plan to land at Gasmata, farther east and closer to air attack from Rabaul, was abandoned. The main objective was Cape Gloucester. At the request of Major-General William H. Rupertus, whose division would attack Cape Gloucester, a proposed paratroop drop was abandoned on the ground that if bad weather, frequent over the island, prevented the drop the plan would be disrupted.

A regiment of 1st Cavalry Division landed round Arawe on 15 December against only a few hundred Japanese. At Cape Gloucester the tested 1st Marine Division landed on 26 December, supported by naval and air bombardment and protected by continuous air cover. After some hard fighting in which the marines lost 310 killed, Imamura ordered the Japanese force in western New Britain, mainly the recently arrived 17th Division and the 65th Brigade, to fall back to Rabaul to help prepare for the expected attack on that base.

MacArthur now decided to make the proposed landing at Saidor, thus putting a force across the route of withdrawal of the Japanese retreating from the Finschhafen area. An American regiment landed at Saidor on 2 January met little opposition and, having established a perimeter, forced the retreating Japanese to move off the main route on to difficult inland tracks, but timidly made no effort to intercept them. Of 13,000 Japanese troops who fought on the Huon Peninsula about 3,000 had been counted dead and thousands more would perish in the retreat. The Australians, now more than ever the masters of the Japanese in bush warfare, lost 283 killed from the landing at Finschhafen onwards. When MacArthur's offensive opened in September Adachi's army was about 90,000 strong. By March 1944, when the retreat to Wewak ended, only some 54,000 remained. It was by far the most costly single defeat the Japanese had suffered so far in their Pacific war.

But the summing-up by MacArthur's Intelligence section of the 1943 operations (reprinted in Willoughby and Chamberlain, *MacArthur 1941-51*) is less illuminating as a judgment on the tactics employed than for the glimpse it gives of the atmosphere of flattery and make-believe that was surrounding the General. It was 'a classic operation on interior lines' in which, after securing Finschhafen,

> the General immediately wheeled to the opposite shore of the vital Vitiaz Strait and established beachheads at Arawe and Cape Gloucester on New Britain. After further swift widening of the breach by amphibious envelopment of Talasea and Gasmata the approach to the Admiralties lay miraculously open, with a Japanese Army one on each flank rendered powerless to hinder the projected breakthrough.
>
> In the context 'miraculous' is a superficial word. To immobilize with a relatively small force the Japanese Eighth Army on the Rabaul flank represents a professional utilization not only of astute staff intelligence but of time and space factors cannily converted into tactical advantage. . . . And through these seemingly scattered actions, there runs a red thread of design, the operative 'leitmotif', the flexible, inexorable advance on the Philippines—somewhere—somehow—sometime.'[1]

The bald facts were that now MacArthur possessed command of the sea and air he could land troops where he chose, whereas the opposing armies on

[1] Willoughby and Chamberlain, pp. 139-40.

each flank could respond only by laborious movement along primitive roads and tracks or perilous coastwise advances in small craft. And it had not been part of MacArthur's own plan to pass Rabaul by; that policy had been imposed on him.

The same environment that produced extravagant private adulation of MacArthur—and equally unmeasured denunciation by those who disagreed with or opposed him—gave rise to what Robert E. Sherwood described later as 'the most unfortunate public relations policy that I have seen in any theatre of war'. Sherwood's comments, written about a visit to MacArthur's headquarters early in 1945, could be applied to the atmosphere of those headquarters from 1942 onwards:

> There are unmistakable evidences of an acute persecution complex at work. To hear some of the Staff officers talk one would think that the War Department, the State Department—the Joint Chiefs of Staff—and, possibly, even the White House itself—are under the domination of 'Communists and British Imperialists'. This strange misapprehension produces an obviously unhealthy state of mind. . . .[1]

From the outset the exaggerations and ambiguities of some of the GHQ communiqués and the efforts of MacArthur's staff to create a picture of a commander of more than human stature had caused resentment among some of the newspaper correspondents and occasionally inspired lampoons that gained wide private circulation. The theatrical nature of the general's own rare press conferences did little to ameliorate the censure. One observer describing a press conference at Brisbane late in 1943 wrote:

> The 30 or more war correspondents and officers present rose as the general made an impressive entry—bare-headed, grave, distinguished-looking, immaculate. His right arm was raised in salute. There was no other introduction. Pacing to and fro almost the length of the conference room, MacArthur immediately began to declaim his statement of the military situation. His phrasing was perfect, his speech clear and unhalting, except for pauses for dramatic emphasis; the correspondents took notes but there was no interruption of any kind. The conference room had become a stage, MacArthur the virtuoso, the other officers the 'extras' in the cast, and the correspondents the audience. It was a dramatic occasion. The statement ended, the general again raised his right arm in salute and strode from the room followed by one or two staff officers. The conference was over. One man alone had spoken—the Supreme Commander. There was no questioning, no opportunity to clarify the meaning of the statement. It had come direct from the lips of General Douglas MacArthur, and as such it was, evidently, beyond question.[2]

[1] Sherwood, p. 867.
[2] D. Gillison, *Royal Australian Air Force, 1939-42* (Canberra, 1962), a volume of the series *Australia in the War of 1939-1945*, p. 569.

Meanwhile, with the war two years old, the long-discussed advance through the central Pacific was under way. Plans and predictions that had foreseen the main American counter-offensive taking years to develop were proving soundly based. On 20 November a convoy carrying 35,000 troops protected by a big naval force descended on Makin and Tarawa Islands in the Gilberts. Makin was lightly defended and was gained with few casualties ashore, but on Tarawa there were 4,500 Japanese with a powerful array of artillery and the invaders lost more than 1,000 killed.

Thus from the outset it seemed likely that an offensive aimed at seizing a trans-Pacific causeway of islands, each defended by enemy forces resolved to die in the last ditch and with no means of escape, would prove expensive. Other handicaps imposed by the policy of advancing along two widely separated routes were now becoming increasingly apparent. Both offensives depended on the support of the Pacific Fleet. If it was committed to a central Pacific operation, a south-west Pacific operation for which plans and troops were ready might have to be postponed. Thus MacArthur was now in January prepared for attacks on Kavieng and Manus in March. But that month the Joint Chiefs had instructed Nimitz to make a full-scale carrier attack on Truk and therefore strong naval support for MacArthur could not be available until April. After subduing Truk Nimitz was to attack the western Marshalls in May and on 1 August either to land on Truk or pass it by and seize the Palaus.

Representatives of the three Pacific areas conferred at Pearl Harbor at the end of January, Sutherland representing the SWPA. The conference agreed that the Marianas were too far from Japan for effective use of B-29s, that Japan would have to be attacked from bases in China and that the formidable base at Truk could be by-passed and the advance carried direct to the Palaus.

In February 1944 MacArthur again pleaded with the Joint Chiefs for a concentration of force along his axis. He said that

> there are now large forces in the Pacific which would place us in the Philippines in December if . . . employed in effective combination. . . . All available ground, air and assault forces in the Pacific should be combined in a drive along the New Guinea–Mindanao axis, supported by the main Fleet. . . . I propose that on completion of operations in the Marshalls, the maximum force from all sources in the Pacific be concentrated in my drive up the New Guinea coast, to be coordinated with a Central Pacific operation against the Palaus and the support by combatant elements of the Pacific Fleet with orders to contain or destroy the Japanese Fleet. Time presses. . . .[1]

King objected, repeating that so far the progress of the central Pacific

[1] Willoughby and Chamberlain, p. 177.

advance had compared favourably with MacArthur's and that strategic control in the Pacific must be naval. It was difficult to see how King could regard progress in the central Pacific, where one group of islands had been seized on the very limit of the Japanese perimeter, as greater than that of MacArthur and Halsey who in 18 months of campaigning had regained the Solomons and the mainland of Australian New Guinea and advanced into New Britain.

In January and February Nimitz made another step forward, landing a force of 54,000 men, including one army and one marine division, on Majuro, Kwajalein and Eniwetok in the Marshalls. Only Kwajalein was strongly defended.

Meanwhile Halsey had been advocating the by-passing of the strongly defended enemy base at Kavieng and the seizure instead of Emirau, which was unoccupied and would provide an air base in much the same position relative to Rabaul as Kavieng. Marshall agreed but King would not. At a conference at Pearl Harbor of representatives of the SWPA, the South Pacific Area and the Central Pacific Area (Sutherland, Kenney and Admiral Thomas C. Kinkaid, who had now replaced Carpender, represented MacArthur) Sutherland announced that MacArthur now wanted Halsey to take Kavieng, not Emirau. Nimitz said that after the carrier strike on Truk he would send two divisions of carriers to operate under Halsey against Manus and Kavieng. When MacArthur learned that he would not be able to attack Manus and Kavieng for some months he decided to occupy the lightly defended Green Islands north of Bougainville and this was done by a New Zealand force on 15 February. A PT boat base was promptly established and in March airfields were in operation.

For the Admiralties MacArthur allotted Krueger the 1st Cavalry Division, a regular formation but now much watered down, plus 12,000 men in air and naval construction units. The Japanese garrison was built round two battalions which were deployed in defence of Seeadler Harbour and Momote airfield on Los Negros, the eastern island of the group.

By 6 February, after weeks of intensive bombing of Momote and Lorengau airfields, no Japanese planes remained. Attacks on the Wewak and Rabaul fields continued, and by 23 February there was good evidence that the battered air force was withdrawing from Rabaul. At the same time it seemed that major naval units had been withdrawn from Truk and there was no likelihood of strong naval or air interference with the landing in the Admiralties.

In these circumstances Kenney and Brigadier-General Ennis C. Whitehead, his deputy, were anxious to advance the date of the attack. Also on the 23rd Whitehead reported that reconnaissance aircraft over the island had seen no signs of an occupying force—no Japanese, no vehicles, no washing hanging out to dry. He recommended that a reconnaissance party be put ashore on Los Negros to occupy and repair the Momote field. If there was strong resistance the party could be withdrawn, if not it could be reinforced.

'If we got ashore and could stick', wrote Kenney afterwards, 'we could forget all about Kavieng and maybe even Hansa Bay. Manus was the key spot controlling the whole Bismarck Sea. That coral strip on Los Negros . . . was the most important piece of real estate in the theater.'[1]

MacArthur was soon persuaded, despite Willoughby's estimate that the Japanese force on the island was 4,000 strong, and on the 24th ordered Krueger to put ashore 800 men from destroyer transports not later than 29 February. MacArthur determined to accompany the force himself. Admiral Kinkaid, now commanding his naval force, had planned to support the landing force with four destroyers, but when he learned of MacArthur's decision he added two cruisers and four destroyers. 'This was necessary because a destroyer had neither accommodations nor communications equipment suitable for . . . MacArthur's age and rank. A cruiser would serve better, but a single cruiser could not go to the Admiralties. Kinkaid's policy forbade sending only one ship of any type on a tactical mission. Therefore he sent two cruisers, and the two cruisers required four additional destroyers as escorts.'[2]

Meanwhile the cautious Krueger, caught between the GHQ estimate that there were 4,000 Japanese on the island and Whitehead's that there were about 300, on the 27th sent in six scouts by flying-boat to the south-east shore of Los Negros. They reported the area to be 'lousy with Japs'. Kenney was not impressed but Kinkaid decided to deliver a stronger naval bombardment than planned hitherto.

On the 28th MacArthur in the cruiser *Phoenix* arrived at Cape Cretin, where Krueger's headquarters were established, determined to land with the reconnaissance force. Krueger urged him not to do so. MacArthur listened, thanked him, and said 'I have to go'. 'He had made up his mind on the subject—and that was that.'[3]

The chosen landing place was the beach of Hyane Harbour, an inlet about a mile wide, just north of Momote field. The first wave of landing craft came under fire while entering the harbour. *Phoenix* and other naval vessels quickly silenced this fire. 'According to Admiral Kinkaid this performance so thoroughly converted General MacArthur into a naval gunfire enthusiast

[1] Kenney, *The MacArthur I Know*, p. 359.
[2] John Miller Junior, *Cartwheel, the Reduction of Rabaul* (Washington, 1959), a volume in the series *United States Army in World War II*, pp. 321-2.
[3] Krueger, *From Down Under to Nippon*, p. 49.

that he became more royalist than the king, and thereafter Kinkaid frequently had to point out the limitations of naval gunfire to the general.'[1]

The first men were ashore by 8.17 and by 9.50 were on the airfield. By 12.50 two howitzers had been landed. MacArthur and Kinkaid went ashore about 4 p.m., MacArthur pinned the DSC on the first man to reach the beach, looked over the positions and ordered General Chase, the divisional commander, to 'hold the air strip at any cost'. Having ignored sniper fire 'wet, cold and dirty, with mud to the ears', he and Kinkaid at 5.30 returned to the *Phoenix*, whence the general sent off orders for swift reinforcement of the reconnaissance force.[2]

Chase wisely pulled his men back for the night to a shorter line about 1,500 yards north-west of the strip. In the darkness the Japanese made a determined attack but the American line held. Chase knew that no reinforcements could reach him until the 2nd. From 5 to 8 p.m. next day the Japanese attacked again but were held. On the following day some 2,000 more troops landed under fire, and that afternoon the cavalrymen secured the airfield and dug in along a perimeter surrounding it. There was no Japanese attack that night—they were concentrating for an all-out effort. This was delivered next night but the enemy was driven off after hours of close contact, leaving many dead. On 15 March the Americans made a successful landing near Lorengau. But it was not until May that the last pockets of Japanese were overcome. The cavalry had lost 330 killed and estimated the enemy dead at about 4,500.

The capture of this valuable base led to yet another army–navy dispute. Nimitz proposed to King that Halsey should develop the base under Nimitz' direction. MacArthur was furious and ordered that work on the Manus base be restricted to providing facilities for his Seventh Fleet plus its Australian units. At a discussion at Brisbane he, in Halsey's words, 'lumped me, Nimitz, King and the whole Navy in a vicious conspiracy to tear away his authority'.[3] Halsey managed to persuade the irate general to countermand his order, but at the same time work on the base was directed by MacArthur's admiral, Kinkaid.

The seizure of Manus completed the isolation of Rabaul, a situation which the Japanese High Command now accepted by adopting a reorganization which in effect left General Imamura's Eighth Area Army, with headquarters on New Britain, forward of the main line of resistance. The Second

---

[1] Miller, p. 326.

[2] Having been awarded the Air Medal for Nadzab MacArthur was awarded the Combat Bronze Star With Arrowhead for his landing in the Admiralties. Probably no other Commander-in-Chief would have allowed his staff to recommend him for decorations in this way or would have shown such boyish delight when he received them.

[3] Halsey and Bryan, p. 189.

Area Army headquarters had been moved from Manchuria to Davao in November. It controlled the Second Army recently moved to Manokwari and the Nineteenth Army based on Ambon. After the loss of Manus and the isolation of Rabaul the Eighth Area Army was placed directly under the command of Imperial General Headquarters, and Adachi's Eighteenth Army transferred to the Second Area Army. In the central Pacific Nimitz faced the Japanese Thirty-First Army, about 50,000 strong, and in the Palaus the augmented 14th Division. The Japanese High Command soon decided in the new circumstances to defend a line from Timor through the Aru Islands to Sarmi, the Palaus and the Marianas, thus placing not only their Eighth Area Army but also their Seventeenth Army in New Guinea outside the perimeter.

In March the Japanese fleet also had been reorganized. It was now primarily a carrier force. Practically every considerable surface ship in the Combined Fleet was concentrated in a First Mobile Fleet under Vice-Admiral Ozawa. It included three carrier divisions each of three carriers. As a result of the heavy losses from the Coral Sea onwards and an inadequate training system the carriers' air crews were mainly replacements and no match for the increasingly efficient American crews. The Commander of the Combined Fleet, Admiral Koga, now had his headquarters at Palau, since the abandonment of Truk as the main base.

The policy of by-passing strong enemy bases and leaving them to wither on the vine, of which tactics some of MacArthur's admirers were inclined to elect him the sole begetter, had in fact been accepted by MacArthur with hesitation. Fortunately for him and his forces the Joint Chiefs had weaned him away from his resolve to attack the immensely strong fortress of Rabaul and the strongly held base at Kavieng. It was the Joint Chiefs and Halsey between them who shaped the by-passing policy, which was one which could have been copied from the Japanese when they, for example, by-passed Bataan and Corregidor and encircled Java before making a direct attack on it. In the light of after-knowledge it was fortunate that MacArthur was compelled to by-pass Rabaul. Though battered by bombing, virtually undefended on sea and in the air, its garrison numbered almost 100,000 first-rate troops with about 900 guns and some tanks. The men were digging formidable fortifications and they and their stores would eventually be sheltered in about 350 miles of tunnels. The reduction of Rabaul would undoubtedly have cost the Allies more than any operation against the Japanese before 1945, and must have delayed for many months MacArthur's advance to the Philippines.

Now a convert to the policy pioneered by Halsey of making longer strides towards the Philippines, MacArthur on 5 March had informed Marshall that he would advance direct to Hollandia, 300 miles beyond Hansa Bay, the former objective, and 200 miles west of the big Japanese base at Wewak. Earlier MacArthur had radioed to Marshall that the forces in the Pacific plus reinforcements scheduled for 1944 could place him in the Philippines in December 'if the forces were employed in effective combination. However, under the plan . . . prepared in Washington, the forces will be employed in two weak thrusts which can not attain the major strategic objective until several months later. . . . '[1]

To a meeting of the Joint Chiefs in Washington on 8 March Sutherland declared that the SWPA needed 'certain naval forces for direct support of its operations' and that MacArthur wished Halsey to be assigned to him as commander of Allied naval forces. But King reminded the conference that at Cairo the Combined Chiefs had decided that the advance should be along two axes; General MacArthur had apparently not accepted this decision, but King did not think that this was a propitious time to change the agreed strategy. The final upshot was a directive by the Joint Chiefs issued on 12 March confirming the policy of isolating Rabaul, ordering the early occupation and development of Manus, the occupation of Hollandia by 15 April and of Mindanao by 15 November. At the same time Nimitz was instructed to seize the southern Marianas on 15 June and the Palaus on 15 September. Formosa, and if necessary Luzon were to be taken in February 1945. MacArthur was to make plans for Luzon, Nimitz for Formosa.

Thus on 20 March a regiment of marines was landed on the unoccupied island of Emirau where a torpedo boat and air base was soon established.

The South Pacific Command had now finished its tasks and the time had come to distribute its forces and terminate the awkward arrangement whereby Halsey was in command of the naval and army forces in the area but under the general direction of MacArthur. Most of the naval units and the 1st and 3rd Marine Divisions were transferred to Nimitz, the Thirteenth Air Force and XIV Corps (25th, 37th, 40th, 43rd, 93rd and Americal Divisions) to MacArthur.

In April and early May the Japanese facing MacArthur suffered a new calamity. Ships carrying some 20,000 troops from Shanghai to Halmahera were attacked by American submarines, two of which sank four transports and drowned about half the soldiers in the convoy.

With Rabaul isolated, Truk emasculated, and the Japanese Eighteenth Army in Australian New Guinea cut off and in retreat, MacArthur could now advance to the Philippines, seizing intermediate bases when and where he

---

[1] Quoted in P. A. Crowl, *Campaign in the Marianas* (Washington, 1960), a volume in the series *United States Army in World War II*.

pleased, confident that he would have the protection of overwhelming air power and adequate naval support. In the next six months, which took his Sixth Army from Saidor to Morotai, the economical nature of an advance along the coast of the land mass of New Guinea rather than from strongly defended island to strongly defended island was demonstrated. Thus in April he took Hollandia and Aitape at a cost of 609 killed. It was a classic victory. MacArthur had by-passed a strongly held base round Wewak where Adachi's still formidable Eighteenth Army, 50,000 strong, was concentrated and had attacked the soft base area round Hollandia, which included the headquarters of the Japanese Ninth Fleet. Of some 11,000 Japanese troops round Hollandia probably only about 1,000 managed to reach Sarmi alive. The 300 officers and men of the Ninth Fleet headquarters perished, including Admiral Endo, who probably committed *hara kiri*. The Ninth Fleet was not reformed. In May and June (when Allied armies were landing in Normandy) MacArthur took Wakde-Sarmi and Biak at a cost of 887 lives, in July Noemfoor (69) and Sansapor (34), and in September Morotai (31).

In the same period Nimitz' forces had secured bases in the Marianas and the Palaus where they were somewhat closer to the Ryukyus, last steppingstone to Japan, than MacArthur's forces. Nimitz had landed two marine divisions on Saipan, which was defended by some 32,000 Japanese, on 15 June and later reinforced them with an army division. The island was secured at a cost of 3,426 dead. While the attack on Saipan was in progress the Japanese Mobile Fleet sought a long-planned decisive battle with the Pacific Fleet which had been supporting the invasion with air bombardment and gunfire. The Japanese sent a force including nine carriers and five battleships against the 15 carriers and seven battleships of the Pacific Fleet. On 19 and 20 June in the biggest carrier versus carrier clash of the war the Americans sank three carriers (two sunk by submarine), inflicted disastrous aircraft losses on the Japanese and lost no carrier of their own. In July a marine division and an army division took Guam at a cost of 1,435 killed, and two marine divisions took Tinian where 389 Americans were killed. The capture of Peleliu and Angaur in the Palaus in September cost the lives of 1,800 troops.

It was a strange anomaly that whereas in the European theatre the American leaders had fought hard for the principles of a single united drive and had opposed subsidiary offensives in the Mediterranean, in the Pacific the jealousies of naval and army leaders made adoption of a single line of advance impossible.

During these six months MacArthur's army and its attendant flotillas of transports and landing craft had developed in confidence and skill. Whereas at the opening of the offensive in mid-1943 he had three American divisions of which two had been in severe actions, he now had 14 American divisions most of which had been in action, some more than once.

Of the three isolated Japanese armies Imamura's Eighth Area Army round Rabaul had done nothing to divert the Allied forces from their objectives, but both Hyakutake's army on Bougainville and Adachi's round Wewak had made resolute counter-attacks. On Bougainville in March Hyakutake launched 15,000 men in an attack on the American perimeter and lost perhaps 7,000 men who were killed in action or died in the subsequent retreat. In July Adachi attacked the Aitape perimeter using 20,000 men plus 10,000 in reserve, and pushed back the defenders' line but was defeated by a force eventually reinforced until it included about three divisions. The reward for these offensives was that in each area two divisions were tied up in defence of American bases.

In the last half of 1944 plans for the semi-final phase of the defeat of Japan had been under keen discussion in Washington and at Hollandia, whither in September MacArthur moved his main headquarters from Brisbane, which was then more than 2,000 miles behind the forward troops.

VIII

The Philippines Regained

1944–45

In June 1944, when MacArthur's leading troops were fighting for Biak and Nimitz' men were preparing to take Saipan, the Joint Chiefs of Staff, contemplating ways of hastening the advance to Tokyo, asked MacArthur and Nimitz for their opinions about advancing the dates of operations against Formosa by 'by-passing presently selected objectives', the implication being that the Philippines might be disregarded. Both Nimitz and MacArthur were emphatic that the existing timetable could not be accelerated unless they were given more power. MacArthur maintained that it would be unsound to attack Formosa without support of aircraft based on Luzon; Nimitz wished no decision to be made about by-passing chosen objectives until later. MacArthur reiterated that apart from military considerations it was necessary to regain the Philippines for political reasons.

> If the United States should deliberately by-pass the Philippines, leaving our prisoners, nationals and loyal Filipinos in enemy hands without an effort to retrieve them at earliest moment, we would incur the gravest psychological reaction. We would admit the truth of Japanese propaganda to the effect that we had abandoned the Filipinos and would not shed American blood to redeem them; we would undoubtedly incur the open hostility of that people.[1]

Marshall's comment was that 'personal and political considerations' should not interfere with the attainment of the main objectives: invasion of Formosa and Kyushu would aid the recovery of the Philippines.

At this time MacArthur's plan provided for an advance via Morotai to Mindanao on 25 October, Leyte on 15 November and finally invasion of Luzon with six divisions on 1 April 1945.

The Joint Chiefs decided that none of the previously selected objectives could be by-passed, but the President, conscious of the unhappy differences

[1] M. Hamlin Cannon, *Leyte: The Return to the Philippines* (Washington, 1954), a volume of the series *Unites States Army in World War II*, p. 4.

between MacArthur and the naval leaders in Washington, had MacArthur invited to Pearl Harbor for a conference with Nimitz on 26 July.

Meanwhile the capture of Saipan and the accompanying Japanese naval losses had caused the fall of the Tojo government, which had rapidly been losing face. Tojo resigned on 18 July from the post of Chief of the Army General Staff and was replaced by General Yoshijiro Umezu, the commander of the Kwantung Army—the army group in north China and Manchuria. He then resigned from the Premiership, being replaced by General Kuniaki Koiso, Governor-General of Korea. The army and navy leaders were still in full control, but were increasingly divided among themselves, and the government began planning to achieve a general peace settlement with Russian cooperation, but nothing came of it.

In the West time was running out for another dictator. On 20 July an elaborate plot to assassinate Hitler was attempted by a group of army officers, but failed.

MacArthur was not informed that President Roosevelt would be at the Pearl Harbor conference but guessed as much. 'As I had never before been invited to sit in on any of the big conferences, and in fact I never was again, I felt that something closely affecting me must be involved. I took no staff officers with me except personal aides-de-camp, and carried no plans or maps.'

Roosevelt was there, and so was Admiral Leahy, his chief of staff, but King had not been asked to attend, nor had Marshall or Arnold. King was of the opinion that, having just accepted nomination for a fourth term as President and with the Democratic National Convention approaching, Roosevelt wished to underline his role as Commander-in-Chief. King had been in Hawaii on the 21st, had briefed Nimitz for the coming conference and had written to MacArthur outlining the discussions between the American and British Chiefs of Staff in London in June. Next day he left Hawaii. Roosevelt had arrived on the 26th. When the conference opened on the 28th Nimitz seemed shocked to learn that MacArthur had not been told of the subject to be discussed or asked to bring staff. In the conference hall MacArthur found himself faced by a 'tremendous paraphernalia of maps, plans, manuscripts, statistics of all sorts and other visual adjuncts. I began to realize I was to go it alone.'[1]

Nimitz explained a plan, which MacArthur guessed was King's, whereby the Philippines were to be by-passed, and all American forces in the SWPA except two divisions and a few air squadrons were to be transferred to the command of Nimitz, who would continue the advance in the central Pacific and invade Formosa early in 1945. As before, MacArthur opposed the plan

[1] *Reminiscences*, p. 197.

on military and political grounds. Possession of the Philippines would enable America to prevent supplies from reaching Japan from the south and 'by paralyzing her industries, force her to early capitulation'. Frontal attacks on Iwo Jima and Okinawa would be costly; they could be neutralized. Formosa with its hostile population might prove of doubtful value as a base for attack on Japan. The Philippines could have been saved at the outset; to sacrifice them a second time 'could not be condoned or forgiven' and would result in the death of thousands of prisoners, including American women and children. When the discussion was resumed next day Roosevelt said that the recapture of Luzon would cause heavier losses than they could endure. MacArthur replied, as he recollected later: 'Mr President, my losses would not be heavy, any more than they have been in the past. The days of the frontal attack should be over. Modern infantry weapons are too deadly, and frontal assault is only for mediocre commanders. Good commanders do not turn in heavy losses.' MacArthur then expounded his own plan: once he had gained the Philippines he would begin to reconquer the Dutch East Indies, using the First Australian Army.

Roosevelt decided in MacArthur's favour and they spent an agreeable day together inspecting troops. Roosevelt asked MacArthur his opinion of the forthcoming presidential election. MacArthur told him that he knew nothing of the political situation at home but that Roosevelt was 'an overwhelming favorite with the troops', and this greatly pleased the President. For some time MacArthur had been talked of as a possible Republican candidate. He had taken pains to deny that he would accept nomination but evidently Roosevelt had his doubts. MacArthur later recorded that when the Australian Prime Minister had been in Washington in April, Curtin had gone out of his way to tell the President that MacArthur had told him 'a dozen times' that he had no idea of running for the presidency. Roosevelt, according to this account, was 'obviously delighted', summoned his Press Secretary and gleefully told him what Curtin had said. 'I am sure', said Curtin to MacArthur on his return to Australia, 'that every night when he turned in, the President had been looking under the bed to make dead sure you weren't there.'

It was not surprising that MacArthur won Roosevelt over. They were old associates and on several occasions Roosevelt had demonstrated his confidence in the general. Both were cast in an heroic mould. Both were patricians. Both were visionaries and were looking ahead, though through rather different spectacles, to the international situation after the war. It may be that his success at Pearl Harbor helped to give MacArthur an excess of confidence in his ability to overcome presidential opposition.

There was more discussion in Washington until, on 8 September, the

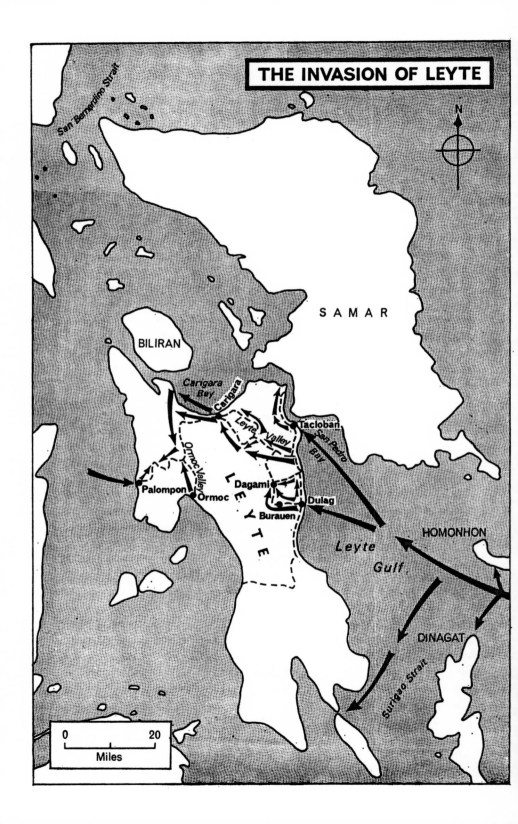

Joint Chiefs agreed to MacArthur's proposal to attack Leyte on 20 December. Then Nimitz stepped in. In the second week of September Halsey's aircraft, preparing for the assault on the Palaus, had attacked Mindanao and places in the Visayan archipelago and had reported that the area was 'wide open'; Filipinos had said that there were no Japanese on Leyte. He urged that his proposed attacks on Yap and MacArthur's on Mindanao be omitted and that MacArthur should assault Leyte with the help of three divisions intended for Yap. Marshall radioed MacArthur asking for his views. MacArthur was on his way to Morotai in a cruiser that was preserving radio silence, but Sutherland took the responsibility of immediately replying that, although the information that there were no Japanese on Leyte was incorrect, the South-West Pacific Command could launch a direct attack on Leyte with two of its own divisions and the three offered by Nimitz.

The notion that there were no Japanese on Leyte had been derived from an American pilot rescued by Filipinos. But MacArthur had better sources of information, including a guerilla network in the Philippines and information brought back by an intrepid naval officer who had first been landed on Mindanao in February 1943 and thence had made trips to Leyte. He knew therefore that in the spring a garrison numbering about 6,000 had been reinforced by the veteran Japanese 16th Division (which had been a main component of the Fourteenth Army in the operations on Luzon in 1941-42) plus 4,000 naval troops. In September his staff believed that there were 21,700 troops on Leyte, that the Japanese Thirty-Fifth Army, with headquarters on Cebu, could reinforce with from five to eight regiments from other islands in the Visayas within ten days and that the enemy could deploy about 800 aircraft over the island.

The directive issued to MacArthur and Nimitz said that all transports, fire support vessels and escort carriers used at the Palaus were to be lent to MacArthur for the Leyte operation.

MacArthur's plan provided that a Ranger (Commando) battalion would seize islands in the entrance to Leyte Gulf on 17 October, and on the 20th the first waves of the X and XXIV Corps would land on the inner shores of the gulf about the airfields of Tacloban and Dulag respectively, some 15 miles apart. In the second phase the X Corps would advance north and west across the island, and a detached regiment would land at the south end. In the third phase the X Corps would advance into Samar and the XXIV would take positions on the west coast. At this stage Krueger, who would command operations ashore, hoped to have driven the defenders into the mountains in disorder.

The plan provided that Admiral Kinkaid would command the amphibious forces until Krueger had established his headquarters on shore. Halsey's

Third Fleet, including Vice-Admiral Marc Mitscher's fast carrier task force, would provide naval protection and Kinkaid's Seventh Fleet close support. Kenney's air forces plus the Australian RAAF Command would attack the Japanese air and naval forces far and wide and give close support. Krueger's Sixth Army would comprise X Corps (1st Cavalry and 24th Divisions) under Lieutenant-General Franklin C. Sibert, and XXIV Corps (7th and 96th Divisions) under Major-General John R. Hodge. The 32nd and 77th Divisions were in reserve. About 174,000 troops were available for the opening phase. Thus this expedition was the largest yet undertaken in the Pacific.

The policy of by-passing whole Japanese armies was exacting its penalties. By the summer of 1944 six of MacArthur's 15 American divisions and other smaller formations were tied to the defence of bases on Bougainville, New Britain and the mainland of Australian New Guinea, now 800 to 1,200 miles behind the forward formations, and soon five other divisions would be on garrison duty or 'mopping up' farther west. To provide adequate forces for the reconquest of the Philippines MacArthur's armies would either have to be substantially reinforced from other theatres or relieved of responsibility for the by-passed areas. In the event both of these steps were taken. As early as March Blamey had foreseen that his troops would be required to take over in all Australian territories and had made tentative plans to allot these tasks to eight militia brigades including two resting and preparing to provide reliefs. This arrangement would leave Blamey's three veteran divisions—6th, 7th and 9th—all of volunteers, for tasks in the forefront of the advance.

On 12 July (when the advance had reached Noemfoor and the planning provided for a landing on Mindanao in October) MacArthur wrote to Blamey that he wished Australian forces to take over in the Solomons on 1 October and in New Britain and the mainland of New Guinea on 1 November. At the same time he told Blamey that he intended to use 'initially' two Australian divisions in the Philippines. Blamey proposed to deploy seven brigades to defend the three areas named by MacArthur, then defended by almost three times as many American regiments, but MacArthur would not agree to such slender forces, and after staff discussions directed that four brigades be deployed on Bougainville, one on outlying islands, three on New Britain and four on New Guinea (including one already in contact with the enemy there). This meant that of Blamey's six combat divisions available for service outside Australia, four including one AIF division would be tied down in the by-passed areas.

It was a puzzling decision in view of the fact that MacArthur was opposed to any offensive operations in these areas—the Japanese were to be left to wither on the vine. A likely explanation is that *amour propre* did not allow him to accept a proposal that three Australian divisions would suffice to carry out tasks hitherto performed by six American divisions.

Meanwhile in September a newly-formed American Eighth Army under Eichelberger had been ordered to relieve Krueger's Sixth Army of its remaining tasks in Dutch New Guinea, the Admiralties and Morotai. By the end of the year the First Australian Army had relieved all American combat formations in Australian territory, with its II Corps in and round Bougainville, 5th Division on New Britain and 6th Division at Aitape. Thenceforward this army operated against the Japanese Eighth Area Army and Seventeenth and Eighteenth Armies virtually independently of MacArthur's headquarters, on which, however, it was dependent for much of its logistical support.

In the second week of October Halsey's aircraft and Kenney's struck at Japanese airfields throughout the Philippines and on Formosa. In the Philippines the attackers destroyed about half the Japanese aircraft there and much shipping. On Formosa about 280 aircraft were destroyed by carrier planes. The Japanese publicly claimed that they had sunk 57 of Halsey's ships. In fact they had sunk none at all. Encouraged by the belief that they had done severe damage to the American carrier forces the Japanese naval leaders planned to fight decisive battles on sea and land in the defence of the southern Philippines. They would not attack the invading convoys on their way to the islands but 'when they were sufficiently close to make retreat difficult, the main strength of the Japanese Army, Navy and Air Forces would descend upon them and deliver a knockout blow'.[1]

At sea the whole strength of the Japanese Mobile Fleet would be employed and in the air a battered but still effective naval and army air force. Field-Marshal Count Terauchi of the Southern Army now controlled four Area Armies whose headquarters were at Rangoon, Singapore, in the Dutch East Indies and at Manila, where General Yamashita commanded the Fourteenth Area Army. Yamashita had been in this appointment only since 9 October, having been transferred to Manchuria after his conquest of Malaya in 1942. He would command ten divisions plus the equivalent of two more in Luzon, and four divisions and two brigades in the southern Philippines; reserves were available from south China and Formosa.

MacArthur wrote afterwards that he knew that Leyte would be 'the crucial battle' of the war against Japan. 'Leyte was to be the anvil against which I hoped to hammer the Japanese into submission in the central Philippines—the springboard from which I could proceed to the conquest of Luzon, for the final assault against Japan itself.'

[1] Cannon, p. 85. The following account of operations on Leyte is based very substantially on this volume and on Krueger, *From Down Under to Nippon.*

From Hollandia MacArthur accompanied the vast convoy of 700 vessels on its two-day voyage. The ships were off Leyte Gulf about midnight. At dawn the naval bombardment opened. As the sun rose MacArthur, on the deck of the cruiser *Nashville*, sighted Tacloban, which he had first known as a young lieutenant. 'It was a full moment for me', he wrote afterwards. He embarked in a landing craft for the left wing of the X Corps and waded ashore, followed by Sergio Osmena, who had succeeded Quezon as President of the Philippine Republic when Quezon died in August. With the small-arms fire still crackling not far ahead, and in drenching rain, he broadcast a radio message to the people of the Philippines. It began: 'People of the Philippines, I have returned. This is the voice of freedom. General Mac-Arthur speaking. . . . People of the Philippines, I have returned', mentioned that Osmena stood beside him, and announced that the seat of government was now on Philippine soil. 'Rise and strike', he exhorted. 'Let every arm be steeled. . . .' Still on the beach he wrote a letter to Roosevelt: the operation was going smoothly; the by-passing of Mindanao would result in saving possibly 50,000 American casualties.

> The Filipinos are reacting splendidly and I feel that a successful campaign of liberation if promptly followed by a dramatic granting to them of independence will place American prestige in the Far East at the highest pinnacle of all times.
>
> Once more, on the highest plane of statesmanship, I venture to urge that this great ceremony be presided over by you in person. Such a step will electrify the world and redound immeasurably to the credit and honor of the United States for a thousand years.
>
> Please excuse this scribble but at the moment I am on the combat line with no facilities except this field message pad.

On the 17th the Japanese commanders learnt of the presence of the American force off Leyte Gulf and knew that Leyte was the objective. The navy promptly put into operation its *Sho* (Victory) plan: one force would steam from the west through San Bernardino Strait and two others through Surigao Strait, whereafter all three would descend on the vulnerable convoy. A fourth force, the Main Body, off the east coast of Luzon, would attempt to draw off fast carriers and modern battleships of the United States Third Fleet, leaving the other forces to destroy Kinkaid's Seventh Fleet, with its seven old battleships, 16 escort carriers and cruiser and destroyer forces. Halsey intercepted and turned back the force, under Admiral Kurita, advancing through San Bernardino Strait, and then, having discovered the presence of the main body to the north, set off to deal with it, whereupon Kurita turned about and advanced unimpeded through San Bernardino Strait and turned south towards Leyte. But meanwhile the Japanese forces moving through the Surigao Strait had been destroyed or put to flight.

Kurita descended on Kinkaid's force, sank one cruiser and three destroyers, lost three cruisers, but then, instead of pressing on against the multitude of transports off Leyte, became fearful of the result of heavier air attacks and steamed north to join the main body, then being mauled by Halsey. What might have been a staggering Japanese success proved a decisive defeat. Finally the Combined Fleet's losses included three battleships, four carriers and six heavy cruisers. The Americans lost three heavy cruisers and three destroyers. Comparable losses had been and would be suffered in naval battles, but never had there been a naval conflict on such a scale.

MacArthur and Krueger considered that if the Japanese squadrons had reached Leyte Gulf the results would have been disastrous, but Halsey, who was widely criticized for accepting the bait offered by the Japanese Main Body, said that with his fleet in being and with Kinkaid's cruisers and light carriers round Leyte the Japanese could have caused only minor damage.

To MacArthur the near disaster off Leyte seemed to demonstrate once more the perils of divided command, a policy that could not be defended, he said later, 'in logic, in theory or even in common sense. Other motives must be ascribed.' He implied that if he had been in supreme command Halsey would have been kept back to protect the invading force. 'This would not only insure my base but would insure his fleet being in the action, as the magnetic attraction of my point of landing would draw the enemy's fleet there.'

Halsey's acceptance of the Japanese bait has been criticized as a tactical error based on faulty Intelligence. But the real blunder was the strategical one committed in Washington when Halsey was given two tasks: the first was to protect the communications of the Leyte force but 'if an opportunity to destroy major portions of the Japanese fleet should arise or could be created, such destruction was to be the primary task of all naval forces from the central Pacific'. It should have been evident to the Joint Chiefs of Staff that the performance of these two tasks might be incompatible and so they proved.

By 23 October the 1st Cavalry Division had secured Tacloban airfield and was advancing north along the coast while the 24th Division thrust west. The infantry pressed on more slowly than had been hoped. It was 26 October before the 94th Division secured Catmon Hill, a long ridge overlooking the gulf and rising to 1,400 feet. Each day from 20 to 23 October MacArthur went ashore from the *Nashville*. Kenney, who landed with him, later described how 'MacArthur calmly walked around wearing his old Philippine marshal's cap, his only weapon the big corn cob pipe he was smoking. We passed a lot of troops lying behind the boles of the palm trees, staring into the bushes and occasionally firing at something. . . . One of the GIs looked up. He nudged the soldier next to him and said, "Hey, there's General

MacArthur." The other lad didn't even look round as he drawled, "Oh, yeah? And I suppose he's got Eleanor Roosevelt along with him."'

It was one thing to announce to the Filipinos that the seat of their government was 'firmly reestablished on Philippine soil' but another to decide how it would be organized. During 1944 this problem had been a subject of debate between the War Department and the Department of the Interior, which wished a civil official representing the High Commissioner to accompany the army. MacArthur was emphatic that he should have undivided responsibility for civil administration and the President supported him. Consequently on 30 August MacArthur had formed a civil affairs unit to conduct the administration in cooperation with representatives of the Philippine Government, one of whose duties would be to arraign suspected collaborators with the enemy. Civil affairs sub-units were placed under the control of the field commanders and these organized local government by Filipinos as soon as military necessities allowed. Meanwhile the civil affairs officers cared for refugees, of whom tens of thousands soon assembled in the larger towns on Leyte, and established dispensaries, hospitals and schools. Genuine guerillas were sorted out from bogus ones eager to jump on the bandwagon, and soon were giving valuable service as scouts and sentries.

In MacArthur's view the Secretary of the Interior, Harold L. Ickes, regarded the Philippines as a possession of the United States and wished to take control. Ickes informed MacArthur that he intended to try disloyal Filipinos on charges of treason. To MacArthur this meant that any Filipino who had cooperated with the Japanese-sponsored government would be executed, and he insisted that any such trials should be conducted in accordance with the Philippine constitution. Stimson supported him and the President decided in his favour. The 'irascible and eccentric' Ickes, MacArthur wrote later:

> never forgave me, and became a leader of a vengeful and abusive faction which has repeatedly misrepresented and falsified my position, opinions, and personal character. The Communists had never ceased their violent attacks against me and, with the liberal extremists joining them, the crescendo was rising.[1]

MacArthur's decision to establish himself at Tacloban, side by side with Krueger, his field commander, was unorthodox and one which might have been actively resented if MacArthur had been a less eminent figure. But he seems to have behaved with tact. He 'did not interfere with General Krueger's prosecution of the battle. But from his headquarters on Leyte he closely followed the progress of the campaign, frequently visited the command posts of the Sixth Army units, and made available to General Krueger

[1] *Reminiscences*, p. 236.

additional troops upon request.'[1] These eventually included the 11th Airborne Division and part of the 38th Division.

By the first days in November Krueger's troops held the vital Leyte Valley and the straits north and south of the island. It remained to dispose of the Japanese concentrated round Ormoc on the north-western lobe of Leyte and separated from the Leyte Valley by the island's mountain spine. Throughout November Krueger's troops were deployed along a front of about 40 miles in these mountains while they strove with little success to advance from north and south into the Ormoc Valley. Krueger now had six divisions in the line or in close support: from the right the 32nd, 1st Cavalry, 24th, 96th, 11th Airborne, 7th. Meanwhile Yamashita had continued to ship reinforcements by sea to Ormoc despite heavy losses as a result of air attacks on his transports.

Krueger was hampered by supply difficulties and delays in constructing adequate airfields in the rain-sodden terrain; 235 inches of rain fell during November. And the American historian of the campaign wrote of 'the natural reluctance of American infantrymen to engage the enemy at close quarters', of 'several instances in which the American attacking force felt out the Japanese positions and then sat back to wait it out . . . if more than minor resistance was encountered, the troops frequently fell back and called for fire from supporting weapons'. The troops were 'too road-bound. Sometimes resistance along the road stopped the advance of an entire division.'[2]

In early December the troops were still making slow progress; a landing on Mindoro was scheduled for the 5th, and Intelligence indicated that Yamashita would launch an offensive on the 10th. Krueger planned to use his last reserve division, the 77th, to make a landing on the west coast. Encouraged by the success of the initial landings MacArthur had returned this borrowed force to Nimitz' command, but when Japanese resistance stiffened and when he learned of the coming offensive MacArthur had had to borrow it back again. The division arrived at Leyte on 23 November; on the 30th MacArthur postponed the Mindoro operation until 15 December.

The west coast landing was a decisive success. The attackers went ashore on 7 December without loss. That morning a Japanese convoy including six transports bringing reinforcements to Ormoc was attacked by aircraft and four transports were sunk. By the end of the first day the 77th Division had established a bridgehead about two miles wide and by the 10th were in Ormoc itself, having suffered fairly light casualties.

But the Japanese leaders were resolved to fight on and Yamashita approved an ambitious plan to wipe out American air power on Leyte by seizing the airfields at and inland from Dulag and at Tacloban. While the

[1] Cannon, p. 244.
[2] Ibid., pp. 245-6.

main strength of his infantry attacked through the mountains from the west, paratroops were to be flown from Luzon and dropped round the inland strips at Burauen. The 16th Japanese Division had lost so heavily that it could find only 500 men for the offensive, and of these only about 150 reached the Burauen strips on 6 December where they were wiped out before the paratroops landed. For five days Japanese infantry and paratroops caused confusion among the air force units, and isolated Fifth Air Force headquarters, but they were eventually halted and dispersed. The aircraft carrying paratroops to the Dulag and Tacloban airfields were all shot down. The Japanese counter-attack caused MacArthur to allot part of the 38th Division to Krueger and these troops took part in clearing the threatened airfields. Thus the Leyte operation, undertaken with an assault force of four divisions with two in reserve, was now engaging all or most of eight divisions, by far the largest force the Japanese had encountered in the Pacific war. But the end was near. Their 16th and 26th Divisions were penned up in the Ormoc Valley, their 1st and 102nd Divisions were facing the 32nd American Division at the northern entrance to the valley. In the third week of December the 1st Cavalry and 32nd Divisions from the north and the 77th from the south cleared the valley. On the 19th Yamashita in effect abandoned the Thirty-Fifth Army to its fate. The survivors withdrew into the mountains west of Ormoc.

On 18 December MacArthur was promoted to the new rank of General of the Army, the equivalent of field-marshal; two days earlier Marshall had been given the same rank; two days later Eisenhower also received it, and the next day Arnold.

On 26 December the Eighth Army took over from the Sixth Army for the mopping-up period, which was to prove long and costly. The operation had attracted far more troops than had been intended at the outset. At the peak there were more than 250,000 troops on the island, including some who were only staging there. From 60,000 to 70,000 Japanese had been engaged, of whom perhaps 48,000 had been killed. The Sixth Army lost 3,049 killed or missing on Leyte; in the mopping-up phase the Eighth Army lost 454. In his message congratulating Krueger on the ending of the Sixth Army's part in the operation MacArthur described the campaign as one with 'few counterparts in the utter destruction of the enemy's forces with a maximum conservation of our own. . . . A magnificent performance on the part of all concerned.' In fact some aspects of the performance had been gravely disappointing: the supply organization had proved unwieldy, the development of airfields slow, and a vastly outnumbered and ill-organized Japanese force had delayed the invaders for two months. But it had proved a crucial operation in ways not foreseen. The Japanese Navy had suffered decisive defeat and its carrier strength had been virtually wiped out; the Japanese air force in the Philippines had been reduced to near impotence; and the army on Luzon had been gravely weakened by the loss of the reinforcements that had been poured into Leyte.

The Leyte operation had again underlined the strengths and weaknesses of the American armies. The organization for putting the troops ashore on hostile territory and protecting and supporting them during the process by naval and air bombardment had been perfected. But once ashore the vast supply apparatus, better suited to operations on the highways of America or Western Europe than in saturated tropical bush, tended to bog down, as happened frequently on Leyte. Dependence of the supply organization on mechanical transport was made heavier by the nature of American tactics. As an American divisional historian breezily put it: 'The Yank style of fighting was to wait for the artillery to come up and let the big guns blast the enemy positions as barren of all life as possible. It saved many American lives and got better results although it took longer.' Their outlook differed from that of the two other infantry forces that fought beside them in the Pacific—the United States Marines and the Australians. 'The marines', wrote S. E. Morison, 'consider that an objective should be overrun as quickly as possible; they follow up their assault troops with mop-up squads which take care of any individuals or strong points.'[1] A Japanese view of the American infantry was: 'The American forces are slow and steady. . . . Generally . . . they advance step by step and will not attack unless they are positive they will not lose.'

The character of a nation's infantry derives from the *mores* of the citizens from whom it is drawn. Training and indoctrination can enhance or diminish militarily useful qualities but cannot create them. The American infantry suffered the grave disadvantage of being recruited largely from those who were left over after the more eager spirits had joined the navy, the marines or the air corps, and after the better educated conscripts had been taken into technical units. Thus whereas in the Japanese and German Armies, for example, the infantry was a *corps d'élite*, in the American Army it was if anything the reverse. Until the end of 1942 the navy and the marines were recruited entirely from volunteers. In 1942 men subject to draft were allowed to volunteer for army service and to choose the arm in which they served, but only five per cent of the total army intake were volunteers and of these most chose the air corps. Of the conscripts, men with trades were as a rule sent to technical non-combat units and the infantry received 'a sub-average portion of the available manpower'. In mid-1943, Lieutenant-General

[1] S. E. Morison, *Aleutians, Gilberts and Marshalls, June 1942–April 1944*, a volume in the series *United States Naval Operations in World War II*, p. 298.

Lesley J. McNair, Commander of the Army Ground Forces, recommended an enlistment procedure that, so far as the infantry was concerned, was 'almost the reverse' of the established practice.

As early as July 1942 Lieutenant-General Ben Lear of the Second Army wrote: 'We are scratching the bottom of the barrel now for officer candidates. We are decidedly short of the right material for non-commissioned officer leaders. We will pay dearly for this in battle.'[1]

But the damage had been done. Far and wide the American infantry often proved slow off the mark and more easily disheartened than the marines or the infantry of their allies or their enemies. As a result commanders had to provide for overwhelming fire power, greatly superior numbers and the possibility that operations would be more drawn-out than plans had contemplated.[2]

During the battle for Leyte MacArthur was concerned with planning for the future rather than with the details of operations in the central Philippines —these were now Krueger's business. Despite MacArthur's conviction that the Roosevelt–MacArthur–Nimitz talks at Pearl Harbor had resulted in a decision in favour of a continued advance through the Philippines rather than concentration on a direct assault on Formosa, by-passing Luzon, debate continued in Washington. King still pressed for the omission of Luzon and 'at least until mid-September 1944 General Marshall leaned toward the Formosa-first strategy and like Admiral King had expressed the opinion that Japan itself, rather than Luzon, should be considered the substitute for Formosa'. Until late September Nimitz favoured attacking Formosa before Luzon. But Halsey advocated seizing Luzon and then Okinawa, by-passing Formosa.

It is noteworthy that, with the possible exception of Nimitz, the ranking Army and Navy commanders in the Pacific—the men responsible for executing or supporting the operation—were opposed to the seizure of Formosa. In general, they favored a program calling for the capture of Luzon and a subsequent jump to Okinawa or Japan. In the face of this opinion of the commanders on the spot, the consensus of most high-ranking Army and Navy planners in Washington—with Leahy and General Somervell as outstanding exceptions—was that the Formosa-first course of action was strategically the sounder and, therefore, the most desirable course for the Allies to follow in the western Pacific.[3]

---

[1] R. R. Palmer, B. I. Wiley and W. R. Keast, *The Procurement and Training of Ground Combat Troops* (Washington, 1948), a volume of the official series *United States Army in World War II*, pp. 10–17.

[2] Perusal of casualty lists and other lists in American divisional and regimental histories reveals that a big majority of officers mentioned bore names of Anglo-Saxon and German origin and a big majority of other ranks names of southern and central European origin.

[3] R. R. Smith, *Triumph in the Philippines* (Washington, 1963), a volume of the series *United States Army in World War II*, pp. 9–10.

But on 21 September after the decision on the 15th to advance the date of Leyte to 20 October, MacArthur told the Joint Chiefs that he could land on Luzon on 20 December, the date originally fixed for Leyte, and again two months ahead of schedule and two months before the proposed invasion of Formosa. Meanwhile the difficulties of the Formosa operation were becoming more evident to the planners in Washington. Nimitz now wanted simultaneous landings in Formosa and at Amoy on the Chinese mainland. As MacArthur had insisted, this would be a perilous business; the available American land and air power might be bogged down interminably in China, and according to the planners this operation would involve immense and perhaps insuperable supply problems, particularly in the provision of the heavy quota of service troops that the American organization demanded. MacArthur continued to argue that Formosa would be costly both in lives and time. On the mainland of China the Japanese deployed one quarter of their army and controlled the railways. The American invaders might expect some support from the aircraft of General Chennault's Tenth Air Force precariously based on fields in south-west China. But already, during the summer of 1944, the Japanese had launched an offensive that by September had driven this air force from the only bases from which it might effectively support operations in south China.

By this time Leahy, Marshall and the senior naval commanders in the Pacific and the army–air force leaders all favoured MacArthur's plan. Among leaders of influence only King remained adamant; he now argued that the fast carriers would be tied up for at least six weeks protecting the Luzon operation and this was unacceptable. Informed of these 'last ditch arguments' MacArthur on 28 September radioed the Joint Chiefs that after the landing on Luzon he would need only a few escort carriers to support the troops ashore until airfields had been made ready for his land-based planes. Kenney's assurance of some two years earlier that his aircraft would provide MacArthur with a substitute for a strong naval power was being realized. MacArthur pointed out that after the initial assault his convoys would arrive from the southern and central Philippines covered by land-based aircraft. Nimitz now declared that he lacked sufficient troops to carry out the Formosa and Amoy operation, and proposed that the plan be shelved and that his forces should assault Iwo Jima in January and Okinawa in March.

Thus on 3 October the Joint Chiefs issued a directive to MacArthur to invade Luzon on 20 December, the date he had proposed, and to Nimitz to carry out the Iwo Jima and Okinawa operations. The Pacific Fleet would provide naval cover for the landing on Luzon and later MacArthur would reciprocate by giving air support over Okinawa.

Thus MacArthur had his way. He would occupy not only a few footholds

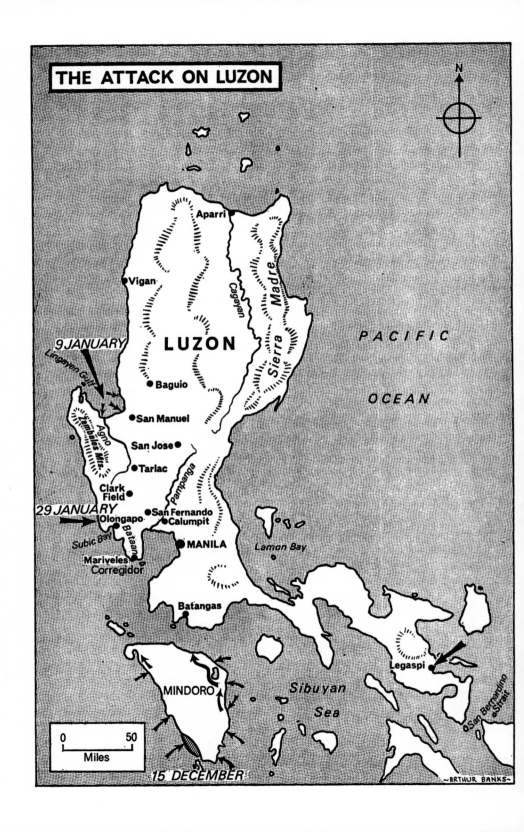

THE ATTACK ON LUZON

Aparri

Vigan

Cagayan

Sierra Madre

LUZON

PACIFIC

OCEAN

9 JANUARY

Lingayen Gulf

Baguio

Agno

Zambales Mts.

San Manuel

San Jose

Pampanga

Tarlac

Clark Field

29 JANUARY

Olongapo

San Fernando

Calumpit

Subic Bay

Bataan

MANILA

Lamon Bay

Mariveles

Corregidor

Batangas

Legaspi

MINDORO

Sibuyan Sea

San Bernardino Strait

0   50
Miles

15 DECEMBER

~ARTHUR BANKS~

in the Philippines but the whole archipelago. But the navy had its way also to the extent that the two final steps towards Tokyo would be taken by forces under naval command operating from naval bases. The policy adopted in the European theatre of concentration on a single line of advance against the main objective was to be disregarded in the Pacific to the very end.

During the planning for Luzon Willoughby's estimate of Japanese strength on the island materially increased. In mid-October he believed that there were four divisions plus three brigades and that the main strength would be deployed between Lingayen Gulf and Manila (as the main American strength had been in 1941). But during the Leyte operation, although reinforcements were sent thither from Luzon, they were more than replaced, and Willoughby estimated that there were or soon would be one armoured division, five infantry divisions, six brigades and two independent regiments with a total strength of 152,000.

Inevitably MacArthur decided, as the Japanese had done three years before, to land his main force at Lingayen, whence it would advance down the central plain to Manila. When this area had been secured the problem would remain of reducing the enemy forces in the south-eastern appendage of the island and in the mountains that flanked the central plain on the west and particularly on the north-east where the mountain spine of Luzon on the west and the Sierra Madre on the east enclosed the valley of the Cagayan River. This rugged northern half of Luzon had been left virtually undefended by MacArthur in the earlier campaign. But experience had shown that the Japanese would fight to a finish and the Cagayan Valley and its protecting ranges offered a big fortress area of great natural strength.

During the planning of the Luzon operation in the last half of 1944, MacArthur's staff gave serious consideration to making preliminary landings at Aparri in the north near the mouth of the Cagayan River and at Legaspi in the south. From these points fighter cover could be provided for the main landing. MacArthur rejected this proposal, which would have required an army corps (the I Australian Corps) to hold a base area 600 miles from the Leyte airfields but only 300 from Formosa, and might have led to complications that would delay the main expedition. The Legaspi proposal was linked with a plan to send the Lingayen convoys round the north of Luzon anti-clockwise. Both concepts were abandoned by October in favour of a plan to establish airfields on weakly defended Mindoro, only 250 miles south of Lingayen, and sail the invading convoy through the Visayas, while the Third Fleet subdued Japanese air power on Formosa.

At this stage MacArthur had hoped to land on Mindoro on 5 December and on Luzon on the 20th, but the demands of the long struggle for Leyte and delays in developing airfields there forced him to postpone Mindoro to 15 December, Luzon to 9 January.

Two regiments were put ashore on Mindoro without opposition on the 15th. The build-up of air power on the island was hampered by air attack and a raid by surface craft. On 26 December when two air strips were in operation Japanese cruisers and destroyers made a night raid and did some damage; later *Kamikaze* suicide aircraft sank a few transports and damaged other vessels. But by 9 January three fighter groups and two of medium bombers were based on Mindoro. In Nimitz' area too the timetable was proving overoptimistic and in November he had persuaded the Joint Chiefs to alter the dates for Iwo Jima (20 January) and Okinawa (1 March) to 3 February and 15 March. And in December, when MacArthur's timetable had been fixed, Nimitz decided that, to give his fleet time for replenishment after Luzon, he would have to postpone Iwo Jima to 19 February and consequently Okinawa to 1 April. This timetable proved final.

The reconquest of Leyte had given new heart to the Filipino guerillas throughout the archipelago and the insertion of Intelligence parties and the delivery of more equipment strengthened their organization and striking power, since 1943 under the control of Major-General Courtney Whitney, a thrustful lawyer-soldier who had spent much of his working life at Manila, and had rapidly become one of MacArthur's most trusted lieutenants and devoted admirers. The guerillas were providing much of the Intelligence on which MacArthur's staff were basing their revised estimates of Japanese strength. These caused MacArthur to increase the size of the Luzon invading force. Initially the plan had been to employ the Sixth Army with four divisions and two more plus a regiment in reserve, and the Eighth Army with one division and two regiments; but by November there were plans to reinforce these in the two months after the landing with five more divisions.

Krueger planned to land his two corps along a wide front, the XIV on the right and I on the left, each of the four divisions using two of its three regiments in the initial assault. Their first objectives were to establish firm flanks and secure crossings over the Agno River about 20 miles inland. Thence they were to thrust south to Manila. Krueger expected that the Japanese would make a strong counter-attack on his left and ordered a regiment and an armoured group to land there and hold firmly astride the coastal plain.

Halsey's Third Fleet would cover the operation from a position within range of both Formosa and north Luzon. Kenney's air forces would be supplemented with escort carriers borrowed from Halsey, and the heavy bombers were to give remote support by attacks on the Japanese homeland and on Formosan ports.

The command arrangements were the same as those already tested in earlier operations: Admiral Kinkaid would command the naval forces including the two amphibious forces carrying the troops and, under MacArthur, he and his subordinates would control the expedition until the moment when the corresponding military commanders could take over on shore.

The assault divisions were assembled from far and wide: the 25th from New Caledonia, the 37th, 40th and 43rd from Australian New Guinea where they had been relieved by Australian troops, the 6th from Sansapor in Dutch New Guinea. On 2 January the minesweeping and survey flotilla that was to prepare the way for the expedition sailed from Leyte Gulf. On the 3rd the Third Fleet arrived off north Luzon from its great base at Ulithi Atoll and next day, off Leyte far to the south, MacArthur boarded the cruiser *Boise*, and the leading sections of the invasion force set out on the hazardous voyage that for some ships would last a week. *Kamikazes* attacked the minesweepers on the 3rd, and on the 4th sank an escort carrier. That day MacArthur radioed to Halsey a request that his carriers should concentrate against Luzon airfields on the 6th. On the 5th 45 *Kamikazes* damaged 11 vessels and the forward squadrons were attacked by submarines, including one midget which ineffectually fired two torpedoes in the direction of the part of the convoy that included the *Boise*. MacArthur watched what was going on from a battery near the quarterdeck and saw old landmarks come into view on the horizon. 'Manila, Corregidor, Mariveles, Bataan. I could not leave the rail. One by one, the staff drifted away and I was alone with my memories. At the sight of those never-to-be-forgotten scenes of my family's past, I felt an indescribable sense of loss, of sorrow, of loneliness, and of solemn consecration.'[1]

On the 6th the Third Fleet's aircraft made disturbing reports that a total of 237 operational planes had been seen on Luzon fields (actually there were fewer than 50); and that day Japanese aircraft, mainly *Kamikazes*, severely damaged two battleships and three cruisers and sank a minesweeper. Admiral Olendorf, commanding the Assault Group, was so alarmed by the damage and the possibility that Japanese surface ships might be encouraged to sally forth that he suggested the whole plan be reconsidered. The upshot was that Kenney's aircraft were concentrated against Luzon fields in greater strength and Halsey agreed that his should hit Luzon again on the 7th. But it turned out that the *Kamikaze* effort was almost exhausted. On the 7th only 20 to 25 attacked; on the 8th, however, a cruiser and two light carriers were seriously damaged; on the 9th 15 *Kamikazes* damaged four naval vessels, one of which, HMAS *Australia*, was hit for the fifth time and

[1] *Reminiscences*, p. 240.

withdrawn. Kinkaid had proposed that the Third Fleet should give close protection to the convoy during the landing but MacArthur agreed with Nimitz and Halsey that the fleet should not be tied to this task but should continue to strike Formosa whence, MacArthur believed, the *Kamikazes* were coming.

The American troops met little opposition on the day of the landing. While the I Corps held in the north the XIV pushed steadily along the plain towards Clark Field and Manila, but as on Leyte progress was slow. By the 17th, having suffered only 120 casualties in nine days, the XIV Corps was barely 30 miles from the beach, but had gained crossings over the Agno River. Krueger's army was again being bogged down by the weight of its transport, which demanded bridges that would support 35 tons or more, and soon he was asking the air force which now commanded the air over Luzon to refrain from attacking bridges ahead of him except when specifically asked to do so.

It was now evident to MacArthur that whereas in 1942 he had withdrawn south-west into Bataan while the Japanese advanced down the central plain to Manila, Yamashita planned to make his major stand in the mountains to the east, covering Baguio where his headquarters were and the Cagayan Valley. Thus I Corps would have to bear the brunt while XIV Corps thrust south to Manila. MacArthur later expressed pride in the speed of the advance but in fact the Japanese imposed far greater delays on XIV Corps than Wainwright's army had imposed on the Japanese. The Americans entered Manila on 3 February, almost four weeks after their landing, the Japanese in 12 days.

Once again Willoughby's estimate of Japanese strength fell far short of the reality: there were some 262,000 not 152,000. Even so MacArthur's staff did not know at the time the extent to which Yamashita's preparations for the climactic battle for the Philippines had been hampered by policies imposed on him by Terauchi, his immediate superior, and Imperial General Headquarters in Tokyo. Early in November when it was evident that Leyte could not be held Yamashita had urged that the reinforcement of that island be halted and all efforts devoted to the defence of Luzon. But Terauchi insisted on draining Luzon's resources in a hopeless endeavour to hold Leyte. And when the Americans landed on Mindoro, Terauchi ordered a counter-offensive there also. But by late December Yamashita succeeded in persuading both Terauchi and Tokyo that it would be a mistake to continue to cling to the central Philippines, and thenceforward he was able to concentrate on the battle for Luzon.

It was evident that as soon as the Americans launched their sea, land and air power against him he would be almost as thoroughly isolated as were the armies in the southern Philippines, New Guinea and the Solomons, and the best he could hope to do would be to fight a defensive campaign that would tie up American forces that might otherwise be employed against more important objectives. Therefore Terauchi decided not to waste much of his strength in what must prove a hopeless attempt to hold the central plain, Manila Bay and the southern peninsula, but to concentrate his main force in the mountainous northern half of the island. Here he deployed 152,000 of his 260,000 troops, including the 2nd Armoured, 10th, 19th, 23rd and 103rd Infantry Divisions and an independent brigade. The southern boundary of this army would embrace Lingayen Gulf on the west and Dingalan Bay on the east. To the south Major-General Tsukada's Kembu Group, 30,000 strong, including 15,000 naval troops, was concentrated from about Clark Field to Bataan. Lieutenant-General Yokoyama's Shimbu Group, 80,000 strong, including the 105th Division, the depleted 8th Division and 20,000 naval troops, held from Manila to the south end of the island. Thus some 35,000 of the troops in the south were naval men concentrated round the naval base. When forced from Clark Field the Kembu Group was to hold out in the Zambales Mountains between the central plain and the west coast. In a few weeks before the American landing Yamashita's men moved thousands of tons of supplies into his fortress area. And as the battle developed Yamashita proposed to move the two divisions in the Shimbu Group into the northern mountains, which would then contain a formidable army built round seven divisions and some 180,000 strong.

The return to Luzon was a time of strong emotion for MacArthur. There his father had reached the climax of his career and there MacArthur himself had spent a great part of his service life and finally had suffered his only big defeat. On the afternoon of the first day he had waded ashore from a landing craft and thereafter often went forward to see what was happening to the infantry. On the 13th he established a command post at Dagupan in the I Corps area. On his excursions he was joyfully welcomed by cheering Filipinos who 'would crowd around me, try to kiss my hand, press native wreaths around my neck, touch my clothes, hail me with tears and sobs. It embarrassed me no end.'[1]

On 17 January MacArthur radioed Krueger that it was imperative to secure the Clark Field area soon. The capacity of the Lingayen Gulf strips was limited and heavy bomber fields were needed from which to support the Iwo Jima and Okinawa operations, to attack Japanese shipping in the Indies and lend weight to the operations on Luzon itself. He urged Krueger to order I Corps to contain the Japanese in the north while the XIV Corps sped on to

[1] *Reminiscences*, pp. 241-2.

Clark. Opposition round Clark would soon be reduced by the forthcoming landing of XI Corps on the coast just north of Bataan. The initial plan had provided for the landing of XI Corps at Vigan north of Lingayen but on 11 January MacArthur had cancelled this operation, fearing enemy air attack from Formosa, and substituted the southern landing. Before receiving MacArthur's orders to press on to Clark, Krueger had made a more cautious plan whereby he would halt the XIV Corps along the Agno until I Corps had removed the threat to his left. This could not be achieved until he could reinforce his right and centre with the 32nd Division, the 1st Cavalry Division and a regiment due to arrive at the end of the month. This plan was based on the estimate of Krueger's staff, fairly accurate as it turned out, that there were 234,000 not 152,000 Japanese on Luzon, and that the Sixth Army's left wing was threatened by 50,000 more Japanese than Willoughby supposed. Krueger had to take into account in his planning that MacArthur was eager to arrive in Manila as soon as possible—perhaps on his birthday, 26 January. Orders issued by Krueger on the 18th conformed to MacArthur's directive. He ordered General Griswold of the XIV Corps to press on southwards first to Tarlac and then to Clark, with I Corps extending its front east and south-east to cover the advance.

In the two weeks after the issue of the new orders I Corps, reinforced by two divisions which arrived at Lingayen on 27 January, had pressed close to the foothills of the mountains to the north and north-east. At San Manuel in the last week of January there had been a long and fierce encounter with a Japanese force over 1,000 strong and a regiment of tanks resolved to make a last stand astride one of the roads leading into Yamashita's stronghold. They were attacked by the 161st Regiment (25th Division) and on the 28th launched a counter-attack by night with 13 tanks. MacArthur later described how, fearing a breakthrough by Japanese tanks, he went forward to the 161st Regiment and joined its commander in steadying the ranks. The enemy attack was halted and later in the day the 161st counter-attacked and practically wiped out the Japanese rearguard. After this episode MacArthur was awarded his third Distinguished Service Cross.

Meanwhile, by the end of the month XIV Corps had secured the Clark Field area and its advance troops were at San Fernando and Calumpit astride the road leading into Bataan; the XI Corps (Major-General Charles P. Hall) had landed three regiments on the west coast on the 29th and advanced swiftly to Olongapo at the head of Subic Bay. One reason why MacArthur decided to land Hall's corps in this area was that the transfer of many of the naval ships supporting the force on Luzon to prepare for Okinawa caused him anxiety lest his base at Lingayen be attacked from Formosa and consequently he decided to secure Subic Bay to provide a second base farther south. At the same time the XI Corps would seal off the Bataan Peninsula.

From late February onwards until early April the XI Corps broke up the Kembu Group, whose commander on 6 April ordered his surviving men to disperse and form guerilla bands. This hotch-potch Japanese force fighting in country favourable to defence had inflicted 2,750 casualties during the mopping-up phase.

By the end of January the XIV Corps had suffered only 750 battle casualties. It was now poised for the final thrust for Manila but Krueger was still concerned lest the Japanese attack from the north-east across his rear. On the other hand MacArthur was still urging him to press on faster. On the 30th MacArthur had driven down the road from San Fernando towards Calumpit and on his return told Krueger that the 37th Division was displaying 'a noticeable lack of drive and aggressive initiative', a comment which Krueger passed down to Griswold and which eventually reached the leading regiment which promptly prepared to cross the Pampanga River.

In the first week of February I Corps succeeded in finally securing the northern flank by capturing San Jose through which for more than a month supplies had been transported into Yamashita's mountain stronghold; and in the process had disabled Yamashita's 2nd Armoured Division. Most of its tanks had been destroyed and the survivors were reorganized as a weak infantry division.

On 1 February the drive on Manila began to speed up. On the left the 1st Cavalry Division organized two flying columns which drove along the eastern road and by dusk on the 2nd were within ten miles of the outskirts of the city. The 37th Division on the western road was a little closer. Krueger ordered Griswold to take Manila as soon as he could and to secure a line embracing the Cavite naval base. The leading cavalry units entered the northern outskirts of the city about 7 p.m. and soon were round the Santa Tomas University where some 4,000 internees were confined.

Meanwhile on 20 January Eichelberger had proposed to MacArthur that the whole of his 11th Airborne Division (two glider-borne regiments and one of paratroops) should be landed south of Manila. MacArthur modified this plan to provide for an initial landing by only one regiment as a reconnaissance in force. If resistance was not strong Eichelberger could then land the rest of the division. Thus a regiment went ashore on the morning of 31 January against negligible resistance and before midday Eichelberger, having decided that the landing of the main body was justified, ordered it to go ashore immediately. The drop of 1,750 paratroops on the 3rd was unopposed, which was fortunate as most of them were put down up to six miles from the intended areas. By the morning of the 4th the division was in good order and advancing fast on Manila past cheering crowds of Filipinos.

MacArthur entered Manila with troops of the 37th Division and hastened through the city with a patrol to try to ensure the safety of his former quarters in the penthouse of the Manila Hotel, reported to be undamaged 'probably because of two vases at the entrance which had been presented to my father by the former Emperor of Japan'. As he neared the hotel the Japanese set the penthouse on fire and

> I watched, with indescribable feelings, the destruction of my fine military library, my souvenirs, my personal belongings of a lifetime. It was not a pleasant moment.
>
> The patrol finally worked forward to the hotel, and flanked by sub-machine-guns, I climbed the stairs toward the top. Every landing was a fight. Of the penthouse, nothing was left but ashes. It had evidently been the command post of a rearguard action. We left its colonel dead on the smouldering threshold, the remains of the broken vases of the Emperor at his head and feet—a grim shroud for his bloody bier.[1]

After the fall of the city MacArthur hastened to visit the camps where internees and prisoners were confined and was deeply moved by their miserable conditions after years of semi-starvation.

As we have seen, a basic feature of Yamashita's plan was to concentrate his main force in north Luzon. Manila was not to be a battlefield. But there were 16,000 naval troops round the city in addition to a small army force, and the commander of the naval troops decided to defend Manila or parts of it to the end. It took eight days after the entry into the northern part of the city for the attackers, now pressing in from north, east and south, to pinpoint the areas where the Japanese were resolved to stand.

> Only when the troops actually closed with the principal strongpoints did they discover where the main defenses were. When XIV Corps began to learn of the extent and nature of the defenses, the plans for a big victory parade were quietly laid aside—the parade never came off. The corps and its divisions thereupon began developing tactical plans on the spot as the situation dictated.[2]

The outcome was a period of bloody city fighting with the Americans reducing one stronghold after another until by the 23rd the surviving Japanese were penned up within the old walled city—the Intramuros. Immense damage was done. MacArthur had set his face firmly against using aircraft, much of whose bombing would be inaccurate and would cause heavy civilian casualties. But when it was evident that the Japanese in the Intramuros would exact heavy casualties from infantry attacking without maxi-

---

[1] *Reminiscences*, p. 247. But R. R. Smith says the Manila Hotel was not occupied until 20 February.

[2] Smith, p. 249.

mum fire support Griswold proposed to Krueger a crushing bombardment, whereupon Griswold substituted seven days of massive artillery fire in which more than 7,400 shells were spent. The infantry attack opened on the 23rd but it was not until 3 March that the last organized resistance ceased. In the fight for Manila the three divisions of XIV Corps lost 1,010 killed, the Japanese about 1,600. The city was in ruins, many of its great buildings beyond repair and the ancient Intramuros flattened. It was estimated that 100,000 of the city's 800,000 people had been killed.

MacArthur had insisted that the same degree of independence should be granted to the Philippine Government as it possessed before the war even while military operations continued and that the 'utmost care should be taken that an imperialist policy not be introduced . . . under the guise of military operations and necessities'. At a ceremony at the Malacanan Palace, once the residence of the Spanish governors, and in the presence of President Osmena and his Cabinet MacArthur on 27 February formally restored the full powers provided by the constitution. For the General this occasion was crowded with memories of men and events in the country where so much of his life had been spent:

> my father, Quezon, Taft, Wood, Stimson, Davis, Theodore Roosevelt, Murphy. In this city, my mother had died, my wife had been courted, my son had been born; here, before just such a gathering as this, not so long ago, I had received the baton of a Field Marshal of the Philippine Army.[1]

Meanwhile the XI Corps had cleared the Japanese out of the Bataan Peninsula after arduous fighting against some 4,000 Japanese who were finally dispersed by 16 February. MacArthur took a close interest in this operation on his old battleground and on the 16th drove along the east coast road five miles beyond the forward infantry. Pilots of the Fifth Air Force decided his group of vehicles were Japanese and sought permission to strafe them but fortunately the divisional commander demanded a check before it was too late.

On MacArthur's orders Corregidor had been under bombardment since 22 January. On 3 February he had ordered Krueger to take the island forces with paratroops or troops landed from the sea or both, and finally approved Krueger's plan to drop the 503rd Parachute Regiment—the same that had made the pioneering jump at Nadzab and had recently been used on Mindoro—and at the same time land a battalion from the 24th Division. It was a risky plan because the dropping areas were so small that the troops would have to be dropped a few at a time and it would take five hours to deliver the whole force of 2,000 men. But MacArthur's staff estimated that there were

---

[1] *Reminiscences*, p. 251.

only 850 men on the island. After heavy air and artillery bombardment the infantry battalion was landed with few casualties and the first lift of paratroops were on the ground, but 270 of those dropped on the 16th were casualties; and the Japanese garrison numbered over 5,000 not 850. However, its counter-attacks were ill-organized and costly: over 300 were killed on the 17th and over 1,200 during the next two days. Thereafter they spent their strength on uncoordinated *banzai* charges. On the 26th the surviving Japanese blew up an underground ammunition store at the narrow eastern end of the island. Debris was thrown a mile in all directions. Some 200 Japanese and 50 Americans were killed. Perhaps 500 Japanese were sealed up in tunnels; only 20 became prisoners.

MacArthur made a characteristically dramatic return to his old headquarters. In four PT boats—the same number as had taken him and his party from the island in March 1942—on 2 March, with all the available people who had left Corregidor with him, he returned to the Rock. He decorated the commander of the paratroops, ordered him to hoist the American flag on the old flagpole, and made a speech in which he declared that the defence of Bataan and Corregidor had made possible all that had happened since. 'Had it not held out, Australia would have fallen, with incalculably disastrous results.' History would record it as 'one of the decisive battles of the world'.[1] But this romantic notion that the relatively small Japanese force that had contained and finally taken Bataan and Corregidor might otherwise have made possible the seizure of Australia will not bear examination.

Thus by the first week of March all the main strategic objectives on Luzon had been taken; the central plain with its airfields, Manila and Manila Bay. The arduous and costly tasks remained of subduing Yamashita's main force round the Cagayan Valley and securing the rest of the central and southern Philippines. In the Australian and Dutch territories to the south MacArthur's policy had been to contain by-passed Japanese forces and let them wither on the vine. But in the Philippines he insisted on an opposite policy of regaining control of the whole archipelago.

In January Eichelberger's Eighth Army had under command for operations in the southern islands five divisions, and from March onwards these were engaged in a series of large-scale operations. The 41st Division secured Zamboanga in western Mindanao and the Sulu Archipelago. In the central Visayas the 40th and Americal Divisions dispersed some 35,000 Japanese of whom about half survived and surrendered at the cease-fire. On eastern Mindanao the X Corps in April, May and June defeated some 30,000 Japanese.

As soon as his troops had entered the outskirts of Manila MacArthur

[1] *Reminiscences*, p. 250.

had instructed Krueger in effect that the destruction of the surviving enemy forces—Yamashita's in Luzon and the relatively weak Shimbu Group in south Luzon—should be regarded as of secondary importance. 'Initially', he wrote on 5 February, 'hostile forces should be driven into the mountains, contained and weakened, and our principal effort devoted to areas where greater power may be applied.'[1]

Thus MacArthur directed Krueger to clear Japanese forces from the south coast of Luzon and from Samar whence with artillery or *Kamikazes* they might threaten the sea route from San Bernardino Strait through the Sibuyan Sea to Manila; and to secure Batangas Bay at the western exit of this passage where MacArthur planned to establish a major base and hospital centre in preparation for the operations against the Japanese mainland. Performance of these tasks would occupy so much of Krueger's strength that it would be impossible anyhow for him to undertake decisive operations against the Japanese in the mountain strongholds. And from February onwards MacArthur substantially reduced Krueger's forces: the 41st Division from New Guinea was given to Eichelberger and so were the 40th and parts of the 24th. This left Krueger with nine divisions, one of which was tied to garrison and police duties round Manila.

To begin operations against the Shobu Group, I Corps had three divisions, 25th, 32nd and 33rd. The Shimbu Group would be dealt with by the XIV Corps with the equivalent of three divisions. Fighting the Shimbu Group continued until June when organized resistance ended and the 15,000 Japanese survivors were mainly engaged looking for food. By April the sea route through the Visayas had been made secure. Meanwhile Krueger advanced against Yamashita's force at first with three divisions and later four. Baguio fell on 26 April. Pressing along the mountain roads and tracks the I Corps steadily forced the withdrawal of the Japanese until by the end of June they occupied a pocket north-east of Baguio some 25 miles by 20. But at the cease-fire 50,500 Japanese would surrender in north Luzon, nearly 40,000 of these being concentrated under Yamashita's command in the last-stand area, and at the end they were still engaging three American divisions and strong Filipino units. In retrospect, to have spent 8,500 lives in securing Luzon and then to spend 5,500 on Iwo Jima, no closer to the Ryukyus, seems a heavy double price to pay for a strategy influenced by concessions to service jealousies.

During the post-Manila phase in the Philippines MacArthur had been preoccupied with other problems. The day on which his troops entered Manila the penultimate conference of the Allied leaders opened at Yalta. There Stalin undertook that Russia would go to war against Japan two or

[1] Smith, p. 362.

three months after the defeat of Germany. In return Russia was promised the Kuriles and the southern part of Sakhalin and a zone of occupation in Korea.

On 19 February three divisions of marines went ashore on Iwo Jima where, after costly fighting, they gained this heavy bomber base, 775 miles from the mainland of Japan. The assault on Okinawa opened on 1 April after an air and naval bombardment of unprecedented weight.

On 6 April the command of the American forces in the Pacific was reorganized but still without unification being achieved. Indeed under the new arrangement there were three not two independent commands in the field. MacArthur was given all the ground forces in the Pacific, which entailed the eventual transfer of forces based on Hawaii including the Tenth Army then on Okinawa. MacArthur's Seventh Fleet was transferred to Nimitz' command. There were three air forces in the field: Kenney's within MacArthur's command, Nimitz' naval air force, and the Twentieth Air Force, with its long-range bombers employed on the grisly task of attacking civilian targets in Japan. This bombardment had opened a new phase a month earlier when some 300 Superfortresses had dropped 1,600 tons of bombs, mostly napalm and other incendiaries, on Tokyo, and killed more than 83,000 people.

On 1 May MacArthur's Australian forces opened the first phase of an operation aimed at the reconquest of the Indies: seizure of Tarakan off eastern Borneo. There had been various proposals for using Australian divisions or an Australian corps in the Philippines but they had come to nothing, a principal reason probably being one given to Blamey by Sutherland in October that 'it was not politically expedient for the AIF to be among the first troops into the Philippines'. At the same time MacArthur did not want to lose his I Australian Corps and when he learnt from Marshall that Mountbatten was asking for an Australian division, MacArthur did not mention the proposal to the Australian Government and advised that the matter be dropped as it would produce heated controversy in Australia. In fact there is evidence that the people and the troops would have welcomed this move. And it seems likely that there were political reasons also why MacArthur wished to use Australians in the Dutch East Indies. When he learnt of a British proposal that a British force of six divisions plus two Dutch divisions should be employed in the Indies MacArthur, with his lifelong interest in American status in the Far East, said that he did not want British forces in the Indies unless they were under US control, since he and King both felt that it might be difficult to dislodge the British once they got in. 'MacArthur, moreover, felt the British should first clean up the SEAC area and then, under his command, should help mop up in SWPA. He did not

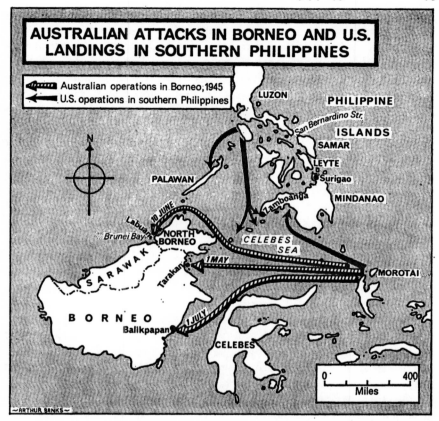

AUSTRALIAN ATTACKS IN BORNEO AND U.S. LANDINGS IN SOUTHERN PHILIPPINES

Australian operations in Borneo, 1945
U.S. operations in southern Philippines

think it fair that the British be allowed to extend SEAC's boundaries later on and reap the fruits of victory in SWPA that they had done so little to merit. In his opinion, it would be destructive of US prestige in the Far East and would unquestionably have a most deleterious effect on future economic trends.'[1]

Plans and preparations for the employment of the Australians in this phàse had led to an acrimonious dispute between MacArthur and Blamey. On 3 February MacArthur had informed Marshall that he considered that he should seize the Borneo oilfields to provide nearby supplies of oil for the operations against Japan, and planned to use I Australian Corps to do this. Marshall replied that ships could not be provided for Borneo and that operations there would have little effect on the defeat of Japan. A few days later GHQ informed Blamey's chief of staff that it was proposed to use the Australian corps of three divisions against Borneo under the command of the

[1] Matloff, p. 495.

Eighth US Army. Blamey protested and as a result GHQ said that the corps would operate directly under the command of GHQ. Blamey thereupon wrote to the secretary of the Australian Defence Department, declaring that 'the insinuation of American control and the elimination of Australian control has been gradual, but I think the time has come when the matter should be faced quite squarely, if the Australian Government and the Australian Higher Command are not to become ciphers in the control of the Australian military forces'. He pointed out that GHQ had asserted its authority to deal directly with the First Australian Army and now intended to take direct control of I Corps, treating Blamey's headquarters—he was still nominally commander of Allied Land Forces—as 'a purely liaison element'.

It was not merely a matter of face and of natural and personal pride. Blamey was in fact and quite properly exerting command of First Army as of other Australian forces, but as he pointed out, the means to secure fully effective control 'were not at his disposal'. One of these was shipping, lack of which was limiting the maintenance of the forces in New Guinea to a painful degree. And in his view control of I Corps from his advanced headquarters was necessary for both operational and administrative reasons. Also, to employ three divisions on Borneo would entail relieving the 6th Division then fully engaged in operations against Wewak. On 27 February Curtin wrote to MacArthur suggesting that MacArthur should adhere to the arrangement to use only two Australian divisions with his spearhead forces, and he reminded MacArthur that it had long been Australia's policy that its forces serving overseas should operate as homogeneous formations commanded by an Australian. On 5 March MacArthur replied with a long letter in which he said that since the Lae operation ground forces had been organized under task force commanders directly responsible to him. He considered it impossible for command of Australian troops in Borneo to be exerted by an officer concerned with command of troops in New Guinea and Australia. 'It is essential that the Task Force Commander remain in the field with his troops and that he have no other duties of any kind. Any other course of action would unquestionably jeopardize the success of the operation and impose a risk that could not be accepted.'

In fact, since the Lae operation, command of the Australian army in the field had been exercised by Blamey; and the First Army at that moment was operating according to his directives which differed radically from the policy MacArthur had adopted in its area.

On 14 March Blamey met MacArthur at Manila and a compromise agreement was reached that I Corps would operate directly under MacArthur's command but 'administrative functions' would be performed by Blamey's advanced headquarters at Morotai. Later Blamey, asked to comment on

MacArthur's letter of 5 March, denied the accuracy of some of MacArthur's recollections, which he could not accept as 'a sincere and complete statement of the matter'. At the same time he questioned the wisdom of the proposed operations in Borneo: the logical move would be to attack the west, not the east coast of the island. It had been MacArthur's policy to let the Japanese in Australian territory wither on the vine, but when discussing current operations in the Philippines he had declared to Blamey that it was essential that no Japanese should remain in the archipelago. Blamey replied that to withdraw Australian troops then in New Guinea (meaning the 6th Division) before they had similarly cleared the Japanese from Australian territory would mean that they would have to go back later on to complete the job. 'In view of the intention of the American forces to destroy completely the Japanese in the Philippine Islands', he wrote, 'it is my considered opinion that further Australian forces should not be withdrawn from New Guinea until such time as Japanese forces on Australian territory are destroyed also. . . . I except from this Rabaul. . . . We should be satisfied to contain it, since we can do so with lesser strength than the enemy force there.'

By this time GHQ had completed the outline plans for Borneo and, despite Marshall's earlier opposition, the Combined Chiefs of Staff had approved them. Plans for Borneo were amended and reamended until they reached a final form in April: Tarakan in May; Brunei Bay in June; Balikpapan in July. Just as the decision to advance west through the Indies had been influenced by a desire to find employment for the Australian Army outside the Philippines, so the decision to seize Brunei Bay seems to have been influenced by a wish to find a separate role, off the main line of advance, for the British Pacific Fleet now concentrating in Australia. The presence of a British fleet in the Pacific had not been welcomed by the American naval leaders, but MacArthur saw it as a means whereby his naval force might be vastly increased. As for the British, having with difficulty won a place in the Pacific team, they had no wish to be sidetracked and the British Chiefs of Staff informed the Joint Chiefs that they considered operations against Borneo inessential and in particular that Brunei Bay was not worth developing as a naval base since it would not be ready until 1946, was too far from Japan, the main objective, and farther from the main base in Australia than, say, Subic Bay. But the Joint Chiefs were adamant: Brunei would be a base for future operations against the Indies. The British chiefs protested but in vain. Resistance to the Borneo operation, which had been disapproved by Marshall in February, adopted by the Joint Chiefs in March, objected to by the British chiefs in April and May, continued even after the opening of the first phase when an Australian brigade group was landed on Tarakan on 1 May.

On the 7th the German forces surrendered. For every one of the Allies except China, India and Australia this event led to a large and prompt diminution of their effort. But unless plans were changed every one of Australia's combat divisions would be in action in the next phase. In proportion to population these were equivalent to more than the total number of American divisions in all theatres. On Blamey's advice the Australian acting Prime Minister (Curtin was ill and later died on 5 July) wrote to MacArthur to say that his government wished the Australian forces to be associated with his command in the advance on Japan but suggesting that the 7th Division be not committed in Borneo. In other words, that the operation against Balikpapan in July be abandoned. MacArthur replied promptly and tartly that

> the Borneo campaign . . . has been ordered by the Joint Chiefs of Staff who are charged by the Combined Chiefs of Staff with the responsibility for strategy in the Pacific. I am responsible for execution of their directives employing such troops as have been made available to me by the Governments participating in the Allied Agreement. Pursuant to the directive of the Joint Chiefs of Staff and under authority vested in me . . . I have ordered the 7th Division to proceed to a forward concentration area and, on a specific date, to execute one phase of the Borneo campaign. Australian authorities have been kept fully advised of my operational plans. The concentration is in progress and it is not now possible to substitute another division. . . . The attack will be made as projected unless the Australian Government withdraws the 7th Division from assignment to the South-West Pacific Area. . . . Withdrawal would disorganize completely not only the immediate plan but also the strategic plan of the Joint Chiefs of Staff.

The notion that the abandonment of an attack on Balikpapan with its ruined oil refineries and abandoned port 2,000 miles from the forward Allied positions would 'disorganize completely' the strategic plan made little sense. But the Australian Government had consistently followed MacArthur's directions even when they differed from those of their own advisers, and on this occasion immediately replied that they agreed to the use of the division at Balikpapan. Thus the 9th Division secured Brunei Bay from 10 June, MacArthur making a point of going ashore with the forward troops on the first day. And he did this again at Balikpapan on 1 July when an amphibious attack involving 33,000 troops—it would have seemed a major operation 18 months before—was initiated. It was the last operation of MacArthur's South-West Pacific Command and, expertly executed, was finished except for patrolling and mopping up by the 21st.

At this stage, after seven months, the long fight on Luzon was still in progress. It was the largest land campaign of the Pacific war, involving finally the equivalent of 15 American divisions plus substantial Filipino forces, compared with, for example, 12 Allied divisions in Sicily, 13 British Empire divisions, mostly Indian, in the final operations in Burma, nine divisions on Okinawa.

Possession of Okinawa was essential to the American plan to bomb the Japanese homeland into submission or failing that to invade it. Occupation of the whole Philippine archipelago did not contribute decisively to the attainment of the final stepping-stones to Tokyo, and indeed MacArthur, from the first, had insisted that the reason for occupying the archipelago was largely political. But this does not mean that a concentrated advance to Okinawa along MacArthur's axis—the New Guinea–Philippine land masses —securing bases at suitable intervals and by-passing major Japanese concentrations (including in particular north Luzon and Mindanao) would not have been more economical and would not have reached the Ryukyus sooner.

Until the end a divided command was maintained in the Pacific. In the planned assault on Kyushu, to take place in the autumn of 1945, Nimitz and MacArthur were to act in cooperation, while the heavy bombers of the Strategic Air Force under General Spaatz would be responsible to General Arnold. The Kyushu operation would have been of unparalleled magnitude. Despite the devastating air and naval bombardment of her cities, factories and airfields, Japan still possessed some 8,000 aircraft to launch against an invader and there was an army of 2,000,000 men in the home islands. The Allied invading force would have been protected or carried by over 3,000 vessels not counting landing craft and would have comprised initially ten divisions with a floating reserve of three more. After this operation a landing near Tokyo was to follow by a force of 14 divisions with 11 more in reserve.

But on 24 July President Truman, then conferring at Potsdam with Churchill and Stalin, authorized the dropping of an atomic bomb on a Japanese industrial city. Spaatz chose Hiroshima. This bomb was dropped on 6 August. On the 8th the Russian Army attacked in Manchuria and on Sakhalin. On the 9th a second atomic bomb was dropped, on Nagasaki. Next day the Japanese sued for peace. On the 12th Truman directed the Strategic Air Force to cease its attacks. On the 15th Japan finally surrendered, and that day MacArthur was appointed Supreme Commander Allied Powers.

IX

SCAP

1945-50

As soon as Japan surrendered, MacArthur established radio contact with Tokyo and ordered the government to send him an envoy competent to receive instructions for carrying out the terms of the surrender. On 19 August, 16 Japanese led by the Vice-Chief of the Imperial General Staff arrived by air at Manila. MacArthur did not attend the subsequent conference but left it to Sutherland and his staff to extract information from the delegation and give them directions: Atsugi airfield near Tokyo was to be prepared for the landing of American troops and the propellers removed from all Japanese aircraft there, armed troops were to be withdrawn from the Tokyo Bay area, vehicles provided to carry staff and troops from Atsugi to Yokohama where the Allies would occupy the New Grand Hotel. There would be a formal ceremony of surrender aboard a battleship in Tokyo Bay.

The Japanese delegates were hesitant about their ability to have Atsugi ready in time, but were told they must do so. At that stage the American staff was not fully informed of events in Tokyo in the last few days. On the night of the 14th four officers of the Japanese 1st Guards Division had demanded of their commander, General Mori, that he cooperate with them in isolating the palace and preventing the broadcast of the Emperor's announcement of the surrender. Mori refused and was shot dead, whereupon the insurgents forged an order to the division to surround the palace and disarm its police guard. General Tanaka, commanding the capital's Eastern Army Group, hastened to the Guards' barracks, harangued the troops and persuaded them to desist. This mutiny collapsed and the four ringleaders committed suicide. But other troops laid siege to the residence of the Prime Minister, set fire to the homes of two senior statesmen, and occupied radio stations. *Kamikaze* pilots based on Atsugi dropped leaflets denouncing the surrender and threatened to bomb the American flagship

Missouri. According to the Japanese diplomat Kase the fanatics were calmed down only a few days before the first American aircraft landed on the 25th.

In March 1945 when, as mentioned earlier, Robert E. Sherwood at the President's request had visited MacArthur in Manila, one of his assignments was to learn something of MacArthur's ideas about the military government of Japan. Sherwood was greatly impressed by the extent of MacArthur's 'understanding of the Orient and the breadth of his views', and his summary of what MacArthur said, in the course of a conversation lasting nearly three hours, is a valuable record of the general's forward thinking at that stage. The destruction of Japanese military power, MacArthur said, could destroy for the civil population the notion of the Emperor's divinity. He went on:

'This will result in a spiritual vacuum and an opportunity for the introduction of new concepts. The Japanese people will have inevitable respect for as well as fear of the instruments of their own defeat. Believing that might makes right, they will conclude that we of the USA must be right. Furthermore, the prestige throughout Asia that we have established by our Philippine policy and which will be vastly increased by conquest of Japan will make us the greatest influence on the future development of Asia. If we exert that influence in an imperialistic manner, or for the sole purpose of commercial advantage, then we shall lose our golden opportunity; but if our influence and our strength are expressed in terms of essential liberalism we shall have the friendship and the cooperation of the Asiatic peoples far into the future.'

It seemed to be General MacArthur's view that the Japanese civil population if treated with stern justice and strength would be more capable of eventual redemption than are the Germans.[1]

Thus the Potsdam Declaration of four months later, which was to be the basis of MacArthur's charter, was not entirely uncongenial to the new Supreme Commander. It prescribed the 'elimination for all time' of those who had led Japan into war, the occupation of points in Japanese territory until a 'new order' had been established, disarmament, the meting out of 'stern justice' to 'all war criminals', establishment of democratic government, and freedom of speech, religion and thought, maintenance of 'such industries as will sustain her economy and permit the exaction of reparations in kind, but not those which would enable her to re-arm for war'. The occupying forces were to be withdrawn when these objectives had been accomplished.

On 29 August, the day before he was due to fly to Japan, MacArthur received a summary of the United States Initial Post-Surrender Policy for Japan prepared by the Departments of State, War and the Navy. It restated and elaborated the terms of the Potsdam Proclamation. The Supreme Commander would possess all powers necessary to carry out the surrender

[1] Sherwood, pp. 867-8.

terms, exercising his authority 'through Japanese governmental machinery and agencies, including the Emperor'. The Supreme Command could require changes in governmental machinery or personnel or act directly but was not committed to support of the Emperor or government in opposition to evolutionary changes looking towards the attainment of United States objectives. Japan was not to have an army, navy, air force, secret police organization or any civil aviation. High military and naval officials and leaders of 'ultra-nationalist and militarist organizations' were to be excluded from 'supervisory and teaching positions'. The Supreme Commander was to favour the dissolution of the large industrial and banking combinations. The Japanese were to provide goods and service for the occupying forces to the extent that this could be done without causing 'starvation, widespread disease and acute physical distress', and at the same time to facilitate the restoration of the economy so as to meet the reasonable peaceful requirements of the people.

From 25 August onwards aircraft had landed engineers and signal teams at Atsugi, followed by infantry of the 11th Airborne Division. Eichelberger who, as commander of the Eighth Army, would lead the occupation force, and was scheduled to land early on the 30th asked MacArthur to delay his own arrival until two days later but MacArthur insisted on flying in that day: 'Years of overseas duty had schooled me well in the lessons of the Orient and, what was probably more important, had taught the Far East that I was its friend.'[1]

Meanwhile, more than 350 ships of the Pacific Fleet and the British Pacific Fleet were converging on Tokyo Bay. The jealousy between the American admirals and generals was being maintained to the last. In war this rivalry had produced unhappy results, now merely comical ones. A 'great crisis in army–navy relations'[2] was averted by the arrangement that the general would take the surrender on Nimitz' flagship, *Missouri*, and, better still, one named after the President's own State. Nimitz would sign the surrender document on behalf of the United States, MacArthur for the United Nations. And a regiment of marines—the 4th, which was the designation of the regiment on Corregidor in 1942—was to be put ashore while army troops were landing at Atsugi. Their commanding officer told Eichelberger with a grin that the 'first wave was made up entirely of admirals trying to get ashore before MacArthur'.[3] And the initial occupation of Japan was to be shared between army and navy. While the Eighth Army and Third Fleet were responsible for Honshu from Kobe eastward, the Sixth Army

---

[1] *Reminiscences*, p. 270.
[2] J. F. Byrnes, *Speaking Frankly* (New York, 1947), p. 213.
[3] Eichelberger, p. 263.

and Fifth Fleet were to occupy western Honshu, Kyushu and Shikoku, the Seventh Fleet and XXIV Corps were to occupy Korea south of latitude 38 degrees North, and the North Pacific Fleet Hokkaido. The Third Fleet was to take over the Yokosuka naval base and, with three battalions plus a battalion from the British and Australian navies, to share in the occupation of the Tokyo area. Ships of the Third Fleet entered Tokyo Bay on the 28th and landed troops at Yokosuka on the 30th. Early on the same day MacArthur and his senior staff officers boarded his Constellation aircraft *Bataan* for the seven-hour flight to Tokyo. On the way he paced the aisle deep in thought. Courtney Whitney has recorded that he paused now and then to dictate notes:

> First destroy the military power. . . . Then build the structure of representative government. . . . Enfranchise the women. . . . Free the political prisoners. . . . Liberate the farmers. . . . Establish a free labor movement. . . . Encourage a free economy. . . . Abolish police oppression. . . . Develop a free and responsible press. . . . Liberalize education. . . . Decentralize the political power. . . .

At 2 p.m. the *Bataan* circled the Atsugi field and landed. MacArthur, in open-neck shirt, without ribbons, corncob pipe in mouth, stood at the door of the aircraft for a moment and was photographed, and then stepped down alone. At a distance Eichelberger was waiting. 'Bob, this seems to be the end of the road. As they say in the movies, this is the payoff', said the Supreme Commander. The new arrivals boarded a convoy of well-worn vehicles and were driven to the hotel at Yokohama along a road lined by Japanese troops with their backs turned as if the Emperor was passing by.

For the first eight days MacArthur's headquarters were at the New Grand Hotel. On the 31st he learnt that Generals Wainwright and Percival had arrived at Manila from prison camp in Manchuria. He ordered that they be flown to Japan to attend the ceremony of surrender, and that night the two commanders arrived, still emaciated as a result of their privations. Wainwright feared that he was in disgrace because of his surrender at Corregidor. 'Jonathan, you can have command of a corps with me any time you want it', said MacArthur.

The ceremony on the *Missouri* took place on 2 September, and on the 8th MacArthur with Halsey, Eichelberger and some of his staff entered Tokyo to establish his headquarters in the United States Embassy. In the embassy grounds a guard of honour from the 1st Cavalry Division was drawn up and a soldier stood at the flagpole holding an American flag that had flown in Washington on the day of Pearl Harbor and on the *Missouri* at the surrender. Standing on the terrace MacArthur said: 'General Eichelberger, have our country's flag unfurled and in Tokyo's sun let it wave in its full glory as a symbol of hope for the oppressed and as a harbinger of victory for the right.'

The Japanese people needed more than a symbol of hope. Never in modern times had a whole country been so devastated by war. Vast city areas were in ruins. Of some 1,850,000 Japanese who had died in the war about 670,000 had been killed in air raids on the home islands. The townspeople were desperately short of food and even clothing. All seemed dejected and apprehensive of reprisals by the victorious Allied soldiery. The merchant fleet had been destroyed. Production of coal was at one-eighth of its peacetime level and winter was approaching. The factories were almost at a standstill. In the next year or so 6,000,000 Japanese, repatriated or expelled from overseas countries, would swell the hungry population. Soon a galloping inflation was cutting the value of wages and of the savings of a thrifty people and breeding organized blackmarketing.

The people's fears of reprisals were soon dispelled when they found that the troops were jocular, friendly and mostly well-behaved, and soon the arrival of ships carrying food for distribution to the needy created more good feeling. MacArthur took it upon himself to establish army kitchens and to begin to bring in 3,500,000 tons of food from his bases throughout the Pacific. A Congressional Committee later sought an explanation and MacArthur provided one in a statement that ended:

> To cut off Japan's relief supplies in this situation would cause starvation to countless Japanese—and starvation breeds mass unrest, disorder and violence. Give me bread or give me bullets.

The next five years are not part of the story of MacArthur as a trainer and organizer of troops in peace or as a field commander, though in addition to being SCAP he was also Commander-in-Chief of the United States Far Eastern Command. But his performance as *de facto* ruler of Japan revealed new qualities, and in this period he reached his highest stature both in his own view and in that of others. 'In Japan', he wrote, 'I had to be an economist, a political scientist, an engineer, a manufacturing executive, a teacher, even a theologian of sorts. . . . Japan had become the world's greatest laboratory for an experiment in the liberation of a people from totalitarian rule and for the liberalization of government from within. . . . The experiment . . . must go far beyond . . . the destruction of Japan's ability to wage another war and the punishment of war criminals. Yet history clearly showed that no modern military occupation of a conquered nation had been a success.'

The staff urged him to summon the Emperor to a meeting but MacArthur decided that 'the patience of the East rather than the haste of the West' was the wisest policy. And in a few days the Emperor himself, through his Foreign Minister, Shigeru Yoshida, sought an interview. MacArthur told Yoshida that his position prevented him from visiting the Emperor but he would be delighted if the Emperor would come to see him at the embassy. The meeting took place on 27 September. They talked, alone except for an interpreter, for 38 minutes. MacArthur put the Emperor at his ease. He had feared that the Emperor might seek to discuss his possible indictment as a war criminal, as had been proposed by Russia and Britain but opposed by MacArthur (though the Emperor knew nothing of this). Instead the Emperor, as MacArthur recalled it, offered himself to the judgment of the Powers 'as the one to bear sole responsibility for every political and military decision made and action taken by my people in the conduct of war'.[1] MacArthur was greatly moved. After this there were other meetings, always in private. In January 1946 the Emperor on his own initiative issued a rescript denying his divinity. Shigeru Yoshida, Prime Minister during most of MacArthur's term, considered that MacArthur's respectful attitude towards the Emperor, and in particular his insistence that the Emperor should not be grouped with the war criminals 'more than any other single factor made the occupation an historic success'.[2]

MacArthur did not travel outside Tokyo except to the airport to receive eminent visitors, and to Manila in 1946 and Seoul in 1948 to be present at ceremonies at which the Philippines and South Korea were declared independent nations. At home and at his office in the Dai Ichi Building he kept himself informed by reading and by questioning his staff and other visitors. Each morning, Sundays included, he worked at his office for six hours or so. In the late evening he read or watched movies at the embassy. This routine, including the movies, somewhat resembled the one followed in Manila in 1935-41.

The Emperor on the other hand soon began to move among his people far more frequently than hitherto. The occupation authorities drastically reduced the Palace staff and volunteer workers helped with domestic chores. It was a singular situation. The hitherto remote and divine Emperor was moving about among his people like an English or Scandinavian king or queen while the Supreme Commander was adopting the posture of a British or Dutch viceroy, remote from and unapproachable by all but a chosen few natives.

Although MacArthur bore the title of SCAP he was in fact the American military governor of Japan under the direct authority of the joint Chiefs of Staff and exerting his power through a virtually all-American team, and one in which key posts were held by men who had served with him on his staff in the south-west Pacific. But there were soon some radical changes among the senior courtiers. Diller, who had for years administered the general's public relations policies, departed and so did Sutherland, who was replaced by a new

[1] *Reminiscences*, p. 288.
[2] Yoshida, *The Yoshida Memoirs* (London, 1961), p. 51.

chief of staff, Major-General Paul J. Mueller.[1] The status of Willoughby, who remained as Chief of Intelligence, and of Courtney Whitney, who was now placed at the head of the 'Government section', seems to have risen. Major-General W. F. Marquat, one-time anti-aircraft commander in the Philippines, controlled the Economic and Scientific Section. For the first three years Eichelberger commanded the Eighth Army, which by the end of the first year had dwindled until it comprised two corps including four divisions —1st Cavalry, 11th Airborne, 24th and 25th—side by side with a British Commonwealth occupation force whose maximum strength was about 40,000. MacArthur's senior diplomatic adviser was at first George Atcheson Jnr, but from August 1947 was William J. Sebald, a former naval officer who had spent ten years in legal practice at Kobe in the 1930s. Sebald won MacArthur's full confidence and became a valued confidant and frank counsellor.

The occupation was organized like a military headquarters with clearly defined channels of command. Directly under MacArthur and his chief of staff were civilian officers in charge of public information, diplomatic and legal sections, but at the next level were 14 staff sections, nearly all concerned with civil administration but headed by soldiers or men holding army rank.

The problem of establishing at least an appearance of international control was solved after much argument by the establishment in Washington of a Far East Commission, agreed to at a conference between the United States, British and Russian representatives in Moscow in December 1945 and comprising representatives of the 11 Allied belligerents in the Pacific war: Australia, Canada, China, France, India, the Netherlands, New Zealand, the Philippines, Russia, the United Kingdom, the United States. The commission was to transmit its decisions to an Allied Council in Japan comprising representatives of the United States, the British Commonwealth (Australians held this appointment), Russia and China. Before the Moscow conference MacArthur had informed the Chiefs of Staff that the proposal for control by a commission was in his opinion not acceptable. He need have had no fear. The representatives of the four senior powers on the commission possessed the veto and this meant that in debates on major problems the commission reached a deadlock and could not radically alter occupation policies or reverse decisions. In the words of one American historian the commission 'gradually settled down to a genteel position of pompous gentility'.[2]

Closer to MacArthur was the Allied Council, which became a thorn in the

[1] In his *Reminiscences*, published in 1964, MacArthur mentions Sutherland rarely and he does not appear at all in the narrative after the Papuan phase. In the same book he does not mention Diller at all.

[2] E. O. Reischauer, *The United States and Japan* (Harvard, 1950), p. 47.

side of the Occupation mainly by reason of the tactics of the Russian representative, General K. N. Derevyanko, who adopted the role of leader of a one-man opposition party determined to embarrass the Occupation to the maximum. From the outset the SCAP administration treated the council with scant respect. MacArthur attended only the opening session, and eventually left the task of chairing the meetings to his senior diplomatic officer. Before the second meeting Derevyanko had complained that some undesirable Japanese had not in fact been excluded from office and asked that the council be informed 'as fully as possible'. When the council met Courtney Whitney attended to reply to the inquiry and filibustered for three hours slowly reading lists of organizations banned by SCAP, using, according to the British Commonwealth representative, Macmahon Ball, a 'sarcastic and contemptuous tone' and with sneering asides. Ball, and no doubt Derevyanko, considered this 'a gross and ill-mannered affront'. 'This second meeting', Ball added, 'showed that it would henceforth be hardly possible for the Council to cooperate in any serious work if an enquiry from the Soviet Member were always to evoke a frivolous, hostile and contemptuous reaction from the representative of the Supreme Commander.'[1] In MacArthur's view the Far Eastern Commission became 'little more than a debating society' and the Allied Council's 'sole contribution' was 'nuisance and defamation'.

But Sebald felt that the council, though powerless, served a useful purpose in providing the Japanese with a view of a forum where SCAP policies were explained and criticized more freely than in the cautious Japanese Diet. He was 'often distressed by MacArthur's sensitivity to the council's discussions of his policies. He appeared to be particularly irritated when the British Commonwealth member asked pertinent questions, which by implication were critical. . . . MacArthur ignored the Council for two years rather than risk unsympathetic comments reported by the world press.'[2]

The Russians had been anxious to share in the occupation of Japan and in particular to have their own area to garrison and control as in Europe. Their manœuvre was successfully resisted. At one stage Derevyanko threatened that Russian troops would be sent into Hokkaido against MacArthur's orders, whereupon MacArthur said that if this happened he would put the Russian Mission in jail. 'By God, I believe you would', said Derevyanko. The Russians took the view that the American policy of repatriation and demobilization of the Japanese forces was too soft. In September the Russian Minister, Molotov, told Byrnes, the American Secretary of State, that the Americans should do what the Russians were doing with their half

[1] W. M. Ball, *Japan—Enemy or Ally* (Melbourne, 1948), pp. 34-5.
[2] W. J. Sebald, *With MacArthur in Japan: A Personal History of the Occupation* (New York, 1965), p. 150.

million or so prisoners in Manchuria: put them to work. Byrnes pointed out that Russia had agreed to the Potsdam Declaration which stated that Japanese troops would be allowed to go home. Despite American protests it was 1949 before some 95,000 Japanese prisoners were returned from Russian custody, and these were men who had been converted to militant communism —a conversion that does not seem to have lasted long after their return and their discovery that conditions in Japan were very different from those their indoctrinators had described. In that year MacArthur reported that according to the Japanese Demobilization Bureau 364,000 prisoners in Russian hands had not been accounted for. In the upshot the ruthless and clumsy Russian policies seem to have greatly aided MacArthur in achieving one of his main objectives: to prevent the establishment of a Russian zone in Japan and subdue the spread of communism there.

As the occupation proceeded the gap between MacArthur and Washington widened. The autocrat in Tokyo tended to interpret his general directives very broadly, often confronting officials at home with a *fait accompli* at times when they thought they should have been consulted. For their part the staff of SCAP resented interference by distant and, they believed, ill-informed officials, and in particular were convinced that Washington regarded Russian ambitions with undue complacency. MacArthur on the other hand never ceased to utter warnings against the threat of Russian and Chinese communism, and at his elbow were even more ardent crusaders, particularly the German-born Willoughby, obsessed by what he described as the menace of 'Imperialist-Mongoloid-Pan-Slavism under the guise of communism'.[1]

When Sebald urged MacArthur occasionally to meet heads of diplomatic missions in Tokyo MacArthur replied that this would serve no useful purpose. 'And why as the sovereign should I? President Truman doesn't do so, nor does the King of England or any other head of state. However I will see any chief of mission who has legitimate business to transact.' One of these days he would 'blast the State Department "wide open"', a remark that persuaded Sebald that someone in Washington was giving MacArthur 'highly distorted information'.[2]

In view of the strenuousness of the party political struggle in America, the aggressiveness of the American Press and MacArthur's long-standing mistrust of some of the leaders in Washington, the widening rift was unfortunate, particularly as it was difficult to picture any other eminent American who would have occupied the post in Tokyo to better effect from the Japanese point of view. Above all MacArthur had provided the bewildered Japanese with the strong and admirable leadership they needed.

[1] Willoughby and Chamberlain, p. 368.
[2] Sebald, pp. 119-25.

His flair for the dramatic, his thundering phrases, his appreciation of the tremendous historical significance of his own acts, all had a strong emotional appeal to the Japanese. Here was a leader who combined emotional depth with firmness of will. General MacArthur became to the Japanese the symbol of perfection, the inspired leader, the knight in shining armor, and they repaid him, foreign conqueror though he was, with unlimited respect and often enough with adulation.[1]

In the words of a Japanese historian, his 'imperious aloofness and lordly graciousness' established the prestige of the Occupation. The Japanese needed the security provided by a new authority and new codes of conduct to replace those that had prevailed during the years of disaster. (In the war Allied interrogators had been surprised at the frequency with which Japanese prisoners at first seemingly stunned by a feeling of disgrace would suddenly begin to cooperate with their captors, exchanging one loyalty for another overnight.) According to a Japanese observer his people's acceptance of the Occupation was 'a voluntary attitude quite apart from any deference to superior power. Some Americans mistook it for good sportsmanship; General MacArthur praised it as the "dignity" with which the Japanese bore their defeat. Elements of sportsmanship and dignity were no doubt present, but to the Japanese there was also a large measure of sheer self-gratification and comfort in conforming to an exacting set of new rules.'[2]

The achievements and shortcomings of the Occupation were discussed at the time and later with a warmth and verbosity only surpassed, in Mac-Arthur's story, by the debate that accompanied and followed the final chapter of his career in the Far East. The following account of the impact of SCAP on Japan aims at being as brief and detached as seems appropriate in a discussion of MacArthur as military commander.

In the view of MacArthur and the uncritical ones among his senior officers the Occupation was an unqualified success in every regard. The disarming of some 7,000,000 troops was smoothly accomplished and the repatriation of those who were overseas was carried out as quickly as provision of ships would allow. About a year passed before the last Japanese troops from the most distant areas were disembarked from overcrowded transports. The general staffs were abolished and their remaining duties performed by Demobilization Bureaux. In general all professional officers were debarred from influential positions. But the folly of including in the Potsdam Declaration and its supplement a provision that Japan should be disarmed until the end of time soon became apparent.

As a prelude to the introduction of the democratic system and in obedience

[1] Reischauer, p. 225.
[2] K. Kawai, *Japan's American Interlude* (Chicago, 1960), p. 6.

to the Potsdam Declaration some 210,000 Japanese were barred from public office, including 167,000 military men, 34,800 politically inclined people, 19,000 businessmen, 18,000 civil servants, and 12,000 engaged in journalism and the like. At the same time an effort was made by imposing a Draconian capital levy, to destroy the power and wealth of the Zaibatsu, the small group of families who controlled nine-tenths of Japanese industry. Mac-Arthur doubted the wisdom of the purge on the grounds that it deprived the government of useful administrators and might breed resentment; he considered it the only measure that was not given full popular support. Others were convinced that the Zaibatsu were so deeply entrenched and so firmly secured by family loyalties that efforts to destroy their power would prove futile. And soon, with the intensification of hostility towards communism, the policy switched from emphasis on banning 'ultra nationalists' to suppression of communists. At length, according to one critic, 'the purge floundered in a morass of contradiction and confusion'.[1]

MacArthur seems to have held the view that the stark facts of defeat and humiliation had sufficed to transform 'the idolatry for feudalistic masters and the warrior class. . . . into hatred and contempt'. For a time perhaps this was so, but cherished national tradition is not blotted out so easily; and before long, in Japan as elsewhere, a vast popular literature would be extolling the feats of wartime heroes.

When MacArthur wrote that one of his roles as Supreme Commander was that of 'a theologian of sorts' he evidently had in mind his decision to disestablish the state religion. In November 1945 he ordered the cessation of subsidies to Shinto organizations. This had the adverse effect of denying public funds to private schools and reducing their ability to supplement and compete with government schools. In the opinion of many observers and even some devoted supporters of Occupation policies the erosion of old loyalties by such measures as this had the unhappy outcome of weakening the restraining influences of religion and family throughout Japan and making room for the adoption of the more tawdry aspects of the American way of life.

Trade unions were encouraged, women enfranchised, the scope of education widened, and a degree of public discussion of politics and administration permitted. Soon trade unions had 5,000,000 members; but when in January 1947 communists gained control of some unions and threatened a general strike aimed at the overthrow of the Yoshida government and demanding a threefold increase in wages sorely eroded by the inflation, MacArthur issued an edict, not through the government, banning 'so deadly a social weapon in the present impoverished and emaciated condition of Japan'. When in the

[1] H. H. Baerwald, *The Purge of Japanese Leaders Under the Occupation* (Los Angeles, 1959), p. 101.

same year communists infiltrated unions of workers in government-operated facilities, MacArthur secured the passing of a law bringing such employees into the public service. From this year onwards Japanese police and American military police suppressed demonstrations more aggressively than hitherto, and sometimes troops were used to overawe strikers. At that stage MacArthur declined to press for the outlawing of the Communist Party. But in 1949 when communists seemed to be gaining strength Yoshida, at his direction, banned the 24 members of the Central Committee of the party from political activity, and later MacArthur suppressed communist newspapers.

Despite the instruction to encourage freedom of speech and to develop. a free and responsible Press, SCAP in fact imposed severe censorship from time to time. Criticism of this policy was banned and importation of books and translation of foreign works controlled. At the same time, for the first four years, very few Japanese were allowed to go abroad, and the people and their leaders were isolated from foreign ideas and influences (except for those provided by the Occupation) to an extent only equalled in communist countries. Perhaps the idea of freedom of speech on the Western model was still uncongenial to Japanese both of the right and the left. Discussion in the Diet was more inhibited than, for example, arguments in the Allied Council, and censorship not widely resented.

Largely the reforms were administered by Japanese in accordance with MacArthur's instructions in governments which represented the pre-war civilian élite which had hitherto been dominated by the military and naval coteries, and in particular by Shigeru Yoshida, the conservative former diplomat who, except for 18 months of liberal governments, was Mac-Arthur's Prime Minister and supported by strongly anti-communist majorities in the Diet. He was a friendly admirer and obedient associate of MacArthur to whom he described himself as 'executor of your directives', and in history they must share the praise or blame for the transformation of Japan in the years before the peace treaty.

It was inevitable that the 'feudal' (idle landlord) arrangements in Japan should come under the American axe. By 1950 5,000,000 acres of land had been bought from the landlords and sold to the peasants; 89 per cent of farm land, MacArthur recorded, was then controlled by the people who worked it. Of all the economic reforms instituted by the MacArthur regime this one seems to have been the most successful.

By 1950 the national income had passed the pre-war level—but the population too had greatly increased. Improved management, technological borrowing from America, education, a rapidly increasing work force and a high percentage of savings were combining to produce spectacular development of Japan as a manufacturing country.

From 1945 until 1948 an International Military Tribunal for the Far East, comprising 11 judges representing the 11 Allied belligerents, and military tribunals far and wide conducted trials of Japanese soldiers and civilians in accordance with the Potsdam Declaration that 'stern justice' should be meted out to all war criminals. Homma, who had been MacArthur's opponent on Luzon in 1942, and Yamashita, his opponent on Luzon in 1945, were among those sentenced to death by military tribunals. Yamashita appealed to the United States Supreme Court, nine of whose 11 justices upheld the sentence, which President Truman also approved. In February 1946 the verdict came before MacArthur for review. Instead of tersely ordering that the sentence be carried out, which would have accorded better with his honour and dignity, he issued a long statement in his customary florid prose, justifying the verdict, denouncing his former antagonist and ordering that before execution Yamashita be 'stripped of uniform, decorations and other appurtenances, signifying membership of the military profession'. What the dissenting judges of the Supreme Court, Murphy and Rutledge, described as 'legalized lynching' was carried out. When reviewing the sentence of death on Homma MacArthur issued a similar statement, but this time declaring that the passing of final judgment was a 'repugnant duty'.

The major war criminals were tried by the International Tribunal. There were 25 of them including four former prime ministers. Seven, including two prime ministers, Tojo and Hirota, were sentenced to death by hanging. Two members of the Tribunal—the Indian and French judges—dissented. When these sentences came before MacArthur for review he again composed a statement giving his reasons for upholding them. Appeals to the United States Supreme Court were denied, the court declaring on 20 December that it had no power to review the sentences. Next day MacArthur sent letters to the four members of the Allied Council requiring them to attend the execution, to take place before dawn on the 23rd. As these unhappy witnesses waited in the execution room with five noosed ropes dangling over a platform before them, there were shouts of *banzai* from within. First Doihara, Matsui, Tojo and Muto were hanged together, and in a second batch Itzgaki, Hirota and Nimura.

In his critical examination of the war crimes trials in general Lord Hankey referred to 'the disconcerting fact that one of the Judges represented a country that could be accused of many of the crimes listed in the indictment'.[1] He could justly have said that several of the judges represented countries that could be accused of some of the crimes with which the defeated Japanese leaders were charged.

When the Occupation began, Japan's first written constitution, bestowed

[1] Lord Hankey, *Political Trials and Errors* (Oxford, 1950).

on the nation by the Emperor Meiji, was but 56 years old. Written under authoritarian German influence, it declared that Japan would be ruled for all time by a 'sacred and inviolable' Emperor. The Diet comprised an appointed House of Peers with powers equal to those of a House of Representatives elected by property owners who at first included only a small fraction of the people. The virtual autonomy of the navy and army was ensured by an ordinance providing that the ministers of the navy and of war must be officers on the active list. In the war the military and naval leaders had in effect formed an oligarchy that proved politically unassailable until Japan was on the verge of defeat. But now that the Emperor was no longer sacred, the military and naval leaders and their powerful civilian supporters had been banished from public life or were in gaol.

From the outset MacArthur demanded of successive prime ministers that they promptly revise the constitution and, in October 1945, when the liberal Shidehara was Prime Minister with Yoshida as Foreign Minister, a committee was formed to draft one. MacArthur was anxious that the Japanese leaders should write their own constitution rather than have an American-style constitution imposed on them. But months passed without the liberals on the committee, who wanted radical changes, reaching agreement with the conservatives who wanted virtually none at all. In February MacArthur decided to wait no longer and gave Whitney and his staff the task. The first general elections were due in April and he wished them to be in effect a vote for or against a new constitution. Within a month, without the knowledge of the Japanese cabinet, Whitney and his staff had put together a new constitution. It was approved by MacArthur and also, grudgingly, by the cabinet. Press criticism of it was suppressed.[1]

At Shidehara's request made in January before the American lawyers began work, the constitution contained an article (IX) which in its final form declared that the Japanese people renounced war 'forever' and would never maintain land, sea and air forces 'as well as other war potential'.[2]

This unpractical article amounted to formal acceptance of corresponding conditions of the Potsdam Declaration. MacArthur took the view that the article did not preclude Japan should she be 'within the orbit of immediate threatened attack' from mounting 'the maximum defensive power' which her resources would permit, an interpretation difficult to follow.

---

[1] Kawai, p. 52.

[2] Article IX reads: 'Aspiring sincerely to an international peace based on justice and order, the Japanese people forever renounce war as a sovereign right of the nation and the threat or use of force as means of settling international disputes.

'In order to accomplish the aim of the preceding paragraph land, sea and air forces, as well as other war potential, will never be maintained. The right of belligerency of the state will not be recognized.'

The Japanese scholar Kawai, though critical of the way in which the constitution had been forced through a reluctant Diet, agreed that it was a good one. 'Although in places its turgidly MacArthurian language was annoyingly un-Japanese and although it was loosely organized and redundant, its provisions did conform to the best standards of a truly parliamentary democracy.'[1]

At the election the voters appeared to approve the new constitution. About 13,000,000 women voted for the first time and 38 women were elected. SCAP decided that only six of the newly elected members could be classed as 'old line politicians'. Substantial numbers of professional people and even farmers were returned. A conservative government was formed with Yoshida as Prime Minister.

The question of concluding a peace treaty was under discussion for six years. As early as March 1947 MacArthur, since he wished the Occupation to end without delay, urged that the treaty be negotiated as soon as possible. But the American Army and Navy Departments, contemplating a Japan that had been required never to maintain any fighting forces and dependent on the United States for defence, wanted it to be postponed. MacArthur, however, saw that the Occupation could do no more than create the climate in which the Japanese themselves might transform their political system. He feared that to prolong the Occupation would lead to the Japanese becoming too dependent on American guidance and resentful of continual supervision, while the Americans would be corrupted by absolute power and develop illusions of grandeur and infallibility. Another reason why he wished to end the Occupation soon was that the young soldiers who began to replace the veterans of the Eighth Army were ill-disciplined and were damaging the reputation the men of the original occupying force had won. Eventually MacArthur would leave Japan before the treaty had been signed.

Between 1945 and 1950, when a new crisis developed, the Occupation forces, with the cooperation of a traditionally docile people, carried out the reformation of Japan with a speed and a degree of moderation that have won the approval of all but the most unfriendly critics. To the benevolent and idealistic autocrat must go much of the credit for the basic achievements: a united Japan free of a Russian zone of occupation; a democratic system; land reforms; and the beginnings of an economic recovery that would attain unforeseen dimensions, when within 25 years after the ceasefire Japan would achieve a gross national product second only to that of the United States among non-communist nations.

Changes of policy derived mainly from pressures external to Japan: increasing American resistance towards Russian aims and a consequent

[1] Kawai, p. 55.

severe repression of communists in Japan; American need for an Asian ally to take the place of China; remilitarization of Japan despite Article IX; warmer support for conservative elements, including big business, and despite the early assault on the Zaibatsu. Kawai wrote that 'the Japanese continue to accord him [MacArthur] a respect, gratitude and admiration which have already [1960] made him a legendary figure in Japanese history', and found the reasons for this high regard in his sincerity, dedication to his mission, intuitive political acumen, power to inspire his subordinates with his own ideals, and the fact that he provided the Japanese with someone to look up to.

But throughout MacArthur's reign as Supreme Commander his critics far and wide outside Japan were acrimonious and persistent. Their onslaughts were of a kind that MacArthur had been largely spared as a military commander sheltered by a military censorship. By nature touchy, autocratic and eloquent, he was unable to let criticism go unheeded. 'The hypersensitive General . . . often replied to the attacks on him, either directly or through personal spokesmen, thus furnishing the press with more copy and adding fuel to the controversy of the moment. Neither MacArthur nor his advisers seemed to understand how often this tactic helped to enlarge and prolong issues that might otherwise have died from under-nourishment.'[1]

This tendency seems to have been fed by MacArthur's recurrent feeling of persecution by the Democratic leaders at home, present since the opening of the war, and a conviction that conspirators in Washington were plotting his downfall. In 1948 MacArthur was put forward as a Republican candidate for the Presidency. At the Wisconsin primary in April he was firmly rejected. In his *Reminiscences* MacArthur said that his name was 'precipitated' into the struggle, that he was not a candidate, and that the 'only tangible result was to bring down on my head an avalanche of political abuse from the party in power. . . . From that moment on it became only a question of time until retaliation would be visited upon me.'[2] But Sebald writes that he learnt later that MacArthur had sought the nomination, and quotes MacArthur's chief of staff, Mueller, as saying that MacArthur was very disappointed at the outcome.

In the first four years of the Occupation MacArthur had been an unhappy observer of the defeat of Kuomintang power in China. American policy had been to persuade the communists and the Kuomintang to form a coalition government, and the Russians supported this policy to the extent that they recognized Chiang Kai-shek's regime and handed over the cities of Manchuria to Nationalist troops, but not before they had stripped them of industrial equipment. In May 1945 Stalin had told Harry L. Hopkins that

[1] Sebald, p. 111.
[2] *Reminiscences*, p. 319.

only Chiang could unify China; no communist leader was strong enough to do so.[1]

In retrospect the contention of MacArthur and many other American leaders that by adopting an uncompromisingly hostile attitude towards the communists and giving maximum material aid to Chiang, America could have made him ruler of all China seems grossly to underrate the moral factor in war and to overrate the material one. Once Japan had been defeated the eventual victory of the Chinese communists was inevitable. On the one hand was the disciplined and sternly indoctrinated army of Mao Tse-tung, on the other the army of Chiang Kai-shek's corrupt Kuomintang plutocracy. As seen during the war by the American general Stilwell it was ill-equipped, ill-trained, ill-fed, led largely by mere job holders and sustained only by its numbers, American support, and a cadre of leaders committed to a dogged defence of old China. There could be no compromise between the new China and the old. The American Government sent out General Marshall to heal the breach. On the way he stayed with MacArthur, who found that he had 'aged immeasurably' since their last meeting. Marshall was soon convinced that a reconciliation of the Chinese parties was impossible. American support for Chiang continued but by 1947 he was on the defensive. In February 1949 the communists entered Peking and at the end of the year the remnants of the defeated Kuomintang armies were pushed out of mainland China to Formosa.

In a press interview on 1 March 1949 MacArthur had spoken of America's line of defence in Asia as running from the Philippines through the Ryukyus, Japan and the Aleutians to Alaska. And in January 1950 the Secretary of State, Dean Acheson, defined America's 'defensive perimeter' in similar terms. No mention of Formosa or Korea.

Since MacArthur's arrival in Japan two rival Korean republics had been established, each claiming authority over the whole peninsula.

A General Order concerning the details of the Japanese surrenders, approved by the United States, Russian and British Governments in August 1945, and issued by MacArthur on 2 September had provided that Russian troops would receive the surrender of Japanese forces north of the 38th Parallel and American troops of Japanese forces south of it. The XXIV Corps formed the American occupation force. There were some 9,000,000 people in the Russian zone, 21,000,000 in the American. A decision by the General Assembly of the United Nations in November 1947 to establish a United Nations Commission to supervise elections throughout the whole country with the object of establishing a national government was made

[1] Sherwood, pp. 891–2.

ineffective by the refusal of the Russians to allow the commission into North Korea. In May 1948 the South Koreans elected a national assembly with the American-educated Dr Syngman Rhee as president, and on 15 August the Republic of Korea was formally established, MacArthur making one of his few visits away from Tokyo to attend. In his address he declared that the barrier between north and south 'must and will be torn down. . . . Koreans come from too proud a stock to sacrifice their sacred cause by yielding to any alien philosophies of disruption.'

On the other hand, in September 1947, the US Joint Chiefs of Staff, then Admirals Leahy and Nimitz and Generals Eisenhower and Spaatz, had advised the Secretary of State that the United States had 'little strategical interest in maintaining the present troops and bases in Korea' and in April 1948, President Truman, on the advice of the Joint Chiefs, approved a statement that an action taken by a faction in Korea or another Power in Korea would not be considered a cause of war by the United States.

A United States Ambassador to Korea, John J. Muccio, was appointed and by June 1949 the last American troops had been withdrawn, except for a military Advisory Group some 480 strong to assist in the training of the Korean Army.

Meanwhile in August and September 1948 North Korea too had elected a People's Assembly and adopted a constitution for a Democratic People's Republic of Korea, which like the Rhee government claimed jurisdiction over the whole country. The North Korean Premier, Kim Il Sung, was a graduate of Chiang Kai-shek's Whamsoa Military Academy, with long service as a guerilla leader with the Communist Chinese.

From this time onwards there were communist demonstrations in South Korea aimed at unifying the country under communist rule. In October 1949 North Korea demanded that the United Nations Commission be withdrawn. The United Nations responded by announcing in March 1950 that it would appoint military observers to report on incidents along the border, where clashes had been frequent.

Meanwhile in South Korea, although it was no longer part of MacArthur's military responsibility, Willoughby had 'quietly' maintained an Intelligence unit, and he was later at pains to point out that it had circulated warnings of warlike preparations by North Korea from time to time, and on 5 January 1950 had reported that North Korea planned an invasion in March or April; on 10 March he reported that North Korea would be ready to attack in June, but qualified this by commenting that it seemed likely that 'overt military measures' would be held in abeyance until Russia had further observed the progress of events in China, Burma and Thailand.

In June John Foster Dulles, as an envoy of Acheson, visited MacArthur to discuss the Japanese peace treaty, and from Tokyo on the 19th went to Korea, where, in an address to the National Assembly, he assured the Koreans that they would be supported if they were attacked. He was driven to the neighbourhood of the 38th Parallel, but was evidently told nothing to suggest that an attack was imminent. Early on the morning of Sunday the 25th the duty officer at MacArthur's headquarters telephoned him in his bedroom at the American Embassy to announce that at 4 a.m. the North Korean Army had attacked across the Parallel and was moving southward fast.

Korea

1950–51

The North Korean Army was drawn from a population of 9,000,000, the South Korean from 21,000,000, but in training, equipment and even mere size the North Korean was by far the more formidable. Syngman Rhee's Korea had been talking of war, Kim Il Sung's had been not only talking about war but seriously preparing for it.

The South Korean Army was 98,000 strong. There was also a constabulary of 48,000, 6,000 in the coastguard force and 1,860 in the air force. The army possessed small arms, heavy mortars, anti-tank guns and, for five of its eight divisions, field artillery. But there were no tanks, no medium artillery, and no fighter or bomber aircraft. There was enough artillery and mortar ammunition for only a few days of action. The army had completed sub-unit training and was engaged in battalion training.

The North Korean Army had been trained by a cadre of Russian advisers which was reputed to have provided up to 15 officers per division. It was about 135,000 strong, about a third being Koreans who had served with the Chinese Communist armies, some of them since 1942 when they had deserted from the Japanese Army in China. There were eight infantry divisions, an armoured brigade 6,000 strong with 120 Russian medium tanks of 1941 vintage mounting an 85-mm gun. The equipment included Russian medium guns and howitzers to which the South Korean Army had no answer. In June the North Korean Air Force had some 180 Russian aircraft including 40 fighters and 70 bombers. There was also a Russian-trained Border Constabulary totalling some 1,800 men.

Thus there were similarities between the two Korean armies and those that had faced one another on Luzon in December 1941. On the one hand a well-trained and indoctrinated force with a strong element of veterans and a full range of equipment; on the other a partly trained force recently developed from a lightly armed constabulary, an army lacking medium

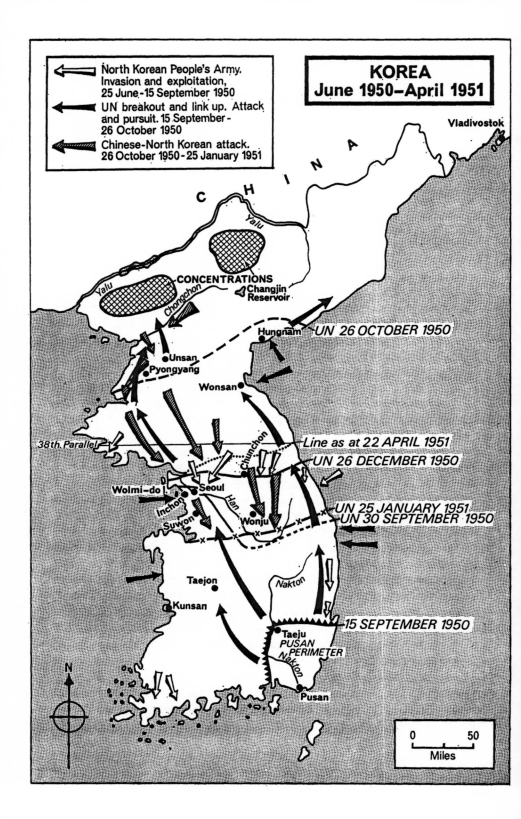

**KOREA
June 1950–April 1951**

North Korean People's Army. Invasion and exploitation, 25 June-15 September 1950

UN breakout and link up. Attack and pursuit. 15 September-26 October 1950

Chinese-North Korean attack. 26 October 1950-25 January 1951

Vladivostok

C H I N A

Yalu

Yalu

Chongchon

CONCENTRATIONS

Changjin Reservoir

Hungnam

UN 26 OCTOBER 1950

Unsan

Pyongyang

Wonsan

38th Parallel

Chunchon

Line as at 22 APRIL 1951

UN 26 DECEMBER 1950

Wolmi-do

Seoul

Inchon

Han

Suwon

Wonju

UN 25 JANUARY 1951
UN 30 SEPTEMBER 1950

Taejon

Nakton

Kunsan

15 SEPTEMBER 1950

Taeju
*PUSAN
PERIMETER*

Nakton

N

Pusan

0   50
Miles

artillery and armour. And in each instance the better force had the initiative.

As in the Philippines in the 1930s and early 1940s, the American cadres had not made the best of their time in training a new army. In September 1947 Lieutenant-General Weidemeyer, after a visit to China and Korea, had reported to President Truman that he expected Russia to withdraw its occupation forces and thus induce a similar American move as soon as the North Korean Government and Army were strong enough to achieve the Russian objectives. If withdrawal of American troops became inevitable, he recommended the formation of a South Korean Army along the lines of the old Philippine Scouts—local troops with mainly American officers. Such a plan would have required the allocation of 2,000–3,000 more officers than the 500 or so who comprised the American military mission in 1950.

By 1950 at least some of these American advisers were happy about the army they were training. Thus Brigadier-General William L. Roberts, the chief of the mission, told newspaper correspondents who had flown to Seoul for the second free general election late in May 1950 that the South Korean troops would 'shoot straight and take care of twice their numbers'. 'I'd kinda welcome an attack', he said.[1]

The North Korean commanders had succeeded in deploying their army for the invasion without the defenders knowing what was happening. On 8 June North Korean newspapers had published a government manifesto declaring that its objective was the election of a parliament for all Korea to meet in Seoul on 15 August, the fifth anniversary of the Japanese surrender and the consequent liberation of Korea. The implication was that in about two months the North Koreans would have occupied South Korea, organized elections and established a new and presumably communist government of the whole country.[2] In ten days from 15 June 90,000 men of seven divisions, the armoured brigade and other smaller formations were along the frontier hitherto manned by some 10,000 troops. The main concentration was astride the roads converging on Seoul from the north. Here four North Korean divisions and the armoured brigade faced two South Korean divisions; and across the eastern roads two more South Korean divisions faced three North Korean divisions. Along the Parallel, with heavy rain falling, the North Korean artillery opened fire at about 4 a.m. on the 25th; it was a Sunday and many officers including all but one of the Americans allotted to forward units in the critical sector were on leave.

[1] R. Macartney, 'How War Came to Korea', in N. Bartlett, *With the Australians in Korea* (Canberra, 1964).
[2] R. E. Appleman, *South to the Naktong, North to the Yalu* (Washington, 1961), a volume of the series *United States Army in the Korean War*.

In the first few days the defenders fought back strongly in some sectors, particularly about Chunchon, where the 6th South Korean Division, no weekend leave having been granted, was at full strength. But by the end of the second day (the 26th) the invaders were nearing Seoul and the two defending divisions were in danger of being outflanked. That evening the South Korean Government began to move from Seoul to Taejon, and on the 27th refugees began to pour out of Seoul, clogging the roads leading south. By evening the first North Korean troops were in the outskirts of the city. About 2.15 a.m. on the 28th, as a result of a blunder for which the chief engineer of the South Korean Army was later executed, the bridges carrying the road and railway out of Seoul across the Han river were blown up, killing thousands of people who were crossing, cutting off a great part of the defending divisions and making it impossible for them to withdraw their vehicles and heavy weapons. Next morning only 7,200 men of the two divisions were along the south bank of the river.

The formations on the right withdrew in better order, but in these last days of June the South Korean Army lost some 50,000 killed or captured. At this stage estimates of the numbers still in organized units ranged from 25,000 to 40,000. The North Korean Army was now poised for the pursuit of a disorganized and largely disarmed opponent.

News of the invasion had reached Washington on the Saturday night (mid-morning on Sunday, Korean time). The Secretary-General of the United Nations promptly called a meeting of the Security Council (where the Russian delegate had walked out in January in protest against failure to make a Communist Chinese delegate the representative of China on the council). Next afternoon the council agreed to a resolution demanding an immediate cease-fire and withdrawal of the North Korean Army to the Parallel, and calling on all member nations 'to render every assistance to the United Nations in the execution of this resolution and to refrain from giving assistance to the North Korean authorities'. That night President Truman conferred with his diplomatic and military advisers and, as a result, the Joint Chiefs of Staff instructed MacArthur, as United States Far East Commander, to send equipment to the South Koreans to prevent the loss of Seoul, and to provide air and naval cover for these replenishments, to evacuate American dependants and to send in a survey party to discover how the South Koreans might be helped.

Next day MacArthur reported that Seoul would soon fall, the South Korean Army was disorganized, and a North Korean aircraft had been shot down by American aircraft. Thereupon MacArthur was authorized to use his naval air forces against targets south of the Parallel. The Security Council on the 27th (Washington time) took a more decisive step, recommending that the member nations 'furnish such assistance to the Republic of Korea as may be necessary to repel the armed attack and to restore international peace and security in the area'. By 29 June 1,527 American nationals and 474 others had been evacuated from Korea in ships and aircraft. Among the evacuees were most of the American officers of the Korean Military Advisory Group.

In accordance with the President's instructions to send a survey party to Korea, MacArthur sent over Brigadier-General John H. Church and 14 other officers and men who arrived at Suwon on the evening of the 27th. He himself took off for Korea in the *Bataan* at 6.10 a.m. two days later, accompanied by seven senior officers including his Chief of Staff, Major-General Edward Almond; Lieutenant-General George E. Stratemeyer, commanding the Far East Air Force; Vice-Admiral C. T. Joy, his naval commander; the ubiquitous Courtney Whitney; and four news agency correspondents. On the flight MacArthur told the correspondents that the Russians were not ready for war and would not intervene if America did so; and while still in the air he instructed Stratemeyer to send an order to the Far East Air Force to bomb the North Korean airfield. At Suwon field he was welcomed by President Rhee, Ambassador Muccio and Church. MacArthur drove on to the Han River along a road crowded with civilian refugees and fleeing Korean troops, and for an hour surveyed the scene from a hill a mile behind the front line. He told Church that he was seeking authority from Washington to send in American land forces immediately.

While MacArthur was in Korea Truman had sent him a directive authorizing him to use American Army forces to hold a fort and air base in the Pusan area, to attack military targets in North Korea with air and naval forces, but to keep clear of the Chinese and Russian borders, to defend Formosa with air and naval forces but at the same time to prevent the Chinese Nationalists from attacking the mainland. The directive added that the instructions did not amount to a decision to engage in war with Russia if Russian forces entered Korea. This directive crossed a report to the Joint Chiefs of Staff which MacArthur had drafted on the return flight from Korea. In it MacArthur described the sorry condition of the South Korean Army and said that efforts would be made to stand on the Han River. He added that:

> The only assurance for the holding of the present line, and the ability to regain later the lost ground, is through the introduction of US ground combat forces into the Korean battle area. To continue to utilize the forces of our Air and Navy without an effective ground element cannot be decisive.[1]

He sought authority to send in immediately a regimental combat team and 'to provide for a possible build-up to a two division strength from the troops

[1] Appleman, p. 47.

in Japan for an early counter-offensive'. Later in the day, after teletype exchanges between MacArthur in Tokyo and the Chief of Staff, General J. Lawton Collins in Washington, and conferences in which the President took part, Truman approved the sending of two divisions from Japan and a naval blockade of North Korea.

Fewer than five years ago, MacArthur reflected, America had been 'militarily more powerful than any military nation on earth'. Now she was being nonplussed by a fledgling Asian nation. American power, MacArthur wrote later, 'had been frittered away in a bankruptcy of positive and courageous leadership toward any long-range objective'. It seemed clear to him that the coming struggle in Korea was to be a major battle against 'imperialistic Communism'.

Also while MacArthur was in Korea the Secretary-General of the United Nations on the 29th sent messages to the member nations asking what help they would give to South Korea. Most of the members promised support of one kind or another, but Russia, Poland and Czechoslovakia declared the motion of 27 June illegal. Already on the 28th the British Government had placed the British naval vessels in Japanese waters under MacArthur's command, and on the 29th the Australian Government informed the Secretary of State that it would make available its two naval vessels based in Japan and a fighter squadron that had formed part of the BCOF and was just preparing to go home. Two days later this squadron was escorting the United States bombers and transports over Korea, the first non-American unit to go into action.

On 2 July the Nationalist Chinese mission in Tokyo sent MacArthur a note offering three divisions for service in Korea. MacArthur passed the offer to Washington where it was declined, probably partly because the divisions would have been ill-equipped and partly because the Koreans would have resented their intrusion.

Already MacArthur was planning a decisive counter-offensive, and on 7 July he appealed to the Joint Chiefs for reinforcement by not fewer than five divisions and three tank battalions to enable him 'by amphibious maneuver' to strike behind the North Korean forces. The Joint Chiefs replied that no increase in the armed services had been authorized; forces elsewhere, meaning mainly Germany, had to be maintained, and there was a shortage of shipping (there were only two divisions in the United States). To MacArthur this meant that, as in 1941-44, the Far East was again at the bottom of the list of priorities. That day the Security Council decided on the form of a United Nations command for Korea under US direction, and MacArthur was appointed its commander-in-chief.

During the Occupation MacArthur had already been wearing three hats.

He was SCAP, Commander-in-Chief of United States Air, Army and Naval Forces in the Far East, and directly commanding the United States Army in the Far East. Also in the western Pacific was the Seventh Fleet (Vice-Admiral Arthur D. Struble). MacArthur's principal military force was the Eighth Army (Lieutenant-General W. H. Walker) which included four of the ten divisions in the United States Army—1st Cavalry, 7th, 24th, 25th—distributed throughout Japan and under-strength, having, for example, only two instead of three battalions per regiment. There were no corps headquarters. At this stage MacArthur ordered that American formations in Korea be brought to full strength by adding Korean troops, and persuaded the Yoshida government to form a 'national police reserve' 75,000 strong, and to increase the coastguard force by 8,000.

MacArthur's naval and air forces promptly gained effective command of the air over South Korea and of the seas round it. And although the roads leading south from Seoul were crowded with fleeing troops and civilians, other South Korean troops were resisting strongly along the Han River, delaying the main North Korean crossing until 3 July. While the surviving South Koreans were still fighting on the Han there was a panic at Suwon, where signal gear was destroyed. This upset a plan of MacArthur's to fly in troops to hold the Suwon airstrip, and finally it was agreed that American reinforcements would be put down at Pusan.

The first little American force to arrive was a two-company group which hastened northward and deployed astride the road south of Suwon. It was attacked by more than 30 tanks and two infantry regiments which were held on the road but soon began wide outflanking movements along the ridges on either side and forced the defenders to withdraw in some confusion. Fewer than half the little American force escaped. But new arrivals at Pusan were building up the American strength, and two fresh battalions from Major-General William P. Dean's 24th Division fought a delaying action astride the road about 25 miles farther south. Again the defenders were forced back with heavy losses of men and weapons. At this stage Walker assumed command of all United States forces in Korea, with headquarters at Taeju where South Korean headquarters were also established. Soon MacArthur informed Walker that at Rhee's request he was to assume command also of the South Korean Army. Thus in the next phase of the war, which saw a fighting withdrawal down the peninsula, the fall of Taejon on 20 July and the withdrawal of the defending force south and east behind the Naktong River, the major tactical decisions were Walker's.

Meanwhile on the 9th MacArthur, after receiving a signal from General Dean which included the comment that the North Korean troops had been underestimated, sent a message of crucial importance to the Joint Chiefs:

the situation was critical; the enemy's armour and infantry were first class; the North Korean force was assuming 'the aspect of a combination of Soviet leadership and technical guidance with Chinese Communist ground elements'. He urged that in addition to forces already asked for he be sent promptly an army including four divisions; 'the situation has developed into a major operation'. Next day he was informed that the 2nd Division and other units had been ordered from the United States to Japan.

In the last week of July the Pusan perimeter was being heavily threatened and it was uncertain whether all the retreating troops would reach it in time. But by 4 August the defending army was within the eastern part of the southern half of Korea with the five surviving South Korean divisions holding the north side of the box and three American divisions the central sector. The whole front, thinly manned in the south-west, extended over some 200 miles.

The 1st Cavalry Division, which MacArthur had hoped to retain for his counter-stroke, had to be sent to reinforce the Pusan perimeter. It and the other divisions were proving unready for action, and for similar reasons that had affected American infantry in MacArthur's and other commands in 1942.

> A basic fact is that the occupation divisions were not trained, equipped, or ready for battle. The great majority of the enlisted men were young and not really interested in being soldiers. The recruiting posters that had induced most of these men to enter the Army mentioned all conceivable advantages and promised many good things, but never suggested that the principal business of an army is to fight.[1]

The Pusan perimeter extended for about 145 miles as the crow flies. The Eighth Army with, at the outset, three divisions in the line—25th, 24th and 1st Cavalry—held the left and more dangerous sector of 65 miles, and I and II South Korean Corps with five divisions the right sector. In these positions with secure flanks and with reserves behind them, the American troops 'showed a stronger disposition to fight' than hitherto when 'self preservation became the dominating factor'.[2]

The perimeter was enclosed by nine North Korean infantry divisions and one armoured division. Within the perimeter in the forward areas were some 47,000 American and 45,000 South Korean troops. The North Koreans were about 70,000 strong (but at the time Tokyo was issuing statements that the United Nations forces were outnumbered four to one).

Furthermore, reinforcements were arriving: between 31 July and 5 August the greater part of the 2nd Division and the 1st Marine Brigade. MacArthur

[1] Appleman, p. 180.
[2] *Ibid.*, p. 255.

had planned to hold back the marines for his counter-offensive, but again considered the situation round Pusan too critical and sent them there. In August six battalions of medium tanks arrived at Pusan from the United States and at that stage American medium tanks in the battle area out-numbered the North Koreans' by five to one. The 3rd Division had now been ordered to Korea, and on 19 August MacArthur asked for personnel to form two corps headquarters. On 24 August the 27th British Brigade arrived from Hong Kong.

MacArthur in late July told the Joint Chiefs that he proposed to visit Chiang Kai-shek in Formosa for military talks. The Joint Chiefs suggested that he send a deputy but gave him the choice of going himself, and this MacArthur decided to do, taking with him Almond, Stratemeyer, Whitney and Willoughby, but not his senior diplomatic officer, Sebald. On his return he made a public statement praising Chiang and his 'indomitable determina-tion to resist Communist domination'. His visit, he said, had been a recon-naissance of the defence potential of the island, and arrangements had been completed for coordinating his forces and Chiang's to meet any attack. This statement caused concern in the State Department, and on 6 August Truman sent a trusted envoy, W. Averell Harriman, to Tokyo to inform MacArthur of America's cautious policy towards Chiang. With Harriman went Generals Larry Norstad of the air force and Matthew B. Ridgway, the Deputy Chief of Staff. Only they, MacArthur and Almond were present when MacArthur described his plan for victory in Korea and what he needed to achieve it. Unless the offensive was launched soon the winter would descend and it would be too late; and delay would increase the danger of Chinese and Russian intervention. MacArthur gave a glimpse of the way in which his ambitions were ranging far beyond the boundaries of Korea. If Communist China attacked Formosa he would assume command there and 'deliver such a crushing defeat it would be one of the decisive battles of the world—a disaster so great it would rock Asia and perhaps turn back Communism'. He prayed nightly that the Chinese would attack, he said. The visitors were convinced, however, of MacArthur's 'loyalty to constitutional authority', and on the way home Harriman declared that 'political and personal con-siderations should be put on one side and our Government deal with General MacArthur on the lofty level of the great national asset which he is'.[1]

On the other hand the impressions MacArthur gained from Harriman disturbed him: at Washington, where foreign influences, particularly British, were powerful, there was no urge to mount an offensive against the com-munists; the policy was a defensive one; Truman had developed 'a violent animosity' towards Chiang Kai-shek. For his part Harriman reported to

[1] M. B. Ridgway, *The Korean War* (New York, 1967), p. 37.

Truman that MacArthur had 'a strange idea that we should back anybody who will fight Communism'.[1] Worse still, on 17 August, at the invitation of the veterans of foreign wars, MacArthur sent a long message to be read at their annual camp. The gist of it was that since World War II America's strategical frontier had moved west to include the entire Pacific Ocean which America controlled from a chain of islands from the Aleutians to the Marianas, and whence her air power could dominate every Asiatic port from Vladivostok to Singapore. In the hands of an enemy Formosa would be a dangerous salient in the centre of this perimeter.

> Nothing could be more fallacious than the threadbare argument by those who advocate appeasement and defeatism in the Pacific that if we defend Formosa we alienate continental Asia. Those who speak thus do not understand the Orient. They do not grasp that it is the pattern of Oriental psychology to respect and follow aggressive, resolute and dynamic leadership—to quickly turn from leadership characterized by timidity or vacillation. . . . The decision of . . . June 27th lighted into a flame a lamp of hope throughout Asia that was burning dimly toward extinction. It marked for the Far East the focal and turning point in this area's struggle for freedom. It swept aside in one great monumental stroke all of the hypocrisy and the sophistry which has confused and deluded so many people distant from the actual scene.[2]

Some days after the speech arrived in Washington for approval MacArthur received a message from the Secretary of Defense that the President directed him to withdraw it because 'various features with regard to Formosa are in conflict with the policy of the United States'. But a comical situation had now arisen. The statement had already been printed in the Veterans' journal and was generally available when MacArthur informed the Veterans' commander-in-chief that he had been ordered to withdraw it. At the same time he insisted to Washington that his message 'was most carefully prepared to fully support the President's policy decision'.

Whitney wrote a few years later that his message 'innocently ran afoul of plans being hatched in the State Department to succumb to British pressure and desert the Nationalist government on Formosa'. Perfidious Albion. In Churchill's time, according to MacArthur's entourage, Roosevelt had been under the domination of British imperialists. Now Roosevelt's successor was conspiring with British socialists.

As mentioned MacArthur had been planning a decisive counter-stroke aimed at cutting the communications of the North Koreans ever since early July. But one by one the fresh formations that he hoped to employ in this venture had been drawn into the Pusan perimeter. On 29 July, after not only the 1st Cavalry Division but the 2nd Division and 1st Marine Brigade had

[1] H. S. Truman, *Memoirs*, Vol. 2 (London, 1951), p. 371.
[2] Whitney, pp. 379-80.

been allotted to Pusan, he informed the Joint Chiefs that he proposed to use his only remaining force—the 7th Division—'along a separate axis in mid-September'. His mind was now firmly set on a landing at Inchon which if successful would lead to the recapture of Seoul and the severing of the roads and railways leading south. At the end of August he had formed X Corps to conduct this operation and had told Almond that he would command it while retaining his present post. He believed that the counter-stroke would swiftly end the war, whereupon Almond would resume his former appointment. Meanwhile Major-General Doyle Hickey would act as chief of staff. The corps would comprise the 7th Division and 1st Marine Division.

From the outset the Joint Chiefs had agreed to the principle of an amphibious landing. It had evident advantages to a commander possessing command of the sea and the air, and it was inevitable that MacArthur's mind should turn to the kind of operation that had carried him from Papua to Luzon. But the Joint Chiefs and their advisers, for a variety of reasons, were not enthusiastic about the choice of a landing place—so far north and at a port with difficult tides. At length the Army Chief of Staff, Lawton Collins, and the Chief of Naval Operations, Admiral Forrest P. Sherman, were sent to Japan to settle the matter.

At a heavily populated staff conference on 23 July the naval objections were stated, concluding with the opinion that the operation was not impossible but not recommended. Collins and Sherman favoured a more cautious landing 100 miles south at Kunsan. Then MacArthur went into action, speaking with his customary eloquence and conviction. A landing at Kunsan was not likely to lead to the cutting of the North Koreans' communications. But seizure of Inchon and Seoul would win great military and political results.

He argued that most of the North Koreans were concentrated around the Pusan perimeter. Inchon was not adequately prepared for defence. An attack at Inchon would achieve the same kind of surprise as Wolfe's at Quebec. The proposed landing at Kunsan would amount merely to extending Walker's perimeter. He concluded with a characteristic peroration. It was apparent that it was in Asia that 'the Communist conspirators' had chosen 'to make their play for global conquest'; if the war was lost to communism in Asia, the fate of Europe would be in danger. 'I can almost hear the ticking of the second hand of destiny.' The notion that the outcome of the world-wide hostilities between America and her allies on the one hand and Russia and her allies on the other would be decided in a Korean war in which so far neither Russia nor China had shown an active interest was far-fetched, yet acceptable no doubt to MacArthur's audience. Sherman agreed to the Inchon plan but Lawton Collins remained doubtful.

It was not until 29 August that the Joint Chiefs finally radioed to Mac-Arthur that they concurred in his plan. And a week before the landing was due MacArthur received from the Joint Chiefs a message seeking his estimate of the 'feasibility and chance of success of projected operation'. MacArthur wondered who in Washington had lost his nerve. The President? Marshall, just appointed Secretary of Defense in succession to Louis Johnson who was proving an unenthusiastic supporter of government policy? Bradley? He reiterated that the chance of success was excellent and the project offered the only hope of gaining the initiative and presenting an opportunity for a decisive blow. The Joint Chiefs replied that in view of this opinion they approved the operation and had so informed the President.

The command set up for the forthcoming offensive provided that Walker's Eighth Army, breaking out from Pusan perimeter, and Almond's X Corps at Inchon would each be directly under the command of MacArthur's head-quarters in Tokyo, and soon MacArthur had to adjudicate between the two subordinates. Walker wanted to retain the 1st Marine Brigade for the break-out but Major-General Oliver P. Smith of the 1st Marine Division insisted that it was essential for it to be added to his force. MacArthur ordered Walker to give his marines to Almond. Intelligence estimated the North Korean strength round Inchon and Seoul as about 6,500, perhaps about 2,500 being at Inchon itself. This proved fairly accurate. The X Corps was 70,000 strong off Inchon on the 15th.

The misgivings of the naval and marine leaders were understandable. The tides in the channels leading to Inchon had a range of over 30 feet. At low tide inner harbour was a mud flat with a twisting narrow channel about 12 feet deep. On 15 September the morning high tide would be at 6.59, the evening tide at 7.19. A tide of 23 feet was needed to enable the LSTs to navigate the flats. There would be no room for error or delay. And as if there were not enough normal hazards, on 3 September a typhoon struck Kobe where the 1st Marine Division was embarking, interrupting the loading and damaging vessels and gear. Soon afterwards a second typhoon was detected moving towards Korea and due to arrive on the 12th or 13th, but it had moved away from the convoy by the 13th.

MacArthur with Almond, Whitney and others, embarked on Admiral Doyle's flagship, the *Mount McKinley*. From 13 September there had been heavy naval bombardments of enemy positions ashore and particularly of Wolmi-do, an island about half a mile off Inchon. In the morning the marines secured Wolmi-do against weak resistance by about 350 men. The main assault had to wait for the evening tide. All day the naval and air bombardment continued. At about 5.30 the forward troops of two marine regiments were landed on two beaches, losing only about 200 killed and wounded that day.

Early on the 17th MacArthur landed with Struble, Almond and others, went forward to a marine battalion and saw about a dozen disabled enemy tanks. He had predicted to Almond that he would be in Seoul in five days; but Almond had said two weeks and he was right. The North Koreans abandoned Seoul on the 28th. Next day MacArthur and his entourage landed on Kimpo airfield and at midday, at a ceremony in the National Assembly hall, on behalf of the United Nations Command MacArthur formally and eloquently restored the seat of government to President Rhee, and led the Assembly in a recital of the Lord's Prayer. He flew back to Tokyo that afternoon. By this time the North Koreans had been in retreat along the southern front for five days. MacArthur's judgment had been proved right. As a military commander it was his greatest moment, though for years afterwards naval and marine historians would continue to insist that Inchon had been an unjustified gamble.

Now the question was whether and how far to pursue the defeated army. The obvious military answer was yes, but fear of Chinese or Russian intervention along the lines of the American intervention—for MacArthur's army contained only token contingents to justify naming it a United Nations force —caused the leaders in Washington to hesitate. Finally the United States Government decided that the Eighth Army should move into North Korea, and on 27 September the Joint Chiefs issued a momentous directive to MacArthur ordering him to destroy the North Korean Army and unite Korea under President Rhee. But, they said, developments might demand that the directive be modified: he was to ascertain whether Russian or Chinese intervention seemed likely, and report relevant information at once. No United Nations troops were to cross the Chinese or Russian boundaries and only South Korean troops were to be used in the frontier area. Mac-Arthur was to submit his plans for operations north of the Parallel to the Joint Chiefs for approval. Indeed it was an 'if' order, that did little credit to the leaders in the Pentagon, and MacArthur rightly objected. He sought freedom to cross the Parallel, to set about destroying what was left of the North Korean Army and to demand surrender. On the 29th Marshall sent him a personal message that the President and he wished him to feel free tactically and strategically in an advance north of the Parallel. Thereupon on 1 October MacArthur sent to Washington a signal seeking approval to make the following statement:

Under the provisions of the United Nations Security Council Resolution of 27 June, the field of our military operations is limited only by military exigencies and the international boundaries of Korea. The so-called 38th Parallel, accordingly, is not a factor in the military employment of our forces. To accomplish the enemy's complete defeat, your troops may cross the border at any time, either in exploratory probing or exploiting local tactical conditions. If the enemy fails to accept the terms of surrender set forth in my message to him of 1 October, our forces, in due process of campaign, will seek out and destroy the enemy's armed forces in whatever part of Korea they may be located.

As a sequel to the directive of 27 September MacArthur had fixed a line beyond which non-Korean troops should not advance. On 17 October, as the pursuit of the thoroughly defeated North Korean Army proceeded, he moved this line forward to one 30 to 40 miles from the Manchurian frontier. Then on the 24th he lifted all restrictions and instructed his commanders to advance to the border, with air support keeping pace with them. This was in disregard of his orders and another step towards his downfall, but the Joint Chiefs, apparently hesitant to impede the advance in any way, did nothing about it.

On 1 October MacArthur had addressed a demand for surrender to the Korean commander-in-chief. That day Premier Chou En-lai, speaking at Peking, issued a warning that China would not stand aside if 'the imperialists' invaded the territory of their neighbours. On the 2nd the Russian delegate to the United Nations proposed a cease-fire and the withdrawal of all foreign troops, and next day the Indian delegate said that his government considered that UN troops should not cross the Parallel. By 9 October there had been no reply to MacArthur's demand for surrender and he repeated it. On the 10th Premier Kim Il Sung broadcast a rejection of the demand.

On 6 October the General Assembly of the United Nations endorsed MacArthur's outlined plan, already approved by the Joint Chiefs, for operations north of the Parallel.

In the coming phase MacArthur was determined to continue the arrangement whereby X Corps operated independently of the Eighth Army. Walker continued to find this arrangement unwelcome but does not seem to have protested strongly. Having made one successful amphibious attack MacArthur now proposed another—at Wonsan on the east coast and again by Almond's X Corps. In the western sector the Eighth Army would advance towards the enemy capital, Pyongyang, while the X Corps moved against it from the east. This would involve a heavy strain on the port of Inchon, whence the X Corps would embark on its new venture, with consequent delay to the supply of the Eighth Army. Walker would have preferred X Corps to advance on Pyongyang, whence the Eighth Army following up would march overland on Wonsan to join the South Korean troops in that sector while X Corps advanced from Pyongyang towards the Yalu. Admiral

Joy considered that if X Corps was to take Wonsan it could get there sooner overland. And Walker was convinced that in any event the South Koreans would be in Wonsan before the X Corps got there. He was right. On 10 October the I South Korean Corps entered Wonsan and the leading division of X Corps—the 1st Marine—did not begin landing there until the 26th. The 7th Division landed unopposed 150 miles above Wonsan from the 29th onwards. If MacArthur had not possessed such great numbers of transports and landing craft he could not have adopted this absurdly elaborate way of redeploying his troops. It was another example of the manner in which an army can be actually handicapped by an abundance of equipment. The plan had been opposed by the naval and divisional commanders 'but none strongly raised his voice, simply because at that time no one was questioning the judgment or prescience of the man who had just worked a military miracle. Had he suggested that one battalion walk on water to reach the port, there might have been someone ready to give it a try.'[1]

MacArthur's October offensive, if successful, would place his whole army in a position where it could not be maintained in sufficient strength to hold against a full-scale Chinese attack. His troops would be 80-120 miles from their bases and supplied mostly along winding mountain tracks.

On 3 October Chou En-lai had informed the Indian ambassador at Peking, K. M. Panikkar, that if the UN forces crossed the Parallel China would send troops to the help of North Korea. But despite these unequivocal statements and his estimate that 24 Chinese divisions were deployed along the Yalu under an army commander of high repute, Willoughby in his Intelligence summary of 14 October declared the Chinese threat to support North Korea as 'probably in the category of political blackmail'.

On 12 October Marshall as Secretary of Defense informed MacArthur that the President wished to confer with him three days later either at Honolulu or on Wake Island. Evidently the object was to adjust MacArthur to American policy concerning the containment of communism, mainly by the maintenance of American bridgeheads in Europe, and to inform him that these had priority over similar bridgeheads in Asia. MacArthur chose Wake as the meeting place. He learned that Truman would be accompanied by a troop of Washington newspaper correspondents, but when he asked if he could bring some Tokyo correspondents in his own aircraft, he was instructed not to do so. MacArthur arrived before the President, having slept only an hour or so. They talked alone for half an hour when, as MacArthur told Whitney afterwards, MacArthur regretted any misunderstandings about his message to the Veterans, and Truman said 'Think nothing more about it'; otherwise they discussed the economic problems of the Philippines.

[1] Ridgway, p. 44.

Then the conference opened. MacArthur had brought Whitney and an aide with him; Truman had a large party including Secretary of the Army Pace, Chairman of the Joint Chiefs Bradley, Dean Rusk and Averell Harriman.

When the conference opened, the President's press secretary noticed that MacArthur's aide was taking notes and told MacArthur that no record was to be made of the discussions. In fact Truman's staff had left ajar a door behind which a woman stenographer was concealed, and she did her best to make a full note which would later be made public and become a subject of widespread controversy. In retrospect this seemed to be playing politics at about its lowest level.

The formal conference lasted about an hour and a half and dealt with uncontroversial matters except towards the end when the question of Chinese intervention was brought up 'almost casually'. MacArthur wrote afterwards:

> It was the general consensus of all present that Red China had no intention of intervening. This opinion had previously been advanced by the Central Intelligence Agency and the State Department. General Bradley went so far as to bring up the question of transferring troops in the Far East to Europe, and said he would like to have two divisions from Korea home by Christmas for this purpose.

MacArthur gave the opinion that 'with our largely unopposed air forces, with their potential capable of destroying, at will, bases of attack and lines of supply north as well as south of the Yalu, no Chinese military commander would hazard the commitment of large forces upon the devastated Korean peninsula. ... There was no disagreement from anyone.' Questioned as to how many troops the Chinese could maintain in Korea, MacArthur said 50,000–60,000—about half the number the UN could deploy for battle. (But in November the Chinese were using about 300,000 troops.)

Thus the error of failing to believe that the Chinese would do what they had plainly said they would do seems to have been shared with MacArthur by all American Intelligence agencies. MacArthur's faulty military estimate lay in his belief that an air force can decisively impede the movement of lightly equipped troops in rugged and wooded country, an error that the American air generals continued to perpetrate for another decade and more, with tragic results.

As for Wake Island itself, the fact that Truman later tried to discredit MacArthur by saying that MacArthur had misled him about the possibility of Chinese intervention seems to justify Courtney Whitney's comment that the conference was a 'sly political ambush'.[1]

After the conference, Truman and MacArthur chatted alone. MacArthur

[1] Whitney, p. 395.

told Whitney afterwards that he asked Truman if he would seek reelection in 1952. When Truman sparred by asking MacArthur if he had political ambitions MacArthur said that if Truman was opposed by a general it would be Eisenhower.

On the airstrip just before their departure Truman read to the assembled officers and newspapermen a citation awarding MacArthur his fourth Oak Leaf Cluster to the DSM: 'for distinguished services to the peoples of the United States and the Republic of Korea, and to the peoples of all free nations'. He had given his forces 'conspicuously brilliant and courageous leadership and discerning judgment of the highest order', and had 'so inspired his command by his vision, his judgment, his indomitable will and his unshakeable faith, that it has set a shining example of gallantry and tenacity in defense and of audacity in attack matched by but few operations in military history'. After describing this scene Whitney, in his book about MacArthur, at this point interpolated a reminder that four years later Truman in answer to a question whether he repented the dismissal of MacArthur replied: 'The only thing I repent is that I didn't do it two years sooner.'[1]

Five days after the Wake Island conference the Eighth Army entered the North Korean capital of Pyongyang. Already for some days Chinese troops had been moving by night into North Korea.

In October and November more Allied units began to arrive in Korea: an Australian battalion, a Thai battalion, a Turkish brigade, a Netherlands battalion, a Canadian battalion, the 29th British Brigade. And the South Korean Army was strengthened by the return from the Eighth Army of most of the Koreans who had been taken into the American Army. There were enough to form a 9th Division. But in Washington, Tokyo and Korea it was believed that the reinforcements would not be needed. In accordance with the Wake Island agreement plans were made to send home the 2nd United States Division; American ships were diverted to Japan or to Hawaii or sent home. MacArthur established a Civil Assistance Command within the Eighth Army to help in rehabilitation.

MacArthur now considered a plan to drop an airborne regiment across the main roads 30 miles north of Pyongyang on 20 October to cut off fleeing North Korean troops and officials, and rescue American prisoners of war. As at Nadzab a little over seven years before MacArthur watched the operation from the air. When he landed at Pyongyang he told reporters that perhaps half the surviving North Korean troops had been trapped, and next day in Tokyo he declared that the war would soon be over; in fact the paratroops were too late and had cut off few troops and no important officials.

The conflict between the autocratic MacArthur and the irresolute Joint

[1] Whitney, p. 390.

Chiefs reached a new stage when the Joint Chiefs learnt on 5 November that MacArthur had authorized the bombing of the Yalu bridge on the North Korean side of the river. The Joint Chiefs made a show of standing firm and reminded MacArthur of a directive banning bombing within five miles of the frontier. MacArthur replied that the bombing was justified and necessary and asked that the President be consulted. Opposition in Washington crumpled; but MacArthur was told not to bomb power plants or dams on the river or to attack Manchurian production.

On 25 October a South Korean division was nearing the Yalu when its leading regiment was attacked and practically destroyed by Chinese troops who seemed to appear from nowhere. The same day Chinese troops struck farther west. In a few days two Chinese divisions had been identified. At the end of the month MacArthur's headquarters were still reporting to Washington that there was no confirmation of large-scale intervention. But by 1 November there was no denying signs of a massive Chinese offensive. The Chinese formations, hitherto deploying by night and with expert attention to concealment during the day, attacked at several points using heavy mortars and firing Russian rockets and blowing horns and whistles. American units were encircled by Chinese who had infiltrated through the mountains and fought their way out. At Unsan, scene of the first powerful Chinese attack, an American cavalry regiment lost half its strength and many of its tanks and weapons. But when Walker reported this setback, MacArthur's headquarters rebuked him for having failed to press on to the Yalu according to plan. On 3 November, however, MacArthur sent to Washington a new impression of Chinese power and intentions. The communist regime, taking over where Chiang Kai-shek had left off, had produced first-class soldiers and were developing competent commanders and staff, and developing 'the character of a united nationalism of increasingly dominant aggressive tendencies'. China had become 'aggressively imperialistic, with a lust for expansion and increased power normal to this type of imperialism'—words which paraphrase those which Peking was hurling at Washington.

That day Peking Radio broadcast an announcement that the operations in North Korea were a threat to China and the Chinese people must combine to resist the United States and help North Korea. Willoughby and his staff conceded that though earlier broadcasts had sounded like bombast this one did not; and on the 5th their Intelligence summary said that China had the means of immediately launching a large-scale counter-offensive. A communiqué that was both bombastic and inaccurate was issued by MacArthur next day: the communists had 'committed one of the most offensive acts of international lawlessness of historic record by moving without any notice of belligerency elements of Communist forces across the Yalu

river into North Korea. . . . ' He recorded the destruction of the North
Korean Army with total casualties of over 335,000, and announced that a new
army now faced them backed by reserves and supplies 'beyond the limits of
our present sphere of military action'. He informed the Joint Chiefs on the
9th that he believed that his air power could prevent Chinese forces crossing
the Yalu 'in sufficient strength to prevent the destruction of those forces
now arrayed against me in North Korea'.

Less important than MacArthur's miscalculation of the strength and
intentions of the Chinese was his overestimate of the power of aircraft to
influence the movement of troops on the ground. MacArthur learnt later
that within a few days of his troops crossing the Parallel on 9 October
Chinese troops began to enter Korea. In perhaps seven days four Chinese
armies each of three divisions were in North Korea. They were commanded
by highly educated leaders, far more experienced in the sort of operations
that faced them than were the Americans. The puzzle remained why
MacArthur and his staff, having the clearest indications of Chinese intentions
and constant evidence of their sincerity, refused to believe. The American
official historian of the campaign finds reasons: Willoughby's belief that the
Chinese were making an empty threat (which in view of Chinese power and
pride was most improbable), the fact that Chinese troop movements were
made by night and therefore not reported by the air force (which should have
occurred to MacArthur and his staff after their four years of war against the
Japanese), and their decision that reports from prisoners and civilians that
Chinese troops were streaming into Korea were not 'adequate confirmation'.

American estimates of Chinese strength and intentions were further
confused when after their series of devastating onslaughts their army broke
contact and disappeared again: no fires were seen, no traffic on the road, no
movement of any kind.

At this stage MacArthur had the choice of advancing, withdrawing or
ordering the army to dig in more or less where it was. He decided that his
forces were too weak to establish a defence in depth astride the peninsula. To
withdraw would be contrary to orders. He decided to press on, and if the
Chinese were in force, to withdraw swiftly, pulling out the X Corps on the
right by sea to Pusan, so as to extend the enemy's lines of supply and subject
them to bombing.

MacArthur flew to the front on 24 November to be present at the launching
of the final offensive. He flew over the area of the coming battle at 5,000 feet
and was greatly impressed by the 'merciless wasteland' below. (After this
flight he was awarded the DFC.)

In Tokyo a message from the Joint Chiefs was awaiting him, announcing
growing anxiety at the possibility of a major clash with Chinese armies;

after advancing to a line near the Yalu MacArthur should use only South Korean forces in the frontier area.

Walker had opened the offensive with misgivings, and while preparing to advance had also been preparing to withdraw again behind the Chongchon River. General Oliver Smith of the marines, advancing on the right through rugged ranges astride a winding single-track gravel road which climbed to over 4,000 feet, was convinced that his task was impossible and moved cautiously, making sure that the high ground on either flank was firmly held. To Smith's right the 7th Division was advancing along a similar mountain track, and the I South Korean Corps along the coast towards the narrow strip of the Russian border.

By the 25th the marines were on the Changjin (Chosin) reservoir, and the Eighth Army was advancing slowly northward from the Chongchon against little resistance. Suddenly on the 26th the Chinese Army launched its second offensive. The Chinese dispersed the South Korean Corps on the Eighth Army's right, and then sent the 2nd United States Division reeling with a loss of 4,000 men and much heavy equipment; it was withdrawn to refit and recuperate. Walker told Tokyo that 200,000 Chinese were attacking. Next, the Chinese in overwhelming strength struck at the marines, but the marines' preparation for such an event served them well, and now, having advanced more cautiously than Almond their corps commander had ordered, they withdrew at a slower pace than he was now urging, bringing out all essential equipment. This was the beginning of what developed into a fine fighting withdrawal which saved the division and brought it finally into a beachhead perimeter near Hungnam.

On the west the withdrawal continued in moderately good order. On 28 November MacArthur had summoned Walker and Almond to Tokyo and authorized a substantial withdrawal. Pyongyang was evacuated on 5 December and the Eighth Army continued to pull back towards the Parallel. The navy lifted X Corps plus many Korean refugees from the Hungnam bridgehead.

Early in December MacArthur was informing the Joint Chiefs that unless the enemy's attention could be diverted and his own resources increased 'steady attrition leading to final destruction can reasonably be contemplated'. At this stage the leaders in Washington seemed to have been spellbound. Already MacArthur had disobeyed one order—to employ only Korean troops in the frontier provinces. What would he do next?

Ridgway has recorded that at a conference in the Pentagon on 3 December he made so bold as to declare that an order should be given to MacArthur to do as he had been told. There was a frightened silence on the part of the Secretaries of State and Defense, the Joint Chiefs and smaller fry present at the conference. On the way from the meeting Ridgway asked the air force general, Hoyt Vandenberg, a close friend, why the Joint Chiefs did not send orders to MacArthur. Vandenberg replied: 'What good would that do? He wouldn't obey the orders. What *can* we do?' 'You can relieve any commander that won't obey orders, can't you?' said Ridgway. Vandenberg looked 'puzzled and amazed' and walked away.[1]

In Korea the withdrawal continued. By late December, when the Chinese armies were nearing the Parallel, the leaders in Washington were filled with anxiety not only about Korea but Japan. They spoke to MacArthur of a possible line of defence halfway down South Korea, and sought his views on a possible withdrawal to Japan, the defence of which was MacArthur's 'continuing primary mission'.

To MacArthur this amounted to acceptance of complete defeat. He replied suggesting that the American Government or the United Nations or both should recognize a state of war with China, whereupon the UN could retaliate by blockading the Chinese coast, destroying Chinese industrial potential by air and naval bombardment, obtaining troops from Formosa to reinforce Korea, and possibly engaging in 'counter-invasion against vulnerable areas of the Chinese mainland'. He believed, he said, that these measures could save Asia from 'the engulfment otherwise facing it'. Evacuation of Korea would have a most adverse effect on the people of Asia. He understood the need for European security but considered that the use of force in the Far East would provide seasoned forces for later employment in Europe.[2]

The Joint Chiefs replied in polite but definite terms. They pointed to the problem of Britain with its big trade with mainland China, the desirability of limiting the war to Korea, and in effect repeated their authorizing of Mac-Arthur to withdraw to Japan if necessary to avoid heavy losses of men and equipment.

MacArthur promptly pointed out that these instructions placed on him the responsibility for a decision that was above a field commander's level. What was American policy: to hold in Korea indefinitely, or for a limited time, or only long enough to achieve an orderly withdrawal? It was not until 14 January that Truman in a personal telegram told MacArthur that there was a desire to demonstrate that the United States and the United Nations (Truman placed them in that order) were resolved to resist communist aggression far and wide and 'to bring the UN through to its first great effort in collective security and produce a free world coalition of incalculable value to the national security interests of the United States'. As for the local situation, some of the main purposes could be served by 'continued

[1] Ridgway, p. 62.
[2] *Reminiscences*, p. 379.

resistance from off-shore islands of Korea, particularly Cheju-Do' if it proved impossible to hold a position in Korea itself.

On 23 December General Walker was killed in a road accident. Some time before, MacArthur had named Ridgway as Walker's successor if one was needed. On the 25th Ridgway reached Tokyo and next morning was in the commander-in-chief's office in the Dai Ichi building. At that stage MacArthur who for some time had been planning for a withdrawal to Pusan, had decided to hold Seoul as long as possible for political reasons. He told Ridgway that his proposals for an attack on China had been rejected by Washington. His objective now was to secure South Korea. His views on the capability of aircraft seem now to have taken yet another somersault. He 'derided the value of tactical air support'. 'It could not', he flatly stated, 'isolate the battlefield or stop the flow of hostile troops and supply.' 'This', added Ridgway in 1967, 'is perhaps a point some active duty officers and their civilian superiors have yet to learn.'[1]

Finally Ridgway asked whether MacArthur would have any objection to his attacking. 'The Eighth Army is yours, Matt, do what you think best', he was told. Ridgway was a soldier of great moral courage, forthright and devoted. He was also to prove again, as he had shown in less senior appointments, a splendid leader and organizer of troops, perceptive, intelligent and decisive. Before he had had time to inspect the army and the terrain he ordered the 2nd Division, still recuperating after its losses at the opening of the offensive, to move forward to Wonju where he saw (rightly as it turned out) a danger of enemy penetration.

Ridgway found his Americans mostly in low spirits, and good leadership lacking; the units were still road bound. With great energy and good sense he began to give new life and purpose to the Eighth Army. There was not much time before the next Chinese offensive, which opened, not unexpectedly this time, on New Year's Eve. The South Korean troops gave way on the right flank and a new retreat began. The Eighth Army fell back across the Han River again. Seoul was evacuated. But the defenders held along a line about 100 miles south of the former one.

Again the Chinese halted and disappeared among the trees, safe from observation or attack by the United Nations aircraft. Ridgway ordered a general attack by his two corps, I and IX (later X Corps, no longer independent, would be added), to test the enemy's strength and be ready to advance to the Han River. At this stage the UN Forces numbered about 365,000.[2]

---

[1] Ridgway, p. 82.

[2] They included I Corps (25 and 3 US Divisions, Turkish Brigade, 29 British Brigade, 1 ROK Division); IX Corps (1 US Cavalry and 24 US Divisions, 27 Commonwealth Brigade (including the Australian battalion), Greek and Philippine battalions, 6 ROK Division and, later, 1 Marine Division); X Corps (2 and 7 US Divisions, three ROK divisions attached); plus I and III ROK Corps.

They were outnumbered by the communist forces, whose total strength was about 486,000. The advance began on 25 January and by 9 February the Eighth Army was on the Han. The Chinese counter-attacked, using massed forces for the first time; they lost heavily in the face of UN fire-power, gained some ground but were halted. Ridgway's reinvigorated army had shown that it could both drive the Chinese back and defeat a Chinese attack. This was the final turning-point in the war.

Another offensive in late February carried the Eighth Army to within 30 miles of the Parallel. The situation had now been reached in which, as MacArthur said in a public statement on 7 March, 'the battle-lines cannot fail to reach a point of theoretical military stalemate'. Ridgway pressed on, took Seoul on the 14th, Chunchon on the 21st and halted a decent interval above the Parallel. The late February offensive and its successor were conceived by Ridgway, under the authority of MacArthur's 'the Eighth Army is yours, Matt'. He was ruffled when, on the eve of the February offensive, MacArthur, having flown in from Tokyo, told a group of correspondents that he had just ordered a resumption of the offensive. 'There had, of course, been no order at all concerning any part of the operation from CINCFE or from the GHQ staff in Tokyo', wrote Ridgway afterwards. Ridgway had another reason for irritation. MacArthur's flights from Tokyo to preside at the opening of any new move were so regularly and well publicized that news of them warned the enemy that something was afoot. Before the March offensive he sent MacArthur a carefully worded message on the subject. MacArthur saw the point and on that occasion postponed his visit until after the attack had begun.

When the Eighth Army had been nearing Seoul MacArthur, according to his postwar recollections, began to contemplate a plan to destroy the Chinese armies in the same manner as he had destroyed the North Korean. From a base line through Seoul he would make devastating air attacks on North Korea 'severing Korea from Manchuria by laying a field of radioactive wastes [the by-products of atomic manufacture] across all the major lines of enemy supply', and, reinforced by troops from Formosa (if this was allowed), would make seaborne and airborne landings on the northern flanks 'and close a gigantic trap. The Chinese would soon starve or surrender.'[1]

On 8 March a Republican Congressman, Joe Martin, wrote to MacArthur informing him that he had urged that Chiang's forces be used in Korea, and proposed to advocate this policy again over the air on 28 March. He would welcome MacArthur's views. On 20 March MacArthur replied, implying that he approved the employment of troops from Formosa and expressing

[1] *Reminiscences*, p. 384.

wonderment that some people failed to realize that in Asia the communists had decided to 'make their play for global conquest, and that we have joined the issue thus raised on the battlefield; that here we fight Europe's war with arms while the diplomats there still fight it with words; that if we lose the war to Communism in Asia the fall of Europe is inevitable; win it and Europe most probably would avoid war and yet preserve freedom. As you point out, we must win. There is no substitute for victory.'[1]

Next day the Joint Chiefs cabled him that a Presidential announcement was being planned that the United Nations was preparing to discuss a settlement in Korea, that a strong United Nations feeling persisted that diplomatic efforts should be made before an advance farther north of the Parallel. The State Department had asked what authority MacArthur should have to give him sufficient freedom of action in the next few weeks to provide security for his forces and maintain contact.

MacArthur replied urging that no further military restrictions be imposed, and on the 24th he issued a long communiqué taunting 'Red China' for its lack of industrial power, inability to maintain 'even moderate air and naval power', complaining again about the restrictions on the activities of his forces, and announcing that he was ready to confer in the field at any time with the commander-in-chief of the enemy forces in an effort to find military means 'whereby realization of the political objectives of the United Nations in Korea, to which no nation may justly take exception, might be accomplished without further bloodshed'. At any time the pronouncement would have been foolish. A military commander gains no advantage by broadcasting boastful and contemptuous references to his enemy. Indeed, by so doing, he is more likely to raise the dander of a proud opponent. And to make this statement, with its implied demand for surrender, when he had just been informed that his superiors were preparing to discuss a settlement was insubordinate. In Ridgway's view the communiqué of 24 March 'cut the ground from under the President, enraged our allies, and put the Chinese in the position of suffering a severe loss of face if they so much as accepted a bid to negotiate'.

> No one in possession of the facts could have been so naive as to imagine that MacArthur was either unaware of what effect his announcement might have or innocent of any desire openly to oppose the President. A little more than three months earlier, on December 6, 1950, President Truman had issued a specific directive to all officials—including General MacArthur—to abstain from any declarations on foreign policy. But a specific directive was actually superfluous. It is never within the province of the soldier, under our Constitution, to make foreign policy. That is solely, specifically, and properly a function of elected officials, regardless of anyone's assessment of the 'rightness' or 'wrongness' of

[1] *Reminiscences*, p. 386.

current policy. Only under a dictatorship does a military leader take council solely with himself in deciding what course the nation should pursue in its intercourse with other sovereign powers.[1]

Then to make matters worse Martin on 5 April, without consulting Mac-Arthur, read his letter on the floor of the House.

Meanwhile on the 24th Truman had decided to relieve MacArthur of his command. By issuing his communiqué 'MacArthur left me no choice— I could no longer tolerate his insubordination', he said afterwards. But he took his time. The first official reaction received by MacArthur was a cable from the Joint Chiefs asking him to observe the order of 6 December that public statements by theatre commanders be approved by Washington.

On 6 April Truman consulted a group of senior colleagues. Averell Harriman said that MacArthur should have been dismissed two years before, Marshall was non-committal, Bradley said that MacArthur was insubordinate and should be dismissed. Both Bradley and Acheson advised seeking the advice of the Joint Chiefs before the next move.

The Pentagon reinforced their spirits by further talks and reading of files. The Joint Chiefs met and supported the decision to dismiss. It was now the 9th. How would the job be done? It was decided that the Secretary for War, Frank Pace, then in Tokyo, should give MacArthur the news at 10 a.m. on the 12th, Wednesday, Tokyo time. Ridgway would succeed him as SCAP. Then Bradley learnt that the Chicago *Tribune* would publish the story next morning. To counter this a Press conference was called in Washington at 1 a.m. 11 April and told that MacArthur had been relieved of his command. Already at 12.30 a.m. the following message had gone to him:

> I deeply regret that it becomes my duty as President and Commander-in-Chief of the United States military forces to replace you as Supreme Commander, Allied Powers; Commander-in-Chief, United Nations Command; Commander-in-Chief, Far East; and Commanding General, US Army, Far East. You will turn over your commands, effective at once, to Lieutenant-General Matthew B. Ridgway. You are authorised to have issued such orders as are necessary to complete desired travel to such place as you select. My reasons for your replacement will be made public concurrently with the delivery to you of the foregoing order.

Unfortunately MacArthur learnt of his dismissal a few minutes after millions of others. One of his aides having heard a broadcast message that 'President Truman has just removed General MacArthur from his Far Eastern and Korean Commands and from the direction of the occupation of Japan', hastened to the embassy where the MacArthurs were entertaining two guests from home. Mrs MacArthur saw him through a doorway,

[1] Ridgway, pp. 154–5.

excused herself and left the room. The aide told her the news. She returned and informed her husband. 'MacArthur's face froze. Not a flicker of emotion crossed it. For a moment, while his luncheon guests puzzled on what was happening, he was sternly silent. Then he looked up at his wife who still stood with her hand on his shoulder. In a gentle voice, audible to all present, he said: "Jeannie, we're going home at last." '[1]

[1] Whitney, p. 471.

Soldier's Return

1951–64

It was a comfort to General MacArthur in the next few days to receive the obviously heartfelt praise and sympathy of the Emperor, Yoshida, Rhee and a host of others round the world. He took off in his own aircraft in the early morning of 16 April, stopped overnight at Honolulu where he was the guest of Admiral Radford, commanding the Pacific Fleet, and then flew on to San Francisco. It was his first return to his homeland since 1935. He had asked General Courtney Whitney to arrange the journey so that he could slip unnoticed into a hotel. But he found the governor and the mayor and thousands of cheering citizens waiting to welcome him at the airport and along the route to the hotel.

Next morning he was given an official welcome at the city hall. In the course of his reply to the mayor's speech he said: 'I was just asked if I intended to enter politics. My reply was "no". I have no political aspirations whatsoever. I do not intend to run for political office, and I hope that my name will never be used in a political way.'

It had been arranged that he should make a speech to Congress and at San Francisco a message arrived that the text must be submitted to the Department of the Army. He protested, and the department cancelled the instruction and apologized. When he arrived in Washington, after midnight, a crowd of some 20,000 welcomed him. Marshall and the Joint Chiefs were in the official party.

Next day, the 19th, the cars of MacArthur and his party, driving to the Congress building, passed more cheering crowds. On arrival he was led to the Chamber of the House of Representatives where he spoke from the rostrum to the members of both houses. The speech, some 3,500 words long, was MacArthur at his best—stately, modest, ornamented as always with flashes of rhetoric. He spoke as 'a fellow American'. The communist threat was global, but he would confine his discussion to Asia. The people of Asia needed guidance and support, food and clothing, and 'realization of the nationalist urge for political freedom'. As a result of the victory over Japan America's strategical frontier had been advanced to embrace the whole Pacific Ocean which America guarded by a chain of islands held by her or by her allies from the Aleutians to the Marianas. But any break in the line would render the other segments vulnerable. Therefore, as a matter of military urgency, Formosa must not fall under communist control.

In general he repeated the arguments he had been using during the last year and more, and wound up:

> I am closing my 52 years of military service. When I joined the Army, even before the turn of the century, it was the fulfilment of all my boyish hopes and dreams. The world has turned over many times since I took the oath on the Plain at West Point, and the hopes and dreams have long since vanished. But I still remember the refrain of one of the most popular barrack ballads of that day, which proclaimed, most proudly, that 'Old soldiers never never die. They just fade away.'
>
> And like the old soldier of that ballad, I now close my military career and just fade away—an old soldier who tried to do his duty as God gave him the light to see that duty.
>
> Goodbye.

When Congress conferred its thanks upon him MacArthur considered that this implied rejection of the policy of appeasement in East Asia. A joint resolution of Congress directed that a gold medal be struck in his honour, bearing the inscription: 'Protector of Australia; Liberator of the Philippines; Conqueror of Japan; Defender of Korea.'[1]

When MacArthur had arrived in Australia in March 1942, fewer than ten years before, Patrick J. Hurley had said to him that the Americans had always had a hero and that now he was it. If he was not the hero then, he was now. The crowds that cheered and poured paper on his motorcade as it drove from the airfield to the Waldorf Astoria, which was to be his home in New York, were larger, the police estimated, than had turned out for any other national hero. And at his suite 20,000 telegrams and 150,000 letters awaited him 'from all over the world, from the high and mighty to the lowly and downtrodden'.

The speech to Congress did not satisfy the thirst for discussion of the great event. It was arranged that the Congressional Committee on the Armed Services and the Committee on Foreign Relations should take evidence about the military situation in the Far East and MacArthur's relief from his command. Between 3 May and 25 June the committee interrogated 13 witnesses,

---

[1] These acknowledgments were destined quickly to be forgotten by the us Government. MacArthur was, for example, not among those representatives of 51 nations invited to San Francisco to the ceremonious signing of the peace treaty with Japan on 8 September 1951.

including MacArthur, who was first to go to the stand; Marshall; and the Joint Chiefs of Staff. MacArthur was interrogated for a total of 22 hours, and the transcript of the whole proceedings amounted to over 2,000,000 words. The policies and differences of opinion of the American leaders were exposed to the world. MacArthur insisted that there had been no disagreement between him and the Joint Chiefs (which was hardly accurate) but there had been basic differences between the policies he advocated and those of the President and Acheson. Marshall, who, whatever his vacillation, was a man who understood the relations of the soldier to the State, put it simply at the Senate hearings.

> What is new and what brought about the necessity for General MacArthur's removal is the wholly unprecedented situation of a local Theater Commander publicly expressing his displeasure at, and his disagreement with, the foreign policy of the United States. [MacArthur] . . . had grown so far out of sympathy with the established policies of the United States that there is grave doubt as to whether he could any longer be permitted to exercise the authority in making decisions that normal command functions would assign to a Theater Commander.[1]

Afterwards MacArthur repudiated charges that he had disobeyed orders and pointed out that at the Senate hearings all the Joint Chiefs had declared that he had not been insubordinate. He resented the abrupt manner of his dismissal, but if it had been delayed while MacArthur defended his actions and Washington criticized them, the whole affair would have been a subject of turgid public debate before as well as after the decision.

MacArthur's policies were in conflict with those of the United States Government and he had made this evident. He had become an embarrassment to the President and had to go. But, in retrospect, the blame for the unfortunate manner of his dismissal rests less on MacArthur than on unfirm and vacillating leadership in Washington. Undoubtedly President Roosevelt would have managed things better.

In the next two years or so, vigorous as ever, with his eloquence undimmed, MacArthur responded to invitations from far and wide throughout the United States to make speeches to admiring audiences of many sorts. He took every opportunity of denouncing communists, fellow travellers and socialists and of deploring corruption in the administration and the heavy taxation imposed by a government that had assumed 'the arrogant mantle of oligarchic power'.

Meanwhile in Korea the war reached the stalemate that MacArthur had predicted; on 27 July 1953 an armistice was signed, both sides having agreed that there was a 'substitute for victory'.

[1] Quoted in Ridgway, p. 154.

Looking back in the early 1960s MacArthur saw the policy that led to his recall as dealing 'a catastrophic blow to the hopes of the free world. Its disastrous consequences were reflected throughout Asia. Red China promptly was accepted as the military colossus of the East. Korea was left ravished and divided. Indo-China was partitioned by the sword. Tibet was taken almost on demand. Other Asian nations began to tremble towards neutralism. . . . It accepted at tragic cost the policy of indecision that in war there can be a substitute for victory.' Soon the United States, with the support of even fewer contingents of United Nations troops than in Korea, would again be deadlocked in conflict with a small but resolute nation— North Vietnam—and MacArthur would become the prophet of those who advocated an unremitting anti-communist crusade in Asia.

His last oration was given at West Point in May 1962 on the occasion of the presentation to him by the Association of Graduates of the Sylvanus Thayer Medal, their highest honour. He died in hospital in Washington on 5 April 1964 aged 84 years.

At this distance it seems likely that MacArthur will be written into history as an advocate of politico-military doctrines and as one-time ruler of Japan rather than as a great captain. Already, in both these roles, his influence has been proving less potent and his policies less far-seeing than many had fancied. But he was a man of his time—a time of great emotional and intellectual confusion among his fellow countrymen.

As we have seen, until 1917, he had had far less regimental experience and staff training than his contemporaries destined for high command at home and abroad. But his self-confidence, the breadth and depth of his thinking and his eloquence and commanding presence ensured that he filled with distinction the senior appointments into which he was swiftly elevated between the wars.

In the Philippines in 1942 he suffered a defeat—the greatest in the history of American foreign wars. For the inadequate preparations that contributed to the speed of this defeat much of the responsibility was his. In his next appointment as commander of the SWPA in the operations on the return journey from Papua to Luzon his judgments were sometimes right, sometimes ill-advised. The credit for the successes rests as much on Admiral Halsey on the spot and on the Joint Chiefs in Washington as on MacArthur. The prescience with which he may at times seem to have been endowed was generally the outcome of the cracking of the Japanese naval code before Pearl Harbor; even then his responses were often too slow or too cautious.

In adversity he displayed a lack of fibre and resilience. In France in 1918 at the times when his division was in sharp action it was as part of an increasingly victorious army. In his next campaign in the Philippines, when he was 62 and commanding forces doomed to defeat, he did not prove an inspiring leader. Then and in the SWPA before the tide turned he was petulant and reproachful, constantly blaming his superiors in Washington, and his subordinate commanders and their troops.[1]

Most great military commanders have possessed an infantry or cavalry superior to that of their opponents. In his operations in Dutch New Guinea and the Philippines and at important times in Korea, MacArthur lacked this advantage and had to rely on manœuvre and overwhelming fire power from land, sea and air forces. When in 1942–43 he had under his command some of the best infantry in the world he was markedly distrustful of their performance. Indeed, much of MacArthur's success could be attributed to good fortune. He was a lucky general. In other countries the commander during a *débâcle* such as in the Philippines in 1942 would not have been given another active command. MacArthur, however, was too eminent a figure and too much a popular hero to be thrust aside without violent repercussions at home, and loss of national prestige. He was lucky again at Inchon.

Throughout the last ten years of his military career his desire for adulation made him prey to devoted followers who flattered his conviction that he was infallible and that people in Washington were conspiring against him. But this was a minor though damaging foible measured against his other qualities: his courage, his patriotism, his ability to inspire his subordinates and others, including anxious Australians in 1942, and the persistence with which he pursued his notion that he was destined to lead a crusade against political decay within America and appeasement beyond its frontiers.

---

[1] In 1956 Marshall in an interview described MacArthur as 'supersensitive about everything. He was conspicuous in the matter of temperament. . . .' (Pogue, *Ordeal and Hope 1939–42*, pp. 374–5).

Bibliography

Appleman, R. E., *South to the Naktong, North to the Yalu*, US Department of the Army, Washington, 1961

Cannon, M. H., *Leyte: The Return to the Philippines*, US Department of the Army, Washington, 1954

Craven, W. F., and Cate, J. L., *The Army Air Forces in World War II*, University of Chicago Press, Chicago: Vol. I, 1948; Vol. IV, 1950; Vol. V, 1953

Crowl, P. A., *Campaign in the Marianas*, US Department of the Army, Washington, 1960

Dexter, D., *The New Guinea Offensives*, Australian War Memorial, Canberra, 1961

Eisenhower, D. D., *Crusade in Europe*, Heinemann, London, 1948

Falls, C., *The First World War*, Longmans Green, London, 1960

Ganoe, W. A., *MacArthur Close-up*, Vantage Press, New York, 1962

Ganoe, W. A., *The History of the United States Army*, Ashton, Maryland, rev. ed. 1964

Gill, G. H., *Royal Australian Navy 1939–42*, Australian War Memorial, Canberra, 1957

Gillison, D., *Royal Australian Air Force 1939–42*, Australian War Memorial, Canberra, 1962

Halsey, W. F., and Bryan, J., *Admiral Halsey's Story*, McGraw-Hill, New York, 1947

Hankey, Lord, *Politics, Trials and Errors*, Pen in Hand, Oxford, 1950

Kawai, K., *Japan's American Interlude*, University of Chicago Press, Chicago, 1960

Kenney, G. C., *General Kenney Reports*, Duell, Sloan & Pearce, New York, 1949

Kenney, G. C., *The MacArthur I Know*, Duell, Sloan & Pearce, New York, 1951

Keogh, E. G., *South-West Pacific 1941–45*, Grayflower Productions, Melbourne, 1965

Killigrew, J. W., 'The Army and the Bonus Incident', *Military Affairs*, Summer 1962

Lee, C., and Henschel, R., *Douglas MacArthur*, Holt, New York, 1952

Long, G., *The Final Campaigns*, Australian War Memorial, Canberra, 1963

MacArthur, D., *Reminiscences*, McGraw-Hill, New York, 1964

MacArthur, D., *A Soldier Speaks* (ed. V. E. Whan), Praeger, New York, 1965

McCarthy, D., *South-West Pacific Area First Year: Kokoda to Wau*, Australian War Memorial, Canberra, 1959

Matloff, M., and Snell, E. M., *The War Department. Strategic Planning for Coalition Warfare*, US Department of the Army, Washington, 1953

Miller, J., Jnr, *Guadalcanal: The First Offensive*, US Department of the Army, Washington, 1949

Miller, J., Jnr, *Cartwheel, the Reduction of Rabaul*, US Department of the Army, Washington, 1959

Milner, S., *Victory in Papua*, US Department of the Army, Washington, 1957

Morison, S. E., *History of United States Naval Operations in World War II*, Little Brown, Boston; Vols III–VI, 1950; Vol. VII, 1951; Vol. VIII, 1953; Vol. XII, 1958

Morton, L., *The Fall of the Philippines*, US Department of the Army, Washington, 1953

Morton, L., 'The Philippine Army 1935–39. Eisenhower's Memorandum to Quezon', *Military Affairs*, Summer 1948

Odgers, G., *Air War Against Japan 1943–45*, Australian War Memorial, Canberra, 1957

Palmer, Frederick, *Newton D. Baker, America at War*, 2 vols, Dodd, Mead, New York, 1931

Palmer, R. R., Wiley, B. I. and Keast, W. R., *The Procurement and Training of Ground Combat Troops*, US Department of the Army, Washington, 1948

Pershing, J. J., *My Experiences in the World War*, Hodder & Stoughton, London, 1931

Pogue, F. C., *George C. Marshall, Education of a General 1880–1939*, MacGibbon & Kee, London, 1964

Pogue, F. C., *Ordeal and Hope 1939–42*, New York, 1966

Rees, D., *Korea: The Limited War*, Macmillan, London, 1964

Reischauer, E. O., *The United States and Japan*, Harvard University Press, Cambridge, Mass., 1950

Ridgway, M. B., *The Korean War*, Doubleday, New York, 1967

Rovere, R. H., and Schlesinger, A., *The General and the President*, Farrar, Strauss & Young, New York, 1951

Sebald, W. J., *With MacArthur in Japan: A Personal History of the Occupation*, Norton, New York, 1965

Sherwood, R. E., *The White House Papers of Harry L. Hopkins*, 2 vols, Eyre & Spottiswoode, London, 1949

Smith, R. R., *Triumph in the Philippines*, US Department of the Army, Washington, 1963

Smith, R. R., *The Approach to the Philippines*, US Department of the Army, Washington, 1963

Stimson, H. L., and Bundy, McG., *On Active Service in Peace and War*, Harper, New York, 1948

Stone, I. F., *The Hidden History of the Korean War*, Monthly Review Press, New York, 1952

Truman, H. S., *The Memoirs of Harry S. Truman*, 2 vols, Hodder & Stoughton, London, 1951

Wainwright, J. M., *General Wainwright's Story*, Doubleday, New York, 1946

Waldrop, F. C. (ed.), *MacArthur at War. His Military Writings*, Bodley Head, London, 1943

Watson, M. S., *Chief of Staff: Prewar Plans and Preparations*, us Department of the Army, Washington, 1950

White, W. A., *The Autobiography of William Allen White*, London, 1946

Whitney, C., *MacArthur: His Rendezvous with History*, Knopf, New York, 1956

Wigmore, L. G., *The Japanese Thrust*, Australian War Memorial, Canberra, 1957

Willoughby, C. A., and Chamberlain, J., *MacArthur 1941–51*, Heinemann, London, 1956

Yoshida, S., *The Yoshida Memoirs*, London, 1961

Index

CPSIA information can be obtained at www.ICGtesting.com
Printed in the USA
LVOW07s0921280615

444164LV00002B/442/P